# IRON MAIDENS *and* *the* DEVIL'S DAUGHTERS

U.S. Navy Gunboats versus Confederate Gunners and Cavalry
On the Tennessee and Cumberland Rivers, 1861-65

# MARK ZIMMERMAN

ZIMCO
Publications LLC

# IRON MAIDENS *and*
# *the* DEVIL'S DAUGHTERS

U.S. Navy Gunboats versus Confederate Gunners and Cavalry
On the Tennessee and Cumberland Rivers, 1861-65

# MARK ZIMMERMAN

*The Tennessee River*

Also by Mark Zimmerman:

*Guide to Civil War Nashville, 2nd Edition*

*God, Guns, Guitars & Whiskey: An Illustrated Guide to Historic Nashville, Tennessee, 2nd Edition*

*Gone Under: Historic Cemeteries of Nashville, Tennessee, 2nd Edition*

Content related to this publication can be found on the publisher's website at:
www.zimcopubs.com

# *Table of Contents*

**Autumn 1861 — MOUND CITY, ILLINOIS**
Three City-Class ironclads — *Mound City, Cairo,* and *Cincinnati* — are built at this shipbuilding and repair riverport, as well as *USS Neosho* river monitor. In 1862, it becomes HQ for Mississippi River Squadron.

**March 25, 1864 — PADUCAH, KENTUCKY**
Forrest attacks this Ohio River port and Union staging area, driving US troops into Fort Anderson. US gunboats inflict casualties and much destruction of property.

ILLINOIS

*Ohio River*

KENTUCKY

**Mound City** ■

Fort Smith

**Smithland**

Fort Anderson

**Paducah**

■ **Eddyville**

**Cairo**
Fort Holt

Bird's Point
**Camp Defiance**

*Cumberland River*

**April 23, 1861 — CAIRO, ILLINOIS**
Cairo occupied by military; serves as headquarters for Western Gunboat Flotilla.

*Mississippi River*

MISSOURI

Columbus (CSA)

**Nov. 7, 1861 — COLUMBUS-BELMONT**
Grant attacks Confederate camp at Belmont, Mo. using gunboat convoy to land troops under sight of rebel fortress at Columbus, Ky. In September 1861, Polk had occupied Columbus; fort abandoned in February 1862.

Belmont
(CSA camp)

*Tennessee River*

*Both Rivers Flow Northward*

**Feb. 6, 1862 — FORT HENRY, TENNESSEE**
Foote's ironclads capture Fort Henry following rebel abandonment of Fort Heiman. Grant's troops occupy the site and later move on Fort Donelson.

KENTUCKY

Fort Henry

Fort Heiman

TENNESSEE

**Feb. 6-11, 1862 — PHELPS RAID**
Three US timberclads steam up Tennessee River as far as Florence, Ala., capturing unfinished Confederate ironclad and destroying the railroad bridge at Danville, Tenn.

Danville

**Union City**

*Nashville & Northwestern R.R.*

**Paris**

*Memphis & Clarksville R.R.*

**1861-1865 — PARTISAN AND GUERRILLA WARFARE**
Irregular warfare exemplified by Col. Thomas Woodward, Jack McCann, and Jack Hinson, wealthy landowner turned deadly sharpshooter, who targeted US gunboat officers on the Tennessee River. In response to enemy harassment, US retaliates by shelling guerrilla-friendly towns.

**Nov. 4, 1864 — JOHNSONVILLE, TENNESSEE**
After capturing US gunboats at Paris Landing and blocking Tennessee River, Forrest's artillery demolishes huge US depot and fortress with great loss of property and stores.

*Mobile & Ohio R.R.*

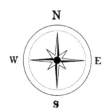

**March 1 and April 6-7, 1862 — PITTSBURG LANDING, TENNESSEE**
*USS Conestoga* skirmishes with CSA troops on March 1; *USS Tyler* and *Lexington* shell the enemy from Tennessee River during battle of Shiloh.

*Mark Zimmerman © 2019*

# US Gunboats vs. Confederate Gunners and Cavalry
## Military Operations on the Tennessee and Cumberland Rivers, 1861-1865

**April 29, 1865 — EDDYVILLE, KENTUCKY**
*USS Moose* repels pro-Confederate attack on
Eddyville in final US gunboat combat.

**Nov. 20, 1861 — CANTON, KENTUCKY**
*USS Conestoga* under Phelps engages Forrest's cavalry
under Kelley in first combat between gunboats and
cavalry. Both sides claim victory in brief encounter.

**Canton**

*Not Shown on Map*
**Oct. 10, 1864 — EASTPORT, MISSISSIPPI**
Kelley's cavalry ambushes Federal expedition at
Tennessee River landing, defeats gunboat escorts.

🏛 **Bowling Green**

**Feb. 3, 1863 — DOVER, TENNESSEE**
Gunboats guarding US convoy assist US garrison at Dover
in repelling Confederate cavalry attack under Wheeler.

**Feb. 14, 1862 — FORT DONELSON, TENNESSEE**
Confederate gunners defeat US ironclads in naval
attack; fort surrenders two days later, however.

KENTUCKY

TENNESSEE

Fort Clark   Fort Terry
Fort Sevier 🏛 Clarksville

**Fort Donelson**

**Dover**

Palmyra

**Feb. 19, 1862 — CLARKSVILLE, TENNESSEE**
US flotilla captures Clarksville with little incident
and occupies Nashville on Feb. 25. Clarksville will
change hands several times during the war.

**Cumberland
City**

Louisville & Nashville R.R.

TENNESSEE

**Charlotte**

Harpeth
Shoals

Fort Zollicoffer   Fort
Negley

Johnsonville

**NASHVILLE**

Fort Hill   Nashville & Northwestern R.R.

**Waverly**

**Nov. 4-15, 1865 — BELL'S BEND, TENNESSEE**
Largest clash between US ironclad and tinclad
gunboats and Confederate cavalry-artillery
as rebels blockade Cumberland River prior to
Battle of Nashville.

Nashville & Chattanooga R.R.

**April 26, 1863 — The Duck River Affair**
White's Battalion unwittingly attacks the infamous Mississippi
Marine Brigade and is chased 12 miles inland, losing their leader.

**Fortress Rosecrans
at Murfreesboro**

**Franklin** 🏛 **Fort Granger**

## *List of Maps*

# Introduction

*Battles between the navy and the cavalry were unheard of—*
*until the Federals invaded Middle Tennessee*

The invasion and occupation of Middle Tennessee by Union forces during the Civil War produced a unique and interesting type of warfare—U.S. Navy gunboats fighting Confederate cavalry. Other similar examples in the annals of military history are difficult to find. There was no gameplan to consult. The rules were created as the battles were fought.

This publication tells the story of how the U.S. Army and U.S. Navy combined forces, along with civilian assistance, to create a unique flotilla of armored river gunboats, essentially from scratch, to fight the gunners in the Confederate river fortifications and the field artillery of the Confederate cavalry.

At the beginning of the Civil War, the Federal authorities faced a dilemma. The blockading of the Atlantic and Gulf coasts (the Anaconda Plan) consumed most of the resources of the U.S. Department of the Navy, including ships, heavy guns, experienced crews, and distinguished officers. But the Lower Mississippi River Valley was in Confederate hands and a major campaign would be needed to wrest control away from the rebels. It was also evident that any invasion route into the Confederate heartland of Kentucky and Tennessee would need to be along the Tennessee and Cumberland rivers. Complicating the situation was the simple fact that the Federals did not possess any gunboats capable of navigating the Western rivers.

On the opposite side, the Confederate authorities considered the defense of their capital at Richmond, Va., as priority number one, with the Western Theater receiving much less attention and resources. This despite the fact that the holding of the Mississippi River was a major Confederate objective along with defending a thousand-mile front from the river eastward to the Appalachian mountains.

There were no plans and few precedents for such an undertaking. Advancements were made in fits and starts. Miscommunications, territorial quarrels, petty jealousies, and other controversies slowed their progress but somehow the job got done through the efforts of men such as James B. Eads, Samuel Pook, U.S. Grant, Andrew Foote, Seth L. Phelps, LeRoy Fitch, and David D. Porter. An invasion route was negotiated via the churning of paddlewheels and the thumping of smoothbores up the Tennessee and Cumberland rivers into the heart of the Confederacy. At first, the fledgling flotilla consisted of three ungainly converted sidewheelers armored solely with thick oak planking. These timberclads performed yeoman's service, patroling the rivers and providing intelligence about enemy defenses.

Facing the Federal "brown water" navy were considerable Confederate fortifications bristling with heavy seige artillery. Confederate cavalrymen led by such famous figures as Nathan Bedford Forrest, John Hunt Morgan, and Joseph Wheeler roamed the countryside, hitting and harassing Federal forces seemingly at will. Battles and skirmishes between the U.S. Navy gunboats and the Confederate cavalry, armed with field artillery, created a unique form of combat during the Civil War. The first such conflict occurred at Canton, Ky. between a lone timberclad and a unit of Forrest's command, fought before Forrest's first acknowledged battle at Sacramento, Ky. The first amphibious landing of troops came at Belmont on the Mississippi River in late 1861, a technique that would be used successfully many times in the coming years of conflict. An ambitious construction program — building armored gunboats from scratch — produced the City Class of casemate ironclads, which battled Confederate gunners at Fort Henry and Fort Donelson, with mixed results. This use of ironclad gunboats (in conjunction with army maneuvers) came a full month before the much more celebrated clash of the USS Monitor and CSS Virginia ironclads at Hampton Roads, Va. In fact, the first ironclad manufactured in the Western Hemisphere was launched in the heartland, at Carondelet, Mo.

Although the Confederacy attempted to build and launch gunboats and ironclads, their efforts were thwarted on the Tennessee and Cumberland rivers. "The lack of a fleet to back up the forts underscores the Confederate defensive problem — you need a navy to fight another navy," stated historian Greg Biggs. Furthermore, there is no known instance of the Federal cavalry fighting a Confederate river gunboat.

As it turned out, the efficiency of the Federal ironclads at Fort Henry and at Fort Donelson could not have been more disparate. The battles at the river forts produced strangely disproportionate effects on both sides.

Between the two river-fort battles, the daring Phelps raid by the three timberclads up the Tennessee River struck terror into the hearts of secessionists and provided support to Union loyalists along the river. The raid, along with the ever-exaggerated rumors of pirate-like behavior on behalf of the ironclad crews, produced literal panic among Mid-South civilian populations along the invasion routes. There were several fortifications between Dover and Nashville that could have given battle to the Federal flotilla, but those battles were over before they had even begun.

One of the major accomplishments of the river invasion of early 1862 was the capture of Nashville, the capital of Tennessee, which became the major staging area and depot for the invasion and capture of Chattanooga, Atlanta, and Savannah. The focus of the struggle on the Cumberland and Tennessee rivers shifted to the logistical necessity of shipping massive amounts of war matériel from the Northern ports of Louisville and Cincinnati to Nashville.

In April 1862, the timberclads played an interesting role at the bloody Battle of Shiloh, a role which is still being debated as to its significance. Few people know, however, that one of the timberclads had clashed with Confederate forces four weeks earlier at Pittsburg Landing in what is called the First Battle of Shiloh. During their routine patrols, the ironclads and other U.S. riverboats often deployed landing parties to project force. The Federal landing party at Pittsburg Landing received quite a surprise.

Traditionally, as depicted in the movies and

other popular entertainment, the cavalry has been called upon to "come to the rescue." In early 1863, however, it was the U.S. gunboat flotilla (escorting a convoy at the time) which came to the rescue of the Union garrison at Dover, which was under attack by Confederate cavalry. Again, the significance of the role of the gunboats is still being debated.

Irregular forces such as partisan rangers, guerrillas, and even lone sharpshooters continued to harass Union shipping on the rivers despite Federal reprisals which grew more frequent and brutal as the fighting lingered on. In this environment, two men rose to the occasion and left their marks, LeRoy Fitch and David Campbell Kelley. U.S. Lt. Commander Fitch devised a system of gunboat escorts for steamer convoys which allowed a steady stream of war goods to reach the front. He also developed and instituted counterinsurgency tactics that discouraged the guerrillas although rarely successful in killing or capturing them. Colonel Kelley, a Methodist preacher serving under Forrest,

became known as the Devil's Parson and became an expert in battling gunboats from the riverbanks and establishing blockades. Another character in this story, a civilian named Captain Jack Hinson, suffered tremendous personal loss, and through patience, skill, and daring, gained revenge against his enemies.

The culmination of U.S. naval combat versus Confederate cavalry came in a series of events in 1864 consisting of Forrest raiding the vital riverport of Paducah, Ky.; an ambush at Eastport, Miss.; the capturing of Union gunboats at Paris Landing; the formation of an ersatz Confederate navy; the destruction of the Federal supply depot at Johnsonville; and a classic series of encounters between Kelley's field artillerists and a host of Union naval vessels at Bell's Bend near Nashville.

The final skirmish between Union gunboats and pro-Confederate forces came in Kentucky in 1865, three weeks after Robert E. Lee surrendered to Grant at Appomattox.

This publication tells the story of the struggle between U.S. naval gunboats and Confederate forces on the Tennessee and Cumberland rivers. It should be noted that both sides placed more emphasis on the conflict over the control of the Mississippi River and its tributaries, not to mention the overall priority of the war in the Eastern Theater and the preferential use of naval forces for the coastal blockades. It should also be noted that the Confederacy did not float any gunboats of its own on the two rivers under study. This publication does not cover in any depth the naval actions on the Cumberland River above Nashville or the Tennessee River above Muscle Shoals. In the author's opinion, however, the importance of the twin rivers as avenues of invasion and routes of supply cannot be overstated. Without the stream of supplies and troops reaching Nashville during 1863-64, there would have been no Atlanta campaign or March to the Sea, much less the subjugation of the Carolinas and final victory in the West.

When all was said and done, the U.S. naval officers and crews on the Western waters served with distinction and little recognition, while the Confederate forces who opposed them fought with bravery and determination, with few tangible results.

Facts can be stubborn things. During the fog of war, commanders tend to overestimate the casualties and damage inflicted upon the enemy and inflate their own contributions and accomplishments, for reasons of vanity, glory, or legacy. Accounts of battle vary as to each witness. Periods of time and estimates of distance become distorted. Victory is claimed by both sides, perhaps for the sake of boosting morale and advancing careers. Victories can come at great cost; defeats can be inconsequential, in the long run. The records and accounts of naval battles included in this publication are no exception to these phenomena. Every effort has been made to minimize these discrepancies or at the very least to make note of them.

Readers are asked to make full use of the many maps in this publication to familarize themselves with the many place names. The last chapter of this publication serves as a brief travel guide to battlefield sites, museums, and interpretive centers the reader can visit to learn more about the subject matter. The author's personal interest in the Civil War was cultivated through participation in groups such as the Civil War Trust, the Civil War Fortification Study Group, and the Battle of Nashville Preservation Society, which are just a few of the organizations, along with state and federal governments, responsible for reclaiming, interpreting, and developing the tourism potential of sites such as Fort Negley, Johnsonville, Bell's Bend, and Fort Defiance-Clarksville. Much of this hard work has been accomplished in only the past two decades. Some of these historic sites had been abandoned, grown over and glossed over, and nearly lost to history.

Also included is a bibliography for further reading. Much of the author's research has come from these publications. A much-welcomed new addition in 2016 was Timothy B. Smith's *Grant Invades Tennessee,* the definitive study of the battles of Fort Henry and Fort Donelson and the Phelps raid. In addition, two scholars should be singled out as significant contributors due to their own works. Myron J. "Jack" Smith Jr., former Professor of Library Science at Tusculum College in Greeneville, Tenn., literally wrote the books on this subject matter, creating reference works on tinclads and timberclads, and biographies of Fitch, the *USS Carondelet,* and all of the naval commanders on the Western waters. Much of the grist for this book, other than the *Official Records of the War of the Rebellion,* comes from this reference material. The other indispensable man is Edwin Bearss, U.S. Marine, Historian Emeritus of the National Park Service, discoverer and savior of the *USS Cairo,* and tour guide extraordinaire. I have had the pleasure of touring Nashville, Chickamauga, and Vicksburg with Mr. Bearss. His book, *Hardluck Ironclad,* with his personal inscription, is one of my most treasured possessions.

Thanks also goes to Middle Tennessee historian Greg Biggs, who was kind enough to read the manuscript and offer many helpful suggestions.

–Chapter One–

# The Rivers

*Any invasion on the rivers from the Ohio would be waged*
*against the current, literally, as the rivers flow northward*

In 1861, the importance of the river system in the Western Theater as a route of invasion into the heartland of the Confederacy and as an avenue of supplying forward bases was self-evident to any military or governmental official who could read a map. The course of the Tennessee River led to northern Alabama and would be advantageous to occupying West Tennessee and cutting vital railway lines. The Cumberland River led to the Tennessee capital of Nashville, a major railway hub and the regional center for agricultural and industrial production. At the beginning of the Civil War, the Age of Steam (river transports and railroading) was in full swing. Steamboat shipping and travel on both rivers, especially the Cumberland, had reached record levels by 1860. The wharf at Nashville teemed with agricultural goods ready to be shipped down the river to the Ohio and then down the Mississippi to New Orleans. Conversely, manufactured goods from as far away as Philadelphia, but mostly from Cincinnati and Louisville, were shipped up the Cumberland and unloaded at the busy river port. Any invasion up the rivers from the Ohio would be waged against the current, literally, as the rivers flow northward, although this was not a major obstacle in the age of steam-powered riverboats. In fact, any gunboats attacking Confederate shore fortifications would have the advantage of drifting downriver out of gunfire range if disabled during a fight. One must take note that in traveling upriver on these waterways one is traveling southward. For example, at Fort Donelson, the upper river battery is actually south of the lower river battery (although it is literally higher in elevation).

# Mileage Upstream from Confluence with Ohio River

## Tennessee River

Patterson's Landing .................... 14.5
Grand Chain of Rocks................. 15
27 Mile Island (foot) ................... 22
Birmingham Settlement ........... 31.5
Birmingham Shoal ..................... 32
Pine Bluff.................................... 55
Panther Island Shoal.................. 60
Fort Henry................................. 60.75
Fort Heiman................................ 62
Paris Landing.............................. 65
Big Sandy Island Shoal .............. 67
Big Sandy Island (head)............. 69.5
Leatherwood Island Bar ............ 72.5
Memphis & Louisville RR........... 78
Green Bottom Bar....................... 88
Reynoldsburg Settlement ......... 92.5
Johnsonville ............................... 94.5
Duck River Sucks........................ 102
Perryville Settlement................. 135.25
Cedar Creek Bar......................... 143
Clifton Town ............................... 154
Saltillo Settlment ...................... 165.5
Savannah Settlement............... 182.5
Crump's Landing........................ 186.5
Pittsburg Landing....................... 192
Hamburg Landing ...................... 196
Big Bend Shoals ......................... 199
State Line.................................... 212.5
Eastport Settlement .................. 223
Chickasaw Settlement.............. 224.5
Colbert Shoals (foot) ................ 232
Seven Mile Island (foot)........... 245.5
Florence RR Bridge.................... 255.5
Great Muscle Shoals ................. 262

## Cumberland River

Smithland.............................. 2
Dooms Landing................ 24.5
Willow Creek..................... 34.5
Eddyville ............................ 43
Ingram Shoals................... 49
Canton................................ 63
Devil's Elbow ..................... 64
State Line............................ 74.5
Tobaccoport ...................... 77
Fort Donelson .................... 88
Dover .................................. 89
Bear Springs Landing ..... 96
Cumberland City............. 104
Palmyra............................. 115
Red River........................... 125
Clarksville ........................ 126
Hogswood Landing ...... 146.5
Harpeth Shoals.............. 152
Harpeth River................. 153
Davidson Landing ......... 173.5
Robertson Island........... 176.5
Fort Zollicoffer .............. 184
Gowers Island ................ 186
Nashville .......................... 190.5
Stones River..................... 206
Drakes Creek ................... 222
Station Camp Creek...... 237
Bledsoe Creek ................ 248.5
Hartsville Landing ......... 279
Carthage........................... 309

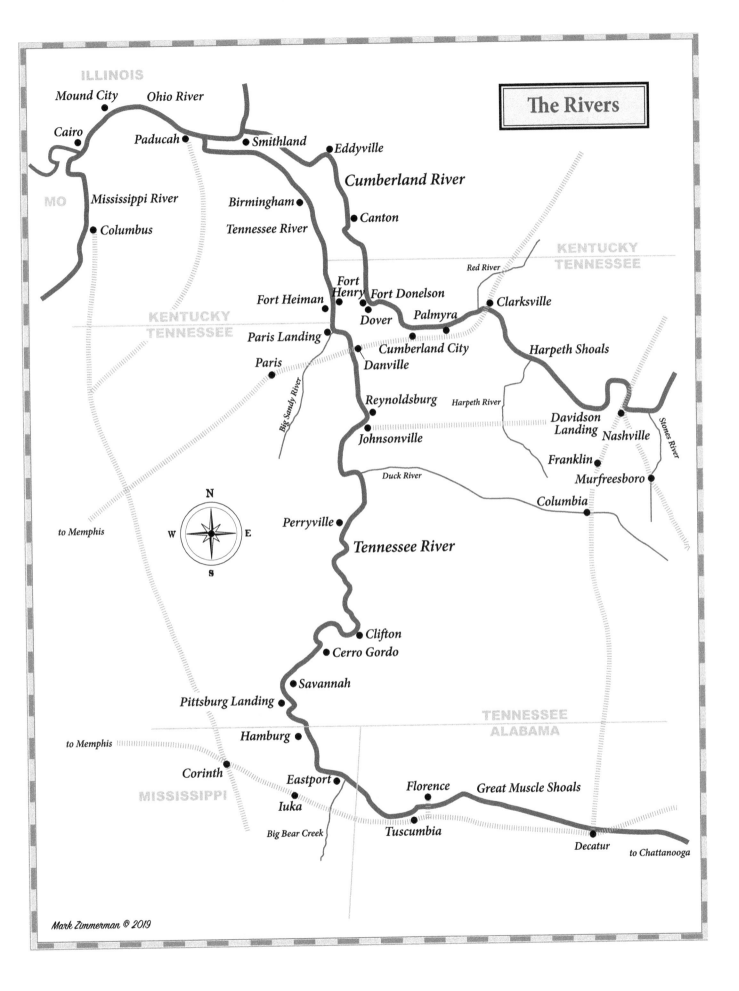

The Rivers

One major obstacle to Union invasion planners in 1861 was the neutrality of Kentucky, a slaveholding border state that did not secede but refused to officially send troops to fight for the Union. This delicate balancing act was thwarted on Sept. 3, 1861 when the Confederates seized the Mississippi River port of Columbus, Ky. (both sides violated the neutrality; the Federals had opened Camp Dick Robinson in that state in August 1861). The Federals had the presence of mind to immediately move upon and occupy the vital Ohio River ports of Paducah and Smithland, Ky., at the mouths of the Tennessee and Cumberland rivers respectively. Thus, the Confederates had gained high ground on the banks of the Mississippi while the Unionists controlled access to the twin river invasion routes.

Ten days after the war began at Fort Sumter in Charleston harbor, Illinois officials ordered the occupation of the town of Cairo at the extreme tip of the state, where the Ohio flows into the Mississippi (the southernmost point of Union territory). This small river port, which suffered from swampy terrain, mud, disease, bad drinking water, and rampant commercialism, would serve as the Union base of operations for naval forces on the Western Rivers until 1862, when headquarters was moved to Mound City, Ill. Other major river ports and shipbuilding facilities for the Federals were located at St. Louis and Carondelet, Mo.; Evansville and New Albany, Ind.; Paducah and Louisville, Ky.; and Cincinnati, Ohio.

Overall, the U.S. Navy's first priority was the coastal blockade of the Confederacy along the Gulf of Mexico and the Atlantic seaboard. The critical need for manpower and naval guns would be a headache for riverine naval forces throughout the war. The next priority was the recapture of the Lower Mississippi River, from Cairo to New Orleans, which was effected with the July 1863 victory at Vicksburg, Miss.

Confederate authorities, headquartered in

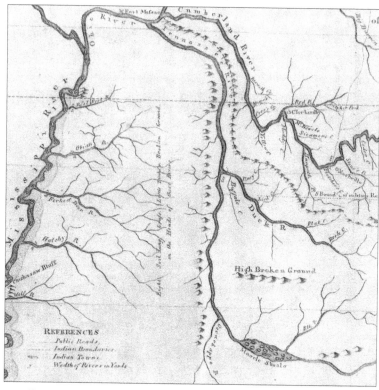

The Tennessee and Cumberland Rivers on a 1799 map by General Daniel Smith, a Cumberland Settlements pioneer.

Richmond, Va., gave top priority to the Eastern Theater. In the West, the neutrality of Kentucky convinced Confederate officials to place an overwhelming priority on Mississippi River defenses. This would have a profound effect on the protection of the twin rivers. Building fortifications on the Tennessee and Cumberland were haphazard, and progressed slowly due to a lack of manpower. For example, at the time the commander of the twin-river forts was pleading for the delivery of a few heavy guns, over on the Mississippi River, Columbus boasted 143 guns, including the largest gun in the Confederacy (a 6.5-inch Columbiad rifle called the Lady Polk), and Fort Pillow, further to the south in Tennessee, bristled with 58 cannon.

## The Cumberland River

Named for the Duke of Cumberland by early explorer Dr. Thomas Walker, the river begins in the eastern portion of Kentucky and flows westward in a southerly direction into Tennessee and then begins a gradual northern movement from Nashville back into Kentucky and drains into the Ohio River at Smithland, Ky. The entire length of the river runs almost 700 miles, but the Union military during the war was mainly concerned with the lower portion of the river from Carthage, Tenn. to the Ohio. Carthage is about 120 miles upriver from Nashville, which lies 190 miles from the Ohio. The initial military objective was to secure Nashville, one of the largest cities in the South, as a forward base of operations. Troops and military supplies would be shipped from Ohio River ports up the Cumberland to Nashville and then transported on the Nashville & Chattanooga Railroad to Chattanooga and Atlanta as the war progressed. After mid-1863, Union supplies were stored at massive Fortress Rosecrans outside Murfreesboro, Tenn. Light-draught gunboats (the tinclads) patrolled the upper river from Nashville to Carthage to prevent Confederate cavalry crossings and to interrupt guerrilla activities.

The Cumberland forms a series of sharp horseshoe bends immediately downstream from Nashville, then flows generally northwestward to Clarksville, a commercial river port and Montgomery County seat (also, the Red River flows into the Cumberland there). En route to Clarksville, about 38 miles downstream from Nashville, was the infamous Harpeth Shoals, a shallow four-mile-long section of gravel bars at the confluence of the Harpeth River (near present-day Ashland City). Many times during the war, riverboats were blocked at Harpeth Shoals due to low water, and at times by guerrillas and Confederate cavalry. Cargo would then have to be hauled by wagon the remaining distance to Nashville. During low-water periods, the depth of the river at the shoals was no more than 15 inches. The shoals was also a notorious gathering place for Southern guerrillas.

Clarksville was the site of two Memphis, Clarksville & Louisville Railroad bridges and Confederate forts Sevier, Clark, and Terry. From Clarksville the river flows westward to the village of Dover, the site of Fort Donelson. Between Clarksville and Dover was the river landing of Palmyra, another notorious guerrilla gathering place. From Dover, the Cumberland River flows northward into Kentucky, past the river ports of

## Rivers Still Treacherous

On Oct. 1, 2012, during a blinding rainstorm and high winds, the former U.S. Navy ship *LST 325* ran aground in the mud of Lake Barkley (Cumberland River) near the Lyon County, Ky. community of Buzzard Rock. The 328-foot flat-bottomed behemoth, piloted by a captain with 35 years experience, drew 8.5 feet of water. Two days later, after several unsuccessful attempts, the ship was floated again through the use of a 4,000-hp towboat, the ship's anchor winch and 1,800-hp engines in full reverse, the ship's Higgins boat pushing, and the filling and refilling of ballast tanks to gently rock the vessel. After a safety inspection, the museum ship sailed back to its home port in Evansville, Ind., concluding a tour of Nashville and Clarksville. The *LST 325* (Landing Ship, Tanks) was built in 1942 and used in World War Two to land Sherman tanks and other military vehicles while intentionally grounded on the beach. The *LST 325* served in Italy and landed at Normandy, France on D-Day 1944 and made 43 supply trips across the English Channel. The surplus ship served in the Greek navy from 1964 to 2000, when she was purchased by The USS Ship Memorial, Inc. and sailed back across the Atlantic. She is currently open to the public for touring. Shipbuilders in Evansville produced 167 LSTs during WWII, two per week at peak production. The *LST 325*, however, was built at the Philadelphia Navy Yard.

MAP of the Tennessee River above Florence, Alabama showing the Muscle Shoals segment of islands, sand bars, shoals, and narrow channels which restricted navigation during the Civil War period. U.S. Navy gunboats required the skills and experience of veteran civilian pilots to avoid river obstacles and contend with the wildly fluctuating river levels.

Canton and Eddysville, and then into the Ohio River at Smithland, site of Fort Smith. From Nashville to the Ohio River, the Cumberland River averaged 600 to 700 feet in width.

## The Tennessee River

The Tennessee River begins at Knoxville in East Tennessee with the confluence of the Holston and French Broad rivers. It flows southwestward in a huge curving movement into northern Alabama, nicks Mississippi, and then flows northward through Tennessee into Kentucky and the Ohio River at Paducah. On the Ohio River, Paducah is 12 miles downstream of the Cumberland River confluence and 30 miles upstream from the junction of the Ohio and Mississippi rivers at Cairo. Interrupting navigation on the Tennessee River at the time was Muscle (Mussel) Shoals, just east of Florence, Ala. The shoals in northern Alabama formed a series of obstructions nearly 40 miles in length, with rock reefs, gravel bars, rapids, log snags, and a shallow channel that caused boats to run aground. The lower river section (256 miles from Florence to Paducah) saw most of the military action by the Federal and Confederate forces. This lower section of the river averaged about 1,420 feet wide.

The city of Florence, on the northern bank, was linked to Tuscumbia on the south bank by a railroad bridge.

Near Eastport, Mississippi, Big Bear Creek flows northward into the Tennessee River at the Mississippi-Alabama state line. Crossing the creek south of the river is the strategically important Memphis & Charleston Railroad bridge. The important river landing of Eastport lies on the west side of Big Bear Creek at the Tennessee River. Twenty-five miles downstream to the north in Tennessee is Pittsburg Landing (Shiloh) and eight miles further on is Savannah (pop. 500). Thirty-two miles further north is the quaint village of Clifton (pop. 300), a frequent river crossing point for Confederate cavalry.

Halfway through Tennessee sat the U.S. river depot of Johnsonville (built in 1863-64) near the confluence of the Duck River.

There is a sharp bend in the river and strong river currents at the Duck River Sucks. Thirty miles further north (downriver) is Paris Landing, near the confluence of the Big Sandy River on the west bank, and five miles further downstream at the Kentucky state line was Fort Henry on the east bank. Across the river and slightly south of Fort Henry was the lofty site of Fort Heiman. Halfway between Fort Henry and Johnsonville the river was spanned by the Memphis and Ohio Railroad bridge at Danville, Tenn. From Fort Henry the river flows 60 miles north through Kentucky to Paducah, site of Union Fort Anderson.

In Kentucky, the Cumberland and Tennessee rivers flow parallel, about ten miles apart, forming the "land between the rivers." Due to the construction of dams by the U.S. Army Corps of Engineers in the 1900s, the Tennessee River is now known as Kentucky Lake; the Cumberland River is Lake Barkley; and the enclosed tract is the Land Between the Lakes National Recreational Area.

(It should be noted that Danville no longer exists;

Steamers lined up at the Nashville wharf in December 1862 with goods unloaded on the river bank. The railroad swing bridge can be seen downriver in the far background.

Eastport was moved to Iuka; and the wartime sites of Fort Henry and Johnsonville are now impounded and mostly underwater. Due to dam construction and navigational aids, the Tennessee River is now passable all the way to Knoxville.)

Most unusual is the northward flow of the Tennessee River once it reaches Alabama. Millions of years ago, the river was thought to have flowed naturally southward into the Mississippi River. Over time, the north-south channel emerged, with the current flowing southward. Even today, most of the tributaries of the river flow into it at a southward angle. Following the geologic effects of the ice age, however, the Tennessee ended up flowing northward into the Ohio. This reversal over time caused sharp northward bends of its tributaries at their confluences.

## Ohio and Mississippi Rivers

The Ohio River runs southwestward from Pittsburg, Pennsylvania 980 miles into the Mississippi River at Cairo, Illinois. Fifty miles upriver is the busy port of Paducah, Kentucky. The important shipbuilding and repair port of Mound City, Ill. lies between Cairo and Paducah. Upriver from Paducah on the Ohio are Evansville, Indiana, the home port of the Union tinclad fleet during the war; Louisville, Ky. at the Falls of the Ohio; New Albany, Ind., another important shipbuilding port; Cincinnati, Ohio; and Pittsburg, site of several major steamboat builders. (The "h" was added to Pittsburg's name in the 1880s.)

Upstream 215 miles on the Mississippi River from Cairo is St. Louis, Missouri, headquarters for Union forces in the Western Theater. Just south of St. Louis is Carondelet, site of the marine works where four City Class ironclads and many other gunboats were built. Downriver on the Mississippi River below Cairo are the wartime sites of Belmont, Island No. 10, Fort Pillow, Plum Bend, Memphis, Vicksburg, Port Hudson, and New Orleans. (The Lower Mississippi naval campaigns, which made heavy use of some of the gunboats which began service on the Cumberland and/or Tennessee rivers, are not covered in this publication.)

## The Age of Steam Arrives

Today on the Cumberland River, a modern paddlewheeler, the *General Jackson,* serves as a showboat for a large tourist destination in Nashville.

The showboat was named in tribute to the first steamboat to reach Tennessee's capital city. The *General Jackson* docked on March 11, 1819, having traveled three weeks from New Orleans. The steamboat was owned by General William Carroll, a friend of General Andrew Jackson, and had been built in Pittsburg. Four years later the first bridge was built across the Cumberland River at Nashville, and five years after that the city wharf was built and graded at the foot of Broadway. By 1830, steamboating was big business on the Cumberland. On Christmas Day 1850, a steamer delivered a significant gift to Nashville's business interests — the first railroad locomotive, *Tennessee.* It took four days for the locomotive to be moved from the wharf to the main tracks of the Nashville & Chattanooga Railroad about four blocks away. Another significant milestone in the Age of Steam had arrived.

By 1854, there were 13 shipping lines in Nashville employing 22 packets (a packet was a steamboat making regular scheduled runs between two river ports). Five years later there were 72 packets. More than one million tons of commercial goods worth $40 million (more than $1.1 billion in today's dollars) were being shipped annually on the Cumberland.

Tennessee became known as the hogs and hominy state. Twenty years before the Civil War, Tennessee was the largest corn producing state in the Union, in addition to producing 4.5 million bushels of wheat. By 1850, the state was the largest hog producer. Tobacco production was high in quantity and quality — 40 million pounds of the leaf by 1860. More than 16,000 hogsheads (a large wooden barrel holding about 1,000 pounds) of tobacco products left Clarksville for New Orleans, plus 17,000 hogsheads of flour and 16,000 hogs.

Prior to the war, the Highland Rim west and northwest of Nashville supplied raw materials for 25 iron furnaces producing more than 37,000 tons of pig iron. Stewart County alone boasted 12 ironworks. The region had abundant ore deposits

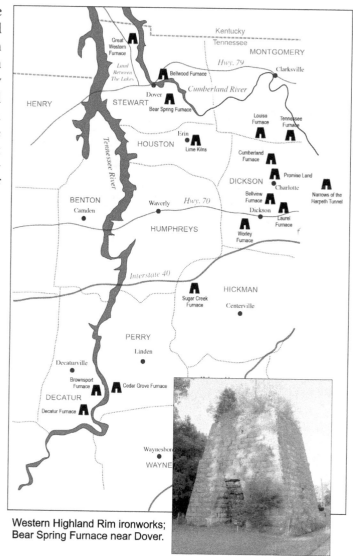

Western Highland Rim ironworks; Bear Spring Furnace near Dover.

near the surface, limestone for flux, timber to make charcoal, access to water supplies and waterways, and cheap slave and immigrant labor. Cannon balls fired by General Jackson's artillerymen at the Battle of New Orleans in 1815 were cast at Cumberland Furnace, Tenn. Another antebellum iron plantation was located at Cedar Grove Furnace, the only double-stack structure still extant, located near the Tennessee River in the southern portion of the Western Highland Rim. This furnace was probably the first in Tennessee to use the "hot blast" method in which the air blast was heated before being blown into the furnace, thus increasing the efficiency of the process and requiring less raw materials. The plantation covered 8,800 acres and "employed" about 100 workers. In 1833 the furnace was producing 40 tons of pig iron a week. The pigs (crude bars of iron) were hauled by ox carts two miles to the river, where they were loaded onto wooden flat-bottomed boats about 65 feet long which could carry several tons. In 1850, rebuilt and under new ownership, Cedar Grove Furnace was producing 1,800 tons of iron. In 1862, the operation was shut down by Union river gunboats lobbing shells into the factory. The ironmaster was ambushed and shot to death shortly thereafter.

Robertson County was the prime producer of whiskey, with a distillery operating in just about every holler (hollow). On some streams, a stillhouse stood every 100 yards. Corn was abundant, with adequate oak and maple for cooperage and charcoal for filtering, and most importantly, iron-free mineral-rich spring water filtered through limestone and flowing at 50 to 56 degrees. On the frontier, whiskey was an anesthetic, disinfectant, and either a stimulant or a tranquilizer, depending on the usage. Distillers sent their product south on flatboats to Natchez, where it sold for $2 a gallon, twice the going rate in Nashville. Whiskey demand always exceeded supply, especially during the war when Union forces banned distilling because corn and other grains were needed to feed both humans and livestock. Whiskey could be had for 25 cents per gallon before the war; afterwards it sold for $3.75 a gallon. In the Confederacy, due to regulations, a gallon went for $6.00 by 1863.

Whiskey was important during wartime. General George Washington had said, "The benefits arising from the moderate use of strong Liquor, have been experienced in All Armies, are not to be disputed."

President Lincoln commented on General U.S. Grant's propensity for drinking: "I wish I knew what brand of whiskey he drinks. I would send a barrel to all my other generals." On the evils of whiskey, Lincoln once noted that "injury from liquor is not from the use of a bad thing but from the abuse of a very good thing."

During the war, high-quality gunpowder was always in demand but not always available. Samuel Watson established Sycamore Mills, located on

*Submarine No. 7* was a twin-hulled salvage boat designed by James Eads to raise steamboat wrecks from the Mississippi River. The vessel was converted to the gunboat *USS Benton*.

Sycamore Creek four miles north of Ashland City, to manufacture gunpowder. In 1842 he sold half-interest in the operation and 5,000 acres of land to Richard Cheatham, at which time the name of the mill was changed to Cheatham, Watson and Company. The operation included a cotton gin, grist mill, and a powder mill. The manufacture of gunpowder was the most important product. As one of only two large gunpowder mills in the South (the other was in Augusta, Georgia), Sycamore Mills became a target for Federal forces in the opening months of the war. The plant was producing 2,800 pounds of gunpowder per day in November 1861. A niter refinery in Nashville produced 3,000 pounds of niter per day for the plant. A smaller gunpowder plant, in Manchester, Tenn., reportedly was producing up to 1,500 pounds per day. All in all, the Tennessee plants supplied 100,000 pounds of gunpowder to the army of Confederate General Albert Sidney Johnston before being shut down. In 1862 Sycamore Mills came under Union control and suspended operations.

Nashville boasted a population of 30,000 in 1860 and served as a regional center for manufacturing and industry, in addition to agriculture and shipping. The Brennan Foundry made cannon tubes, and at the beginning of the war, the company literally beat plowshares into swords. Several highly skilled gunsmiths in the city produced fine weaponry.

*"Fighting is nothing to the evils of the river — getting on shore, running afoul of one another, losing anchors, etc."*
—Admiral Farragut

The copper percussion caps used by the victorious Confederate troops at First Manassas (July 1861) in Virginia had been manufactured in Nashville.

Although steamboating was highly profitable, the business wasn't all sweetness and light. The rivers could be killers. Torrential freshets were unpredictable; strong currents and the water levels were uncontrollable in the everchanging channel. An experienced pilot was needed to maneuver through the rocks, shoals, rapids, sand bars, sucks, and other natural obstacles. There was always the possibility of running aground, colliding with another boat, or becoming stranded upstream due to low water. Typically, the steamboating season began with the "spring rise" and then dropped in the summertime. The low water period began in June and ended the last of September. Water conditions varied greatly with the weather. The Cumberland River rose and fell with such rapidity that a difference of eight to twelve feet in 24 hours was not uncommon. There were ten major shoals (serious impediments to navigation) on the Lower Cumberland alone. At times, it seemed that Federal naval commanders were more worried about being stranded by shallow waters than combat with the enemy.

The rivers also featured many islands where the main channel would pass only on one side although both waterways might be navigable in high water periods. The river current beside the islands was much faster than normal.

Steamer transports were not built for heavy duty. Tree trunks and other debris were a constant danger. They could easily rip apart the flat bottom of most steamboats. There were planters (tree trunks embedded in the river bottom with branches jutting upward just below the surface), sleepers (waterlogged trees floating just below the surface), and sawyers (trees bobbing on the surface).

The night before the attack on Fort Henry, a terrible storm struck, causing the commander of one ironclad gunboat to write: "The swift current brought down an immense quantity of heavy

Downtown Nashville

## Deluge of the Century

Although much less prevalent today, flooding still occurs on the Cumberland River despite the building of dams and other navigational infrastructure by the U.S. Army Corps of Engineers. On May 1-2, 2010, an average of 15 inches of rain fell over large areas of Middle and West Tennessee, with some areas receiving as much as 20 inches, the equivalent of 420 billion gallons of water in just two days. The Cumberland River crested in downtown Nashville at 51.86 feet (flood stage is 40 feet), with flood waters reaching as far inland as Fifth Avenue. The previous record had been 47.6 feet on March 15, 1975. Two dozen people were killed and 1,500 homes destroyed. Nearly 2,800 businesses and 14,500 employees were affected, costing $3.6 billion in revenue losses.

driftwood, lumber, fences, and large trees, and it required all the steam power of the *Carondelet*, with both anchors down, and the most strenuous exertions of the officers and crew, working day and night, to prevent the boat from being dragged downstream."

Then there was the danger of a steam boiler explosion in which sailors and/or passengers might be scalded to death—a painful way to die—or forced into the river to drown. By 1848, there had been more than 100 boiler explosions on steamboats on the Western waters, according to *DeBow's Review*.

–Chapter Two–

# The Flotilla

*The building and equipping of a riverboat flotilla
was a work of almost insuperable difficulty*

On a busy bustling day in 1833 at the river wharf in St. Louis, Missouri, a passenger steamboat approached for a routine landing when suddenly the boat's chimney inexplicably collapsed and the matchbox vessel burst into flames. Eight passengers lost their lives and many were injured. A 13-year-old boy named James Buchanan Eads from Indiana, along with his mother and two sisters, survived the conflagration with only the clothes they were wearing. Unfortunately, such tragedies on the frontier were much too common in those days. Six years later, aspiring mud clerk Eads was serving on the steamer *Knickerbocker* when it hit a snag in the turbulent Mississippi River and sank with a large loss of cargo. Three years after that, 22-year-old Eads walked into the St. Louis offices of Case and Nelson shipbuilders, showed them his plans for a salvage boat and diving bell, and offered them partnerships in his new business if they would build the equipment for free. After building his first salvage boat, *Submarine No. 1,* Eads traversed the mucky bottom of the Mississippi River in his diving bell, hunting for wrecks to salvage. In 1849, two dozen steamboats in close proximity were consumed by flames and sank at St. Louis, providing a windfall for Eads' salvage business. Soon, Eads devised boats with pumps and winches capable of raising sunken steamboats and cargo. During the 1850s, Eads bought snag boats from the government and converted them into salvage vessels, then formed a syndicate of 50 insurance companies to finance his operations.

In 1857 at age 37, Eads retired with a personal fortune of $500,000, having raised and set afloat approximately 50 sunken vessels. In April 1861, following the attack on Fort Sumter, Eads wrote to his friend, Attorney General Edward Bates, that "vigorous action must be taken to defeat the South." Bates had the ear of Lincoln, and he told Eads to expect a reply shortly. Eads was summoned to Washington, D.C. to discuss plans to form an inland navy of ironclad gunboats. Up to that point, the Anaconda Plan, proposed by Army Chief General Winfield Scott, had been adopted to blockade the coastline of the Confederacy, preventing the exporting of cotton by the South and the importation of vital goods, especially weaponry and machinery. Due to the extensive length of the Southern coastline (Atlantic and Gulf), the blockade placed a severe strain on the Union's supply of ships, guns, officers, and sailors. A secondary, yet important, part of the plan was to open trade on the Mississippi River from the Ohio at Cairo to the Gulf at New Orleans and in the process split the Confederacy. Besides the blockade and the advance upon the Confederate capital at Richmond, another part of the overall Union military strategy was to invade the Confederate heartland and force open a corridor roughly from Nashville to Chattanooga to Atlanta to Savannah.

On April 29, 1861, Eads forwarded his thoughtful proposal to form a riverine Union navy of gunboats that would retake the lower Mississippi. All of the officials in Washington, including Navy Secretary Gideon Welles, approved of the plan, with the exception of Secretary of War Simon Cameron.

Eads proposed using Cairo, Illinois, as the base of operations on the Western rivers and converting one of his mightiest salvage boats, the double-hulled *Submarine No. 7*, owned by the Missouri Wrecking Company, into a gunboat that would prevent the Confederates from establishing gun batteries on the banks of the river.

Just ten days after the fall of Fort Sumter, Federal forces occupied the small river port of Cairo in a region of southern Illinois known as Little Egypt (the region was prone to flooding and featured Indian mounds that somewhat resembled the pyramids). The city featured ample wharfs on the banks of the Ohio River (where the current was slower than on the Mississippi River) and served as the terminus of the Illinois Central Railroad. Cairo would be the headquarters and staging area for the Federal fight on the Mississippi and home port for what

James Buchanan Eads

U.S. Secretary of the Navy Gideon Welles

Commander John Rodgers (post-war photograph)

would be called the Western Gunboat Flotilla.

War Secretary Cameron later reversed himself and gave his approval to the plan, mainly because he wanted the U.S. Army in control of inland river operations and not the U.S. Navy under Welles.

[At the beginning of World War Two, when it was proposed that army commander General Douglas MacArthur be placed in command of all U.S. forces in the southwest Pacific, including naval forces, Admiral Ernest King would have none of it, arguing that the U.S. Navy should be in control of its own ships.]

After several fits and starts, and trips between St. Louis and Washington, Eads was directed to consult with Major General George McClellan in Cincinnati about forming an inland navy. Welles ordered Commander John Rodgers to Cincinnati to assist in the endeavor, under orders from McClellan. Esteemed naval designer Samuel M. Pook was directed to examine the proposal. It was

## Jefferson's Gunboats

The U.S. Navy used gunboats in great numbers in the early 1800s, although they were much smaller and used exclusively for coastal defense. The wooden gunboats were sail-powered, about 75 feet in length, crewed by 20 to 30 men, and featured a single 32-pounder cannon in the bow. On Sept. 8, 1804, the first American-built gunboat was driven in a storm from her moorings in Georgia high and dry into a cornfield, where she lay stranded for two months. Of the 278 gunboats authorized by Congress, only 176 were built in 1805 to 1807. The gunboats were favored due to their success in fighting the Barbary Coast pirates in their home ports in North Africa and as a less-costly alternative to larger warships such as frigates. Each gunboat cost about $10,000 to build, while a frigate such as the *USS Constitution* cost more than $300,000. The gunboat program was supported by President Thomas Jefferson and his Republican Party. The gunboats along the East Coast could only be used for defensive purposes (one British frigate had 40 times the gunpower as one U.S. gunboat), and the shallow-draught gunboats proved to be effective only in calm waters. The program was quietly abandoned by the James Madison administration. When war against Britain was declared in 1812, the U.S. Navy possessed seven frigates, four schooners, four ketches, and 170 gunboats to pit against the greatest naval power in the world.

determined that the naval equipment for the boats, plus armament and officers and crews, should be fulfilled by the U.S. Navy. It was most likely the largest naval building project since the construction in the early 1800s of the first U.S. naval gunboats under President Jefferson.

Rodgers rejected Eads' proposal to convert *Submarine No. 7* into a gunboat. The "submarine"

*(Continued on Page 20)*

**TYPES of U.S. NAVY GUNBOATS**

**Timberclad:** *USS Conestoga*

**City Class Ironclad:** *USS St. Louis*

**Casemate Ironclad (non-City Class):** *USS Essex*

**River Monitor:** *USS Neosho*

**Light-Draught Tinclad:** *USS Fairplay*

## Dimensions and Specifications of Selected U.S. Navy Gunboats

| | Length | Tonnage | Draught | Speed | Armor | Armament |
|---|---|---|---|---|---|---|
| **Timberclads** | | | | | | |
| *USS Conestoga* | 170 ft. | 279 | 6 ft. | 12 knots | 5-in. thick oak | Four 32-pounder smoothbores |
| *USS Lexington* | 178 ft. | 362 | 6 ft. | 7 knots | 5-in. thick oak | Two 32-pdr smoothbores; four 8-in. Dahlgren smoothbores |
| *USS Tyler* | 180 ft. | 420 | 6 ft. | 8 knots | 5-in. thick oak | One 32-pdr smoothbore; six 8-in. Dahlgren smoothbores |
| **Ironclad-City Class** | | | | | | |
| *USS St. Louis* | 175 ft. | 512 | 6 ft. | 6 knots | 2.5-in. iron plate | 30-pdr Parrott rifle; three 42-pdr rifles; three 64-pdr SB; six 32-pdr SB |
| **Ironclad-Casemate** | | | | | | |
| *USS Essex* | 250 ft. | 640 | 6 ft. | 5.5 knots | 1-in. iron plate | Three 9-in. Dahlgren SB; one 10-in Dahlgren SB; one 32-pdr SB; one 12-pdr howitzer |
| **Ironclad-River Monitor** | | | | | | |
| *USS Neosho* | 180 ft. | 523 | 4 ft. | 12 knots (max.) | 6-in. iron plate (turret) | Two 11-in. Dahlgren smoothbores |
| **Light Draught Tinclads** | | | | | | |
| *USS Fairplay (17)* | 155 ft. | 156 | 5 ft. | 5 knots | Half-inch iron plate | Four 12-pdr smoothbore howitzers |
| *USS Moose (34)* | 155 ft. | 189 | 5 ft. | 6 knots | Half-inch iron plate | Six 24-pdr smoothbore howitzers |
| *USS Brilliant (18)* | 155 ft. | 227 | 5 ft. | 5 knots | Half-inch iron plate | Two 12-pdr Dahlgren rifles; two 12-pdr Dahlgren smoothbores |
| *USS Silver Lake (23)* | 155 ft. | 236 | 5.2 ft. | 7 knots | Half-inch iron plate | Six 24-pdr smoothbore howitzers |

boat was actually a twin-hulled salvage vessel used to recover cargo from underwater wrecks. Later, the army would accept the salvage vessel and convert it into the *USS Benton,* the most powerful ironclad afloat at that time.

At the outset of the Civil War, the business of steamboating on the inland rivers dropped considerably, to say the least. Most of the transport fleet, built

Unloading heavy ordnance at the Cairo, Ill. naval base in 1861

and owned by Northern interests, were moored and unused. There were plenty of boats for the Union military to purchase and convert into gunboats, which was faster and easier than building gunboats from scratch. Unfortunately, river steamboats were built strictly for function, were not very sturdy, and did not last long.

On June 8, 1861, Rodgers purchased three steamers at Cincinnati for conversion into gunboats and charged the expense to the navy, generating a rebuke from Navy Secretary Welles. He sternly advised that the army would foot the bill; that the navy would supply only guns and crews. This dictate in effect put the U.S. Army squarely in charge of what would become the Western Gunboat Flotilla. This "unified" command would remain in effect until September 1862, when the U.S. Navy took over all riverboat flotilla operations.

This was the beginning of a unique, sometimes contentious, cooperation between the army and navy which would reap many dividends. The joint command also necessitated the cooperation of skilled civilians, including that of the river pilots required on each gunboat to navigate the tricky Western rivers.

The first three gunboats were the timberclads *USS Conestoga, USS Lexington,* and *USS Tyler* (sometimes mistakenly called *Taylor*). These were river steamboats converted into lightly armored (five inches of oak planking) and heavily armed gunboats. They were sidewheelers, powered by coal-burning steam engines, and recognizable by their tall twin chimneys (smokestacks). Derisively they were called stinkpots and bandboxes.

The initial conversion of the timberclads left much to be desired. Rogers said the project "was more like the work of Irish laborers than mechanics." More work was required, and repairs on the timberclads would hinder their operations for many months.

On Aug. 12, 1861, the *USS Conestoga* completed its maiden trip down the Ohio and anchored at Cairo. Her captain, Lt. Commander Seth Ledyard Phelps, shook hands with Col. Richard Oglesby of the 8th Illinois Regiment, the first face-to-face encounter between the leaders of U.S. Army forces and the U.S. Navy flotilla.

Besides Eads, Rodgers, and Pook, the establishment of the Western Gunboat Flotilla can also be credited to the efforts of two other men — Brigadier General Joseph G. Totten, who was directed by General Scott to prepare a study of "boatbuilding facilities, distances, steamers for transportation, gunboats, coal supplies, and the like" on the rivers; and John Lenthall, chief of the navy's Bureau of Construction.

Following his inspections, Totten advised that there were 400 steamers available on the rivers for transporting troops, 400 coal barges, and 200 freight barges. Boatbuilding facilities were available at Pittsburg, Pa.; Wheeling, Va.; Cincinnati; Madison and New Albany, Ind.; and Mound City, Ill.

Lenthall drew up plans for what a Western river gunboat would look like — a flat-bottomed sidewheeler about 170 feet long and 28 feet wide that was double-ended, so that the boat could change directions without turning about. Totten suggested that ten to twenty gunboats be built at an average cost of $20,000 each, without public bidding so as not to alert the Confederates as to their intentions.

## The Stevens Battery

Unpropelled artillery batteries or floating gun platforms had been used by the French during the Crimean War in 1855 but prototypes of gigantic proportions dated even further back in time. In 1842, New Jersey engineer Robert Stevens persuaded the U.S. government to invest the unearthly sum of $250,000 and more than two years to develop such a watercraft. By the outbreak of the Civil War, the vessel with six large guns was still not completed although $586,717 had been expended. The semi-submersible boat was 420 feet long and displaced more than 6,000 tons, with sloped iron plating nearly seven inches thick. Eight steam-powered engines producing 900-hp drove two screw propellers and machinery situated below the water line. The boat contained a 1000-ton coal bunker and could make 20 knots (estimated). The death of Stevens in 1856 brought construction to a halt at the Hoboken, N.J. site. Although two brothers offered to finish the project at their own expense, the government declined the offer. The *New York Times* of August 1861 questioned the decision: "If the Government really intends to have an inferior article at a greater cost, the public would be pleased to know some of the reasons. If the Naval Engineers approved of the Stevens Battery it would probably be finished." After the war, the Stevens estate bequeathed the project to New Jersey along with $1 million to complete it. George McClellan was named superintendent and plans were drawn up to convert the battery into a turret ram. Although the million dollars were spent and new engines installed, Congress finally put a halt to the project, and the behemoth was scrapped in 1874.

General Scott approved the report and forwarded it to Secretary of War Cameron on June 10, 1861, recommending that 16 gunboats be built and be ready for service by September 20 of that year. Cameron turned the proposal over to Quartermaster General Montgomery Meigs, who requested that Commander Rodgers have naval designer Pook and his engineers study the proposed designs for suitability of production and operation of gunboats on the Western waters.

Pook consulted builders, engineers, and river captains in the Cincinnati area and then revised Lenthall's design extensively. The gunboats would be 175 feet long and 50 feet wide and draw six feet of water. The flat bottom would have three keels. The double-ender concept was abandoned. The hull would support a casemate (superstructure) that would feature sloped sides and house 20 naval guns. The sides of the casemate and around the steam engines and boilers would be clad in iron plate. Specifications for the steam engines, which would be powered from coal-fired tubular boilers, were drawn up by A. Thomas Merritt and approved by chief naval engineer B.F. Isherwood. A proposal for a gunboat using a screw propeller system was rejected as impractical for the shallow, debris-ridden inland rivers. The sidewheeler concept was rejected in favor of a single enclosed paddlewheel at the stern of the boat. Named for their designer and the appearance of the sloped walls of their casemates and low-lying hulls, these ironclad gunboats would be called "Pook's turtles."

On July 15, 1861, three prominent men from St. Louis wrote to Meigs that their city would be a favorable site for the construction of the proposed gunboats—drydocks were in place; machinery could be manufactured locally; skilled mechanics were available; and its location on the Mississippi allowed for the greatest usage relative to river levels. Three days later, Meigs advertised proposals for bids for the construction of the gunboats. When the seven bids were opened on Aug. 5, 1861, the low bid was by James Eads, who proposed building four to 16 gunboats at $89,600 apiece and delivering them to the government at Cairo in 59 days (by October 5). Subsequently, Eads signed a contract to build seven gunboats for $89,600 each, on or before October 10. For every day he missed the deadline, Eads would forfeit $250 per boat.

The specifications called for casemate ports for 20 guns, an enclosed paddlewheel, 75 tons of protective iron plating, five boilers 25 feet long, a firebox lined with firebrick, and two chimneys 44 inches in diameter and 28 feet high. At some point, the armament requirement was lowered to 13 guns per boat (three bow, four starboard and port, and two astern). The boat's two steam engines would have cast-iron cylinders inclined at a 15-degree angle with a bore of 22 inches and a stroke of six feet. The piston would be attached to a driving rod four inches in diameter and nine feet long. Hartupee and Company of Pittsburg was subcontracted to build and supply the gunboat engines and boilers.

Eads leased the Carondelet Marine Railway and Drydock Co., just south of St. Louis, for the construction site. Meigs named the engine designer Merritt as overall superintendent of the project; Rodgers named John Litherbury to oversee the construction of the gunboats at Carondelet.

Commander Rodgers wrote to the chief of naval ordnance that he needed 35 rifled 42-pounders and 70 nine-inch Dahlgren smoothbores to arm the gunboats, a request that was tentatively denied. The Secretary of the Navy recalled that the War Department had promised to provide 35 rifled 42-pounders for the gunboats and requested they be sent to St. Louis posthaste. Eagle Iron Works of Cincinnati won the contract for providing the wooden gun carriages and implements.

When rumors circulated that Southern sympathizers had vowed to burn the gunboats before they could be launched, Rodgers persuaded Major General John C. Fremont, newly appointed commander of the Western Department at St. Louis, to post a regiment of soldiers at the marine ways. Then, some of the skilled workers at Carondelet threatened to strike for higher wages, but the threat was subsequently averted. At the time, 200 men were working on the four vessels under construction, being paid $2 for a ten-hour day, with 25 cents per hour of overtime. Many of the workers came from boatbuilding ports such as Louisville, Cincinnati,

Lt. Commander Henry Walke

Jeffersonville, and New Albany, and many were recent immigrants.

Due to time constraints, Eads decided to build the remaining three gunboats at the Marine Railway and Ship Yard owned by Captain William Hambleton and located at Mound City. By the end of August, an additional 130 carpenters and workers had been hired, and construction at Mound City commenced immediately. Eventually, 800 men and 13 sawmills in five states would be working on the boats. Two large iron rolling mills in Cincinnati worked day and night for two weeks to produce

*(Continued on Page 27)*

THE COMMANDERS of the Federal gunboats on the Western waters were colorful characters even as they fulfilled their duties in a professional manner. Henry Walke, the commander of the *Carondelet*, was somewhat of a maverick who also developed a talent as a fine artist and illustrator, depicting many of the battles in which he participated. Involuntarily retired in 1855 by the infamous Naval Retiring Board set up by congressional legislation, he was returned to duty (but during the war received only half of the pay due his rank). In early 1861, while commanding the store ship *Supply* off Pensacola, Florida, he elected to remove personnel from the guardian forts and navy yard rather than allow them to become POWs. His actions technically violated previous orders, resulting in a court-martial, complimentary reprimand, and temporary banishment to the post of lighthouse inspector at Williamsport, N.Y. On Sept. 6, 1861, Secretary Welles ordered Walke to St. Louis.

Commander William D. Porter (pictured) was known as Dirty Bill for his "scandalous private life and ability to quarrel with almost anyone." Porter was constantly in debt, a notorious womanizer, and convinced he had secret enemies who were sabotaging his career. The son of the famous War of 1812 naval officer Commodore David Porter and the brother of Rear Admiral David Dixon Porter and step-brother of Admiral David Farragut, Porter was also known as an expert in ship design and naval ordnance. In his diary, Secretary of the Navy Gideon Welles wrote of him, in so many words, like all the Porters, he was a courageous, daring, troublesome, reckless officer. Porter served well in the Mexican War, organized the U.S. Light-House Service, was court-martialed for being absent without leave and was placed on the retired list from 1855-59 but was reinstated and placed in command of the *USS St. Mary's* in the Pacific. Porter commanded the ironclad *USS Essex*, having converted it from the tinclad *New Era* and naming it for his famous father's sailing ship (without permission). The *Essex* was severely damaged at Fort Henry, and Porter was wounded. Later, the *Essex* would duel with the *CSS Arkansas* near Vicksburg.

Timberclad commander William Gwin was later wounded in action on December 27, 1862, while commanding the *USS Benton* in the Battle of Haines Bluff on the Yazoo River. He died from his wounds on Jan. 3, 1863, on board a hospital ship on the Mississippi River. In reporting his death to the Navy Department, Gwin's squadron commander, Rear Admiral Porter, remarked: "The country has lost one of its bravest officers."

At the beginning of the Civil War, Thomas O. Selfridge Jr. helped with efforts to destroy the untenable Norfolk (Va.) Navy Yard. He then escaped from the burning and beleaguered base in the *USS Cumberland,* helping to save the sloop of war for the Union Navy. He participated in the capture of the Hatteras forts and was on board the *Cumberland* on March 8, 1862 when she was sunk by the Confederate ironclad, *CSS Virginia*. He then briefly commanded the *USS Monitor* after Lieutenant John L. Worden was wounded; and then commanded the *Alligator*, an experimental submarine, in testing operations based at the Washington Navy Yard. In August, he joined the Mississippi Squadron, and subsequently commanded the *USS Cairo* and the *USS Conestoga* when those ships were sunk in action.

ILL

MISSISS

Illinois Central R.R.

O H I O

CAIRO

O

Ft Cairo

Confluence of the Mississippi
and Ohio Rivers

CAIRO

Illinois Central R.R.

Prob.

Note: *The Soundings are expressed in feet, and represent a stage of the
River, approximately 12 feet above extreme low water.
The dotted lines indicate sections of the bottom at depths of
6,12 and 18 feet,— thus,*————*6 ft*-------*12 ft*------*18 ft.*

KENTUC

# Mound City

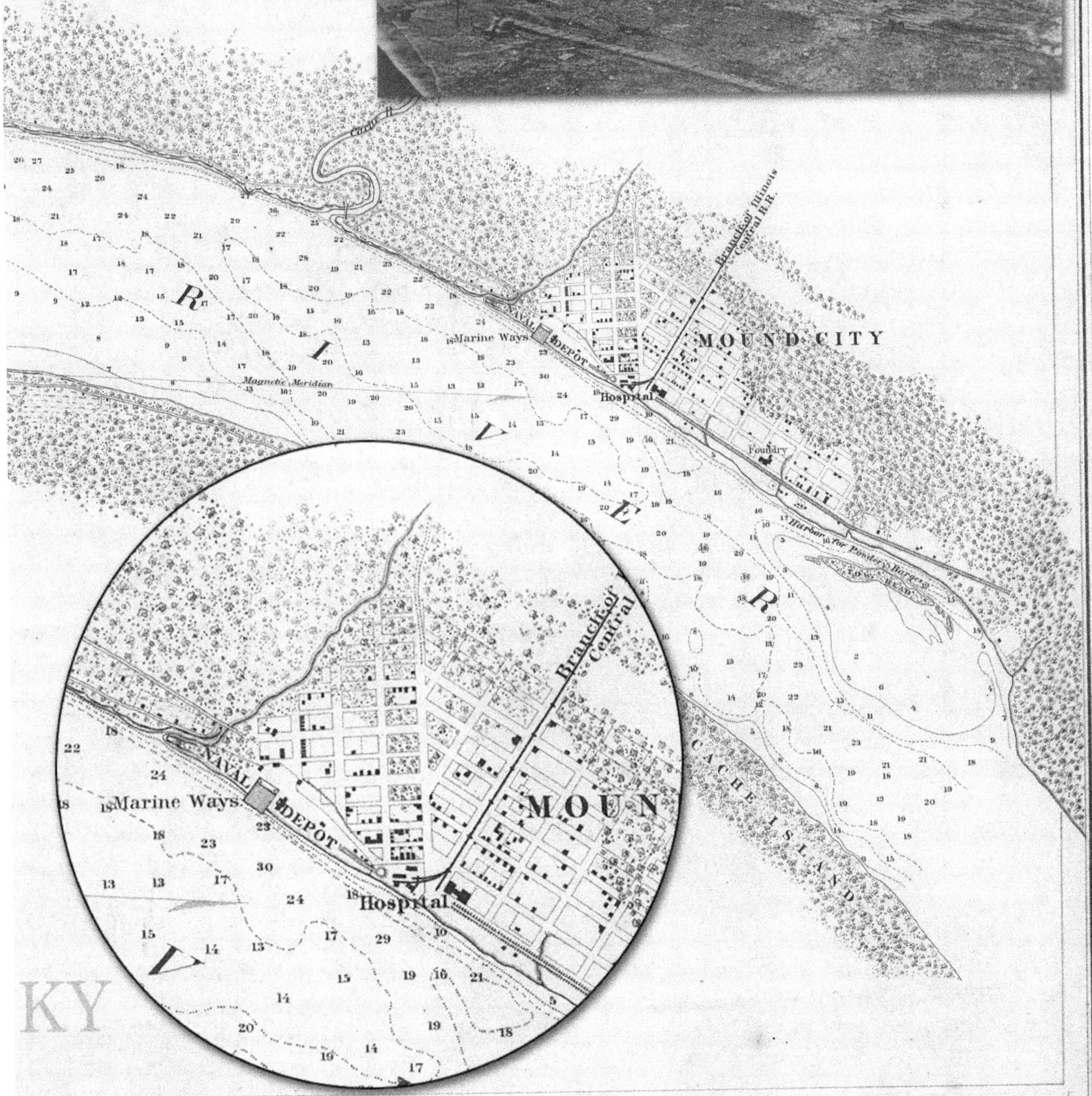

INOIS

KY

MOUND CITY

Branch of Illinois
Central R.R.

Creek

RIVER

Magnetic Meridian

Naval
Marine Ways
DEPÔT

Hospital

Foundry

Harbor for Powder Barges

CACHE ISLAND

MOUN

Marine Ways

Naval DEPÔT

Hospital

Branch of
Central

*Headquarters and Shipbuilding Center for U.S. Gunboat Fleet*

# Cairo, Mound City vital to Western Gunboat Flotilla

Cairo was laid out along the peninsula formed by the confluence of the Mississippi and Ohio rivers, with buildings and docks aligned along the Ohio River side, which boasted a three-mile-long levee 14 feet high. Steam engine pumps worked at keeping out the seepage but the city streets remained muddy at all times. More than 1,000 soldiers from Illinois toiled under the hot summer sun building breastworks along the shore. Several six-pounder brass cannons were the city's only defense. On June 10, 1861, several large 32-pounder cannons arrived from Pittsburg and were positioned and tested. Camp Defiance was beset not only by the steamy weather but disease in the form of fever and diarrhea and poor drinking water supplies. Life at Camp Defiance was hard, tough, and boring. "The inhabitants seemed to revel in dirt," observed one distinguished British reporter. The 42nd Wisconsin Regiment served as the garrison force at Cairo during the war. One Wisconsin volunteer wrote, " I have witnessed hog pens that are palaces compared with our situation here." Residents pronounced the name of their town *ker-row*. Visitors stayed at the St. Charles Hotel. A riverfront store advertised "Family Whiskey, Tar & Feathers, Cowhides, Bowie Knives and Slow Poison," while next door at the dispensary a concoction of whiskey, water, prune juice and caramel coloring sold for 25 cents a shot and came with a free lunch of cheese, cold cuts, rye bread, pickles, and hard-boiled eggs. The town boasted of 90 saloons, one for each 200 residents, and one murder per week. When a new tavern opened, the owner threw the key into the river to signify that the door was always open. In October 1861, General John McClernand ordered the saloons shut down. The headquarters of the Western Gunboat Flotilla, commanded by Captain A.M. Pennock, USN, was housed in a wharfboat owned by Graham & Halliday Co.

Ohio Street ran along the wharf and featured the quartermaster's office and warehouse, post and district headquarters and the Ohio Building (Grant's headquarters).

Three years before the war, Mound City, named for a nearby Indian mound, merged with Emporium City, a planned riverport that had gone bust. The shipyards and marine ways were purchased by Hambleton, Collier & Co. and were leased to the U.S. government for $40,000 a year. The naval yard was the largest of the war, home port for 100 gunboats and 200 other vessels. Three of the Eads City Class ironclads were built there, and many gunboats received repairs there during the war. Fifteen hundred men were employed at peak times. The *USS Red Rover*, the first hospital boat of the United States Navy, was commissioned at Mound City in June 1862. More than 1,500 patients were treated aboard the boat from 1862 to 1865, and 157 died on board. One of the warehouses built by the Emporium Company was converted into the Mound City Naval Hospital in 1861. Two thousand Union casualties from the battle at Shiloh were treated there. The hospital was staffed by the Nursing Sisters of the Holy Cross, St. Mary's Convent, of South Bend, Ind. The hospital building burned down in 1976.

Today, the once-thriving commercial district of Cairo resembles more of a delapidated ghost town, having seen its better days. Fort Defiance State Park lies at the confluence of the rivers and offers a good view and little else. In Mound City, all that remains of the marine ways from the Civil War era are some sliding ramps, rails, and some concrete foundations. The small riverport is the site of the Mound City National Cemetery. Both ports do serve barge traffic today, mostly dealing in grain shipments.

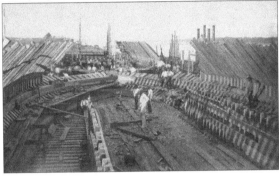

Construction of the City Class casemate ironclads at the Carondelet Marine Railway and Drydock Co., near St. Louis, Mo. Upper left shows four gunboats constructed simultaneously. Left shows the timberwork and slanted sides of the casemates. Above shows the five boilers, each three feet in diameter and 24 feet long.

the iron cladding. Gaylord, Son and Company in Portsmouth, Ohio, and Newport, Ky. rolled 700 tons of iron into 2.5-inch-thick plates for the cladding. In building the boats, Eads determined that each boat would require not the 75 tons of ironcladding specified, but actually 122 tons, an increase of 63 percent in weight.

By the second week of September, the engines

Map of Cairo, Ill. shows the unique routing of the railroad.

and boilers were almost ready for delivery, but Eads had run into a problem — the government had not been paying him for the work completed as agreed upon in the contract. He had spent $700,000 on the project so far and had not received a penny from the government. Sub-contractors were pressuring him for payment. The government forked over about $44,000, which was not nearly enough, Eads said, to prevent him from "being cramped and annoyed for money."

As work progressed, the builders became curious as to the strength of the ironcladding and set up a test range on the sandy Mississippi shore opposite the Carondelet boatyards. Lt. Albert R. Buffington of the St. Louis Arsenal oversaw the firing of two 10-pounder Parrott rifles into sheets of gunboat iron securely fastened at a 35-degree angle to oak blocks 16 inches thick. At 800 yards it was difficult to hit the target, but one shot dislodged a bolt fastener and made a "raking" mark. At 500 yards, the solid shot made a one-inch indentation. Moving ever closer, at 200 yards, the shot made a deep indentation but no sign of cracking or breaking. Finally, at 100 yards (point-blank range) and the iron set up perpendicular, the projectile knocked

(Continued on Page 30)

# MOUND CITY

on the Illinois shore of the Ohio River, in addition to being headquarters, served as a major refitting and repair center for the gunboats of the U.S. Navy's Mississippi Squadron and the site of a major military hospital.

THE MARINE WAYS

DURING THE CIVIL WAR THE NAVAL DEPOT OF THE WESTERN RIVER FLEET WAS LOCATED AT MOUND CITY. HERE THE KEELS OF THREE OF THE FAMOUS EADS IRONCLAD GUNBOATS WERE LAID, AND A LARGE FORCE OF WORKMEN WERE EMPLOYED TO KEEP THE FLEET IN FIGHTING TRIM. THE MARINE WAYS, STILL IN OPERATION, ARE 400 YARDS SOUTH OF HERE.
ERECTED BY THE STATE OF ILLINOIS 1935.

the target down and splintered it into a thousand pieces. Commander Rodgers concluded, "The iron resisted beyond all expectations, and proved to be of a very superior quality." The performance of the iron in actual combat, they would later learn, would be a different experience.

On Sept. 4, 1861, the same day that Brigadier General U.S. Grant established his command at Cairo, the Confederates made a stupendous strategic blunder. Gen. Leonidas Polk, the "fighting bishop," directed a 1,500-man rebel force to occupy the Kentucky town of Columbus on the Mississippi River. This movement, in effect, violated the state of Kentucky's tenuous neutrality (the state would remain in the Union but had two state capitals during the war). The high cliffs at Columbus were subsequently fortified with so many big guns that it was called the Gibralter of the West. Realizing what was happening, Grant immediately moved to occupy Paducah and Smithland, at the mouths of the Tennessee and Cumberland rivers, respectively.

Work progressed on the ironclads until at last the glorious day arrived, on Saturday afternoon, Oct. 12, 1861 (two days past the deadline) when the first ironclad gunboat in the Western Hemisphere was launched at Carondelet with so much care and consideration that, according to newspaper reports, "not even a lady was frightened." This first gunboat would be named the *Carondelet*. The second vessel, the *St. Louis,* was launched three days later, and the other two, the *Louisville* and the *Pittsburg*, would slide into the river the third week of October. Thus were born the City Class of ironclad "casemate" gunboats, named after ports on the rivers.

The *St. Louis* would be the first of the gunboats to be fitted out and, by the end of 1861, ready for combat. When the flotilla was turned over to the U.S. Navy in October 1862 the name of the *USS St. Louis* was changed to *USS Baron deKalb* because the Navy already had a ship named *St. Louis*. The ironclad was named for Baron Johann DeKalb, a German officer and major general in George Washington's Revolutionary War army. The other ironclads were not commissioned until January 1862. These included *Mound City, Cairo,* and *Cincinnati*, all built at the Mound City works.

Flag Officer Andrew H. Foote

On Sept. 6, 1861, command of the Western Flotilla was taken from Rodgers and assigned to Captain Andrew Hull Foote, a naval veteran who was soon elevated to the rank of Flag Officer. It was Foote who rejected the original names for the ironclads (Eads suggested naming the ironclads for generals and prominent officials) and named them for cities along the river. Foote was a competent and able seaman, highly disciplined, religious, and vehement in his disgust for liquor. While other sailors might be issued a well-earned dram of whiskey, Foote would not allow alcohol to be consumed in his command. Hardworking, Foote died during the war, in June of 1863. The attending surgeon would tell Foote's brother, "Your brother

*(Continued on Page 32)*

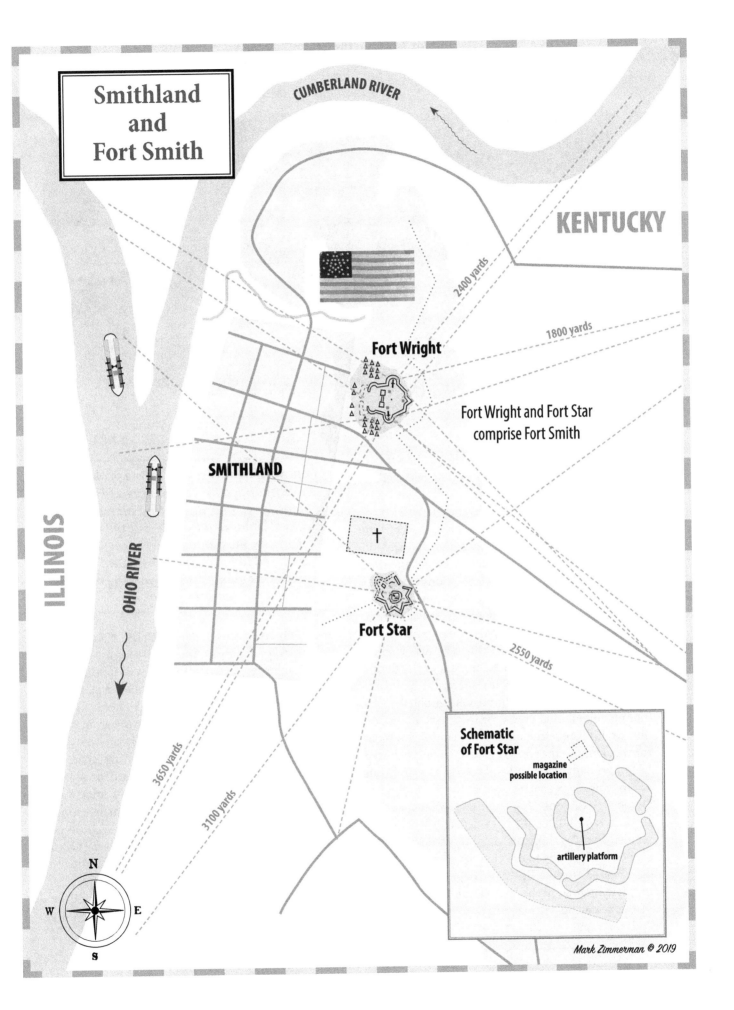

Smithland
and
Fort Smith

CUMBERLAND RIVER

KENTUCKY

Fort Wright

Fort Wright and Fort Star
comprise Fort Smith

SMITHLAND

2400 yards

1800 yards

ILLINOIS

OHIO RIVER

Fort Star

2550 yards

3650 yards

3100 yards

N
W        E
S

Schematic
of Fort Star

magazine
possible location

artillery platform

Mark Zimmerman © 2019

Gundeck of a U.S. City Class ironclad gunboat.

has literally worn himself out in the public service. He is truly a victim of this war as if he perished on the battlefield."

Foote noted in his diary the difficulties of establishing the flotilla: "The service on the Western rivers was anomalous. The officers of the Navy in charge of the vessels being transferred, for the time being, to act under the general directions of the War Department, with the want of navy-yard facilities, and having but a single navy officer to each vessel, superadded to the want of navy equipments and stores, especially in the ordnance department, rendered the building and equipment of the flotilla a work of almost insuperable difficulty."

One of Foote's most immediate problems was finding able-bodied crews for the boats, a mission that would plague the naval command throughout the war. Duty on the gunboats was generally believed to be too dangerous and not nearly as glamorous as working on a seafaring ship. By the middle of October 1861, only 100 men had volunteered to serve. A month later, the navy department sent 500 seamen from Washington to Cairo. When mustered a week later, it was found that 58 men had simply disappeared enroute. The naval department warned that few men could be spared due to the increase in the seafaring saltwater fleet. Foote claimed he

*One of Foote's most immediate problems was finding able-bodied crews for the boats, a mission that would plague the naval command throughout the war. Duty on the gunboats was generally believed to be too dangerous and not nearly as glamorous as working on a seafaring ship.*

needed an additional 1,100 men. The navy shifted the burden of supplying men to the army. General McClellan ordered General Henry W. Halleck (who had succeeded Fremont as commander in St. Louis) to detail 1,100 soldiers stationed in St. Louis to man the gunboats. The army insisted, however, that the army men, labelled "marines," would answer only to army officers. By January the now-commissioned gunboats averaged only 60 men onboard, one-third of the actual crew needed. Freedmen of color were allowed to serve on the gunboats much sooner than they were allowed to enlist in the U.S. Colored Troops infantry. They drew the same pay ($18 a month, almost half that of infantrymen) and were employed as gunners, cooks, and coal tenders.

Foote complained about the need for manning the gunboats, noting that he had enough crew for only

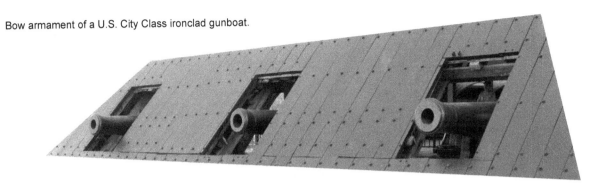

Bow armament of a U.S. City Class ironclad gunboat.

seven of the existing eleven gunboats. Grant suggested converting men from the brig into sailors, and Foote did not object. Infantrymen who were trouble for their commanders were offered up for gunboat service along with men such as the 4th Illinois Cavalry, mostly Norwegians and Germans who could barely speak English. Also, one man accused of trying to kill his lieutenant who chose gunboat duty instead of a court-martial.

Meanwhile, Eads was petitioning the government for the $150,000 in payments owed to him according to the contract. During construction, the government had not kept up with its partial payments. Quartermaster Meigs reminded Eads that the gunboats had not been completed on time; the government was due damages. Eads wrote: "The Govt. failed to pay me according to agreement, and I failed to build the boats in time — Question, am I liable to forfeiture?"

As it would happen, the Union military attacked Fort Henry in February 1862 using gunboats that it legally did not own. Meigs assigned a staff member to investigate all claims and his subsequent report was generally favorable to Eads, who had not been paid promptly and had to deal with changes in specifications and additional workload. The Union victory at Fort Henry also aided Eads' cause. In mid-February, $234,781 in government bonds were issued to Eads as final payment.

It was after the war that master engineer Eads

> COMMANDING the seven ironclads and the three timberclads, plus the *Essex*, were:
>
> USS *Cairo* — Lt. James M. Pritchett initially, then Lt. Nathaniel Bryant by the time of Fort Henry
>
> USS *Louisville* — Lt. Commander Benjamin M. Dove
>
> USS *Cincinnati* — Lt. Commander Roger N. Stembel
>
> USS *Carondelet* — Lt. Commander Henry Walke
>
> USS *Mound City* — Lt. Commander Augustus H. Kilty
>
> USS *Pittsburg* — Lt. Commander Egbert Thompson
>
> USS *St. Louis* — Lt. Commander Leonard Paulding
>
> USS *Essex* — Lt. Commander William "Dirty Bill" Porter
>
> USS *Conestoga* — Lt. Commander Seth Ledyard Phelps
>
> USS *Lexington* — Stembel, then Lt. Commander James W. Shirk
>
> USS *Tyler* — Walke, then Lt. Commander William Gwin

accomplished his most impressive projects. In 1874, the Eads Bridge, named after its designer and engineer, opened in St. Louis, the first bridge over the Mississippi River. In a test of strength, Eads placed 14 railway locomotives on the bridge at one time. After renovations in the late 1900s, the Eads Bridge still stands and is in use today. Eads then tackled the problem of deepening the channel at the mouth of the Mississippi, proposing and then building jetties as a solution. In the five years after the new channel was opened, cargo shipping from New Orleans increased 6,500 percent. Eads died in 1887, still advocating his plan to build a ship railway across the Panama isthmus. In 1932 the Deans of American Colleges of Engineering named Eads as one of the five greatest engineers of all time.

Late in the fall of 1861, itching to take action, Grant and Foote devised a plan to attack the Confederate camp on the Mississippi River at Belmont, Missouri, opposite Columbus. On Nov. 7, 1861, the timberclads *Tyler* and *Lexington* escorted five troop transports to a landing site just upstream from Belmont. While the U.S. troops attacked the Confederate camp, the gunboats engaged in a shooting match with the Columbus batteries, evading hits as moving targets. Grant's troops drove the rebels from the camp but then began looting the campsite. The rebels circled around and, with newly arrived reinforcements from Columbus, nearly surrounded Grant's men. Grant pushed his men through the entanglement and hightailed it back to the transports just in time to avoid a terrible defeat. The men were hastily evacuated under the protection of the timberclads. Grant's expedition wasn't much of a victory, but he did demonstrate the usefulness of joint army-navy operations, the use of transports and gunboat escorts for unopposed amphibious landings of troops, and his willingness to meet the enemy and engage. It was Grant's first taste of combat in the Civil War.

On Jan. 15, 1862, following the required inspections, the seven City Class ironclads were accepted into service by Flag Officer Foote.

Following the successful invasion of Middle Tennessee up the Tennessee and Cumberland rivers, many of the heavy gunboats spent most of their time on the Lower Mississippi and its tributaries. Military occupation called for constant patrols and the guarding of cargo transport convoys from Cincinnati and Louisville to Nashville. What was needed was a faster light-draught gunboat — the tinclad. The first tinclad was built out of the necessity for faster, more maneuverable light-draught gunboats to patrol the rivers such as the Tennessee and Cumberland. The timberclads had been built as an expedient; the ironclads were just too slow and expensive to build. Steamers could be purchased for about $10,000 each and cheaply converted into tinclads. In contrast, the cheapest ironclad on the rivers cost more than $92,000. The

The business end of a 32-pounder naval gun.

failure of the ironclads during the disastrous White River expedition in June 1862 drove home the point. The tinclads were all converted from existing steamboats, heavily armed yet lightly armored. The term "tinclad" was coined by the newspapers because the boats were clad in thin iron armor, enough to protect against small arms and light artillery. There was no tin involved. Much of the protection came from heavy wooden bulkheads.

No two tinclads were similar in appearance. All were numbered in sequence. Of the 72 total, 49 were stern-wheelers; the other 23 were highly maneuverable side-wheelers. The tinclads were usually 150 to 175 feet long and armed with six to eight cannon, typically shiny Dahlgren brass howitzers.

The first tinclad was the 86-ton stern-wheeler *Alfred Robb,* a former Confederate transport discovered on April 21, 1862 in Crane Creek near Florence, Alabama, in good condition. It was armed and clad at Cairo, manned with a crew of 30, and put under the command of Master Jason Goudy.

Put in charge of purchasing and equipping the light-draught fleet, nicknamed the Mosquito Fleet, was Commodore Joseph B. Hull, who had served in the U.S. Navy since 1813. Naval constructor Edward Hartt from the New York Navy Yard would serve as the actual construction superintendent.

# –Chapter Three–

# The Gunboats

*Pook's turtles, stinkpots, bandboxes, the seven sisters,*
*hasty conversions, rotting hulls, and other hardluck vessels*

The Western Gunboat Flotilla began as three timberclads — the *Conestoga*, *Lexington*, and the *Tyler* — which were converted steamer transports armed with a variety of heavy guns and armored with heavy oak timbers and planks. These three gunboats performed yeoman's service during the entire war and saw action on all the inland waters. None were seriously damaged in combat but they were often in need of repair due to their hasty construction.

The first gunboats designed and built from scratch for riverine service were the seven City Class casemate ironclads designed by Samuel Pook and built by James Eads. Essentially identical in construction, they also served for most of the war. They were instrumental in the Cumberland and Tennessee river invasions at the beginning of the war, then served mostly on the Lower Mississippi River and its tributaries. To patrol the rivers and escort supply convoys, a lighter and faster craft was needed. Lightly armored and adequately armed, drawing a shallow draught, the tinclads performed well in those duties. All were converted from steamers and no two were the same design. Late in the war, another craft was seen in action, the river monitor. The *USS Neosho* was one of only two ironclad, low-board paddlewheelers sporting a twin-gun revolving turret in the bow. These vessels were extremely powerful and virtually indestructable, although costly to build and difficult to maneuver.

# Age of Steam on the Rivers

Many of the steamboats converted into tinclads had originally been built in Cincinnati, Ohio or New Albany, Ind., but most probably were built in the Pittsburg, Pa. area where the Monongahela and Allegheny rivers meet to form the Ohio River. Fully one-third of all steamboats on the western waters were built in this area, particularly Bridgeport and Brownsville. From 1825-1903, more than 700 steamboats were built in this area.

"The western river steamer was a particularly American invention that became a symbol of national pride, technological progress, and economic growth," according to historian Louis C. Hunter. "The fact that boiler explosions made steamboats dangerous in some ways added to their allure. To most people, though, the benefits of steamboats to commerce were much greater than the costs of accidents."

Hauling cargo by flatboats and keelboats had been tedious. Boats arriving downriver at New Orleans were scrapped for their lumber and the crews hiked or rode back home. As early as the 1780s the idea of developing a river steamboat had occurred to several inventors, including John Fitch, who operated the first American steamboat on the Delaware River in 1786. Robert Fulton of Lancaster, Pa., operating his *Clermont* on the Hudson River in 1807, was aware that the real impact of steamboats would be in the West. In 1811, Fulton and associates launched the *New Orleans,* which traveled two thousand miles from Pittsburg to New Orleans in two months. The first roundtrip was made by the *Enterprise,* captained by Henry Shreve. In December 1814, the boat brought arms and ammunition to General Andrew Jackson's soldiers at New Orleans. Shreve manned a cannon himself during the battle. The trip to Louisiana took 14 days; the return trip upriver took 54.

The *General Jackson,* built in 1817 in Pittsburg for $16,000, was the first steamboat to arrive in Nashville, to great fanfare, on March 11, 1819, marking the beginning of a new era. On Christmas Day 1850, the first railroad locomotive, *Tennessee,* arrived in Nashville, at the wharf aboard a steamer.

Initially, steamboats utilized one steam engine to drive a stern paddlewheel. Later it was advantageous to use two steam engines. When dual engines were used to power separate sidewheel paddles, the riverboats became much more maneuverable. During the 1840s, experiments using four steam engines (two engines each powering one-half of the stern paddlewheel) proved to be unsuccessful.

It is interesting to note that the Nashville Bridge Co. (NABRICO) produced dozens of warships in the form of barges, mine sweepers, tugboats, and destroyers at the city's wharfs during World War Two. In Evansville, Ind. on the Ohio River, Missouri Valley Bridge & Iron produced 167 huge LSTs (Landing Ships-Tank), which were used to land Sherman tanks, motorized vehicles, and troops during amphibious landings in North Africa, France, and the Pacific.

Today, the tourism giant Opryland USA operates the modern *General Jackson* showboat between its riverside hotel site and downtown Nashville. NABRICO continues operations as Trinity Industries at Ashland City, Tennessee.

Typical 1850s steam transport

## The Timberclads

As of June 1, 1861, there were 60 steamboats on the rolls at Cincinnati, 53 of which were idled. Another 50 were available at Wheeling, Va. and Pittsburg, Pa. After a brief survey, Navy Commander John Rodgers and associates decided on three side-wheelers, the *A.O. Tyler*, the *Conestoga*, and the *Lexington*. They were sold to the government for $62,000 or two-thirds their original price. Renovations would be made by Daniel Morton of Marine Railway and Drydock Co. of Cincinnati at a cost of $41,000, with a deadline of June 27. The conversion of steamboat transports into gunboats would be an unprecedented process; there were no existing written or drawn plans. Most, but not all, of the subsequent gunboats, either constructed or converted, would be stern paddlewheelers.

The *Conestoga* was the smallest, least expensive, and the fastest of the three timberclads, and would serve as the timberclad flotilla's flagboat. The *Lexington* was the newest, the most expensive, the slowest, and would become the best-known due to her extensive wartime service. The *Lexington's* twin chimneys were located near the bow of the boat while the chimneys on the other two boats were amidships. The *Tyler* was the oldest, largest, and heaviest but one knot faster than the *Lexington*. Earlier, in January 1861, as a transport, she had been fired upon at Vicksburg, sunk, and then salvaged.

The purchases raised a firestorm because Rodgers had exceeded his orders. The naval man was reprimanded by the War Department, which reserved the right to acquire the inland river gunboats. Without going into the tedious details, Rodgers had also failed to cultivate good relations and file timely reports with his superiors, resulting in his ultimate replacement.

Due to the unprecedented nature of the conversion work, along with commonplace greed and incompetence, the work on the three gunboats was done poorly and with inferior materials. Green wood was used which eventually shrank and opened up seams which had to be caulked. The main decks and cabins required a complete overhaul. Some of the painting and carpentry was not finished by the time Rodgers needed to send the timberclads downriver to Cairo, due to the falling of the water level. Some of the work would not be completed until October.

The timberclads patroled the twin rivers at the beginning of the war and participated in the battle at Belmont, the captures of Fort Henry and Fort Donelson, and Shiloh. The timberclads conducted the daring Phelps Raid up the Tennessee River in February 1862. Afterwards, they served the remainder of the war on the Lower Mississippi. For a brief period, the converted steamboat *New Era* served as the fourth timberclad, cruising the Tennessee in the fall of 1861 before her conversion to the ironclad *Essex*.

### USS Conestoga

The *Conestoga* was the smallest, least expensive, and fastest (12 knots) of the timberclads, and served as Commander Seth L. Phelps' flagboat. Built in 1859 at Brownsville, Pa., the vessel weighed 279 tons. Due to lack of documentation, her exact dimensions are not known. She could be differentiated from the *Lexington* by the fact that her twin chimneys were centered instead of forward, and from the *Tyler* by a different pattern wheelbox. Her two sidewheels were powered by two single-cylinder high-pressure reciprocating-beam steam engines. The cylinders were two feet in diameter; the length of the piston stroke was seven feet.

The *Conestoga* participated at Lucas Bend in September 1861, Canton, Fort Henry and Fort Donelson, the Phelps raid, Island No. 10, the disastrous White River and Red River campaigns, and scouting on the Black and Ouchita rivers. She was accidentally rammed and sunk on March 8, 1864 by the *USS General Price,* the only timberclad lost during the war. The *Conestoga* was commanded by Lt. Commander Phelps, Lt. George Blodgett, and Lt. Commander Thomas O. Selfridge, Jr.

### USS Lexington

The *Lexington* was 183 feet in length, 40 feet wide, and seven feet deep in the hold, and weighed 362 tons. She was built by L.M. Speer at Belle Vernon, Pa. in 1860. Recognizable by her chimneys located near

*(Continued on Page 40)*

# TIMBERCLAD
## USS Tyler

The *USS Tyler* was the largest of the three so-called timberclads, the earliest of the Western river gunboats, measuring 178 feet in length. The photo at upper left shows wash day onboard, with laundry hung out to dry. The larger photo displays a few of the crew out in a skiff and the gunboat's most prominent features—the tall twin chimneys amidship, the twin side-mounted paddlewheels, and the thick oak bulwarks and open gunports.

the bow, she was regarded as the slowest (7 knots) of the three timberclads. Three boilers lowered in the hold worked a pair of 30-foot waterwheels. The boat drew 4 feet, 7 inches of water. There were three 4.5-foot bulkheads running the entire length

of the hold, with crosswise bulkheads, forming 35 watertight compartments under the main deck. The eight-foot-tall above-deck bulwarks were pierced for eleven guns, five on each side and one astern, all 32-pounder and 64-pounder smoothbores. The *Lexington* served at Columbus and Belmont, Fort Henry, the Phelps raid, and Shiloh. In January 1862 she assisted in the capture of Arkansas Post. In June 1862, she served in the White River campaign, and on the Yazoo River late that year. From February to May, 1863, she escorted convoys and fought guerrillas on the Tennessee and Cumberland. In 1864, she participated in the Black, Ouchita, and Red river campaigns and helped defeat an attack on White River Station. She was commanded by Commander Roger M. Stembel, Lt. Commander James W. Shirk, and Lt. Commander George M. Bache.

### USS Tyler

Built in 1857 in Cincinnati, the *A.O. Tyler* sank and was salvaged in 1861. In January 1861, the steamer transport was fired upon by batteries near Vicksburg on the Mississippi River during what one historian calls the first shots of the Civil War. Converted to a timberclad, the gunboat was the largest of the three, measuring 178 feet long with a 45 foot beam. The modified steamer displaced between 420 and 575 tons (the heaviest timberclad), drawing 6 to 7 feet of water. Her two-cylinder engine produced a speed of 8 knots. She was sometimes erroneously referred to as the *Taylor*. According to one account, the gunboat consumed 1,000 bushels of coal on a trip from Memphis to Cairo. The *Tyler* crew numbered 67 officers and sailors (the number of crew for the other two timberclads is not known). The

*Tyler's* armament included six 8-inch guns and one 32-pounder. In 1863, three 30-pounder Parrotts replaced the 32-pounders, augmenting the 8-inch guns. Still later, four 24-pounders were added. The ship often carried a 12-pound howitzer for landing duties. In one of the earliest contests between Federal and Confederate warships, the *Tyler* and *Lexington* exchanged shots with a rebel gunboat on the Mississippi River off Hickman, Ky. on Sept. 4, 1861. The *Tyler* supported U.S. Grant's landings and assault on Belmont, Mo., in November 1861. Following Shiloh, the *Tyler*, along with the other timberclads, operated against Confederate positions around Vicksburg. While patrolling the Yazoo River on June 15, 1862, in conjunction with the *USS Carondelet* and the *USS Star of the West*, the *Tyler* came under fire from the *CSS Arkansas*. With the *Carondelet* taken out of action and the *Star of the West* in retreat, the *Tyler* alone faced the rebel ironclad. The *Tyler* was damaged but managed to reach the safety of the main Federal fleet. The *Tyler* spent the rest of the war patrolling the Lower Mississippi. The *Tyler* was captained by Commander John Rodgers II, Commander Henry Walke (Sept. 1861), Lt. William Gwin (Dec. 1861), and Lt. Commander George M. Bache.

### The Ironclads

The seven City Class casemate ironclads built by James Eads at Carondelet, Mo. and Mound City, Ill. in the fall and winter of 1861 were the first U.S. ironclad gunboats ever built. Several of the "seven sisters" participated in the captures of Fort Henry and Fort Donelson, and the *USS Cairo* led the flotilla which captured Nashville. The *Carondelet* participated in the Battle of Nashville in December 1864; otherwise, the City Class ironclads participated in the various campaigns of the Lower Mississippi for most of the war. The dimensions and specifications for the City Class ironclads were virtually identical; only the color of the bands near the top of their chimneys were different.

The ironclads were sometimes called Pook's turtles due to their appearance and to their designer, Samuel Pook. Each ironclad was 175 feet long and 51 feet wide with a draft of only six feet and displaced 888 tons. The flat bottom had three keels. The estimated weight of the hull and casemate was 350 tons plus 122 tons of charcoal-iron plating (armor) at 2.5 inches thick. However, the plating covered only the bow and halfway back the sides of the casemate. The casemate was sloped 35 degrees on the sides and 45 degrees on the ends. The exterior was painted black and the interior white-washed. The contract cost for each boat was $89,600. The actual cost was $101,808.

The behemoths were capable of only six knots and consumed one ton of coal per hour. Often, the ironclads had to be towed or lashed to another vessel. Some towed their own coal barges as sources of fuel. Despite the enormous number of bushels of coal that had to be loaded aboard each ironclad, in addition to the bags of gunpowder, artillery shells, rations, and numerous other types of gear, the gunboats did not have a hatch — all supplies had to be loaded through the gunports!

Each ironclad was armed with 13 big guns — four on each side, three in the bow, and two in the stern. These consisted of:

- Three 42-pound army rifles
- Three 64-pound navy smoothbores
- Six 32-pound navy smoothbores
- One 32-pound Parrott gun

The crew of a City Class ironclad numbered 175, composed of the commander and 16 officers, 27 petty officers, 111 seamen, 4 or 5 landsmen, 1 or 2 apprentices, 12 firemen, and 4 coal heavers.

One of the most important men aboard the gunboat did not belong to the military at all—the river pilot. "The contract river pilots aboard the river gunboats," stated historian Myron "Jack" Smith, "have often been singled out for special praise as they were, collectively, perhaps the bravest men aboard. Their position was completely anomalous, being civilians subject to military authority and able to legally exercise no authority save that concerning navigation. Despite Confederate sharpshooters attempting to kill them and thereby disabling the boats they were guiding, many came forward for the positions, even knowing the danger." One courageous pilot would be awarded the Medal of Honor.

When they were not standing patrol, keeping the vessel shipshape or busy with other menial but necessary tasks, the crew was subject to constant drill to the point where they could conduct their duties in their sleep. Each gun required a crew of 12 to operate it in combat. "During their drills," stated Smith, "especially those at the guns, sailors stepped lively, or faced abuse—usually verbal—from the officer in charge or their own mates. Serving a cannon in a slipshod manner could mean death. Safety and speed were essential; uniform (often just bell-bottom trousers and undershirts) and decorum were less important than proficiency. In fact, Flag Officer Foote ordered that all vessels under his command be ready to open fire within five minutes." Although the gun crews were trained to be quick and efficient, reports indicate that the gunboat commanders constantly emphasized the accurate and steady aiming of the heavy guns. Rarely were they discharged without a specific target in their sights. The strident Foote lectured on the evils of "wasted ammunition," noting that each firing of a gun cost the government eight dollars.

One British correspondent noted of the Union sailors, "It will run hard against the Confederates when they get such men at work on the rivers—for they seem to understand their business thoroughly."

Although seasoned seamen (man-'o-war men) were sought and used well, most of the sailors came from Philadelphia and Boston and were untrained. The seamen included Maine lumbermen, New Bedford whalers, New York liners, and Philadelphia sea lawyers. Crews consisted of foreigners, mostly Irishmen, but some English, Scots, French, German, and Scandanavian. Unlike the Union army, black freedmen or runaway slaves (contraband) could serve on a gunboat, usually as coal heavers.

## USS Cairo

Built at Mound City, her chimney bands were gray.

*(Continued on Page 43)*

| | **24-Pdr. Heavy** | **12-Pdr. Heavy** | **12-Pdr. Light** | **12-Pdr. Small** | **12-Pdr. Rifled** | **20-Pdr. Rifled** |
|---|---|---|---|---|---|---|
| **DAHLGREN BOAT HOWITZERS (US NAVY)** | | | | | | |
| **Bore Diameter** | 5.82 in. | 4.62 in. | 4.62 in. | 4.62 in. | 3.4 in. | 4 in. |
| **Bore Length** | 58.2 in. | 55.23 in. | 44 in. | 35.7 in. | 55.23 in. | 58.2 in. |
| **Chamber depth** | 6 in. | 5.23 in. | 5.23 in. | 5.23 in. | 5.23 in. | 6 in. |
| **Overall length** | 68.2 in. | 63.5 in. | 50.95 in. | 42.5 in. | 63.5 in. | 68.2 in. |
| **Diameter at breech** | 11.42 in. | 9 in. | 8 in. | 7.6 in. | 9 in. | 11.42 in. |
| **Diameter at muzzle** | 8.82 in. | 7.24 in. | 6.42 in. | 6.42 in. | 7.24 in. | 7 in. |
| **Weight** | 1,310 lbs. | 760 lbs. | 430 lbs. | 300 lbs. | 870 lbs. | 1,350 lbs. |

*Pictured is a 12-Pounder Howitzer on a boat carriage; wheeled carriages were available for duty on land.*

# Federal Gunboats Armed with Variety of Heavy Ordnance

The timberclads and the City Class ironclads were self-propelled, floating gun platforms. The ironclads sported 13 heavy pieces of artillery each, mounted on wooden carriages and requiring a gun crew of 12 to operate. All these guns were muzzleloaders. The most popular gun was the 32-pounder smoothbore, dating to the 1840s, and cast of bronze. According to this specification, the projectile weighed 32 pounds. Smoothbores fired round shot (solid balls), shells (hollow and filled with explosive, with a fuse), grapeshot, canister, and shrapnel. The last three charges consisted of small solid shot or pieces of metal; they converted the cannon into a giant shotgun, used against enemy personnel at short ranges. A newer cannon was the rifle, which fired an enlongated cylindrical shell or bolt through grooves or twists cut into the bore. The bolt came out of the muzzle spinning, which gave it more distance and far more accuracy than a smoothbore. Some cannons were designated by the diameter of their bore, e.g., a 9-inch Dahlgren. The weight of the cannon tube was expressed in the British measurement of hundredweight (cwt.), which equals 112 pounds. Thus, a 32-pounder of 42 cwt. fired a 32-pound shell from a tube weighing roughly 4,700 pounds. The 32-pounder guns came in 27, 32, 42, and 57 cwt. A 32-pounder of 42 cwt. with a six-pound gunpowder charge could hurl a 32-pound cannonball 1,656 yards (one mile = 1,760

yards) at five degrees elevation in six seconds.

The Dahlgren gun was invented by Rear Admiral John A. Dahlgren (pictured) and incorporated a smooth, rounded design (they were called soda bottles) that minimized the risk of explosion. They were made of cast iron and could be smoothbores or rifles. There were many different models. The 8-inch Dahlgren came in 55 or 63 cwt. The tubes weighed 7,000 pounds. With a 9-pound charge it could fire a 51.5-lb. shell more than a mile at five degrees elevation in 6.32 seconds. The river monitor *Neosho* sported two 11-inch Dahlgrens in her turret.

The Parrott rifle was designed by Captain Robert Parrott, superintendent of the West Point, N.Y. Foundry. The cast and wrought-iron gun is distinguished by the thicker band of metal wrapped around the breech end, a reinforcement meant to prevent accidental explosions. This gun also came in many variations. Many of the tinclads mounted smoothbore howitzers, usually 12- or 24-pounder brass Dahlgrens, until they were replaced by larger guns, usually Parrott rifles. The howitzers could be placed on wheeled carriages for shore duty, when necessary.

The first convoy of transports filled with blueclad soldiers which reached Nashville on Feb. 25, 1862 was led by the *USS Cairo*. On Dec. 12, 1862 on the Yazoo River in Mississippi, the *Cairo* became the first boat to be sunk by an electrically detonated underwater torpedo (mine). The sunken boat was discovered in 1956, and the pilothouse, cannon, and other artifacts were recovered in 1960. Much, but not all, of the structure was raised in 1964, and the restored ship was put on permanent display in 1977 at the Vicksburg National Military Park, where it can be seen today. Please refer to the special section on the *USS Cairo* for much more information.

## USS Carondelet

Built at Carondelet, Mo., she was the first City Class launched. Her chimney bands were red. Commanded by Commander Henry Walke (Jan. 1862-Jan. 1863), she was the first vessel to run past the Confederate batteries at Island No. 10 on the Mississippi. She was known as the slowest of the City Class ironclads. On Feb. 12-13, she bombarded Fort Donelson on her own and sustained moderate damage on February 14. After repairs, she guarded the river crossings at Pittsburg Landing during the battle at Shiloh. In July 1862 she battled the *CSS Arkansas* near Vicksburg, and was refitted. After numerous operations on the Lower Mississippi, she participated heavily in operations at Bell's Bend near Nashville in December 1864, and helped turn Hood's right flank during the Battle of Nashville. After decommissioning in 1865, her engines were placed in the towboat *Quaker* and her hull served as a wharfboat at Gallipolis, Ohio. In 1873 a flood washed the boat 130 miles downriver and grounded her at Manchester Island, Ohio. In 1981, the noted underwater explorer and author Clive Cussler located the wreck but before salvage operations could begin, a dredge boat unintentionally mashed over the site and ruined the remains of the *Carondelet*.

## USS St. Louis

Built at Carondelet, her chimney bands were yellow and a Masonic emblem hung between the stacks. The *St. Louis* participated at Fort Henry and Fort Donelson. She was commanded by Lt. Leonard Paulding (Jan.-April 1862). Upon transfer to the U.S. Navy in September 1862, she was renamed the *USS Baron de Kalb* because the Navy already had a *USS St. Louis*. She participated in many operations on the Lower Mississippi. On July 13, 1863, she struck a mine on the Yazoo River in Mississippi and sank. Her guns and other equipment were salvaged; then she was blown up underwater.

## USS Louisville

Built at Carondelet, her chimney bands were green. The *Louisville* participated at Fort Donelson and sustained heavy damage. She was commanded by Commander Benjamin M. Dove (Jan.-Sept. 1862). She had a distinguished career on numerous operations on the Lower Mississippi. She sustained heavy damage at Columbia, Ark. in June 1864. After the war, she was decommissioned, and sold for scrap in November 1865.

## USS Cincinnati

Built at Mound City, her chimney bands were blue. She participated at Fort Henry, firing the first shot, and was heavily damaged. She was commanded by Commander Roger N. Stembel. After repairs, she participated in Lower Mississippi operations. At Plum Point Bend in May 1862, she was rammed and sunk while guarding a mortar boat. She was raised and on May 27, 1863, she was hit by shore batteries at Fort Hill near Vicksburg, Miss. and sunk again, with 40 casualties. She was set fire by rebels; her guns were removed to outfit Battery Selfridge. In August 1863 she was raised and refitted. After the war, she was sold in 1866 and later that year sank near Mound City.

## USS Pittsburg

Built at Carondelet, her chimney bands were brown. The *Pittsburg* participated at Fort Donelson and was heavily damaged. She was commanded by Commander Egbert Thompson (Jan.-Sept. 1862). She participated in numerous operations on the Lower Mississippi. She was sold in November 1865 and used as a wharf boat. She was abandoned on a bar above Smithland, Ky. in 1870.

## USS Mound City

Built at Mound City, her chimney bands were orange. She was the only City Class ironclad that did not participate in operations covered in this publication (she served on the Lower Mississippi).

## USS Essex

Built in 1856 in New Albany, Indiana as the steam ferry *New Era*, the vessel was converted into the 355-ton timberclad gunboat *New Era* and took part in the Cumberland River expedition in November 1861. She was converted into a 1,000-ton ironclad and renamed *Essex*. Nearly 200 feet long and 58 feet wide, she drafted 6 feet, 10 inches and made 5.5 knots. She was armed with one 10-inch and three 11-inch Dahlgren smoothbores, one 12-pound howitzer, and one 32-pound rifle. Known as the *S.X.*, she was a hardluck ironclad. The ironclad participated at Fort Henry and sustained heavy damage. During repairs, she was upgraded and participated in operations at Vicksburg and fought the *CSS Arkansas*. She bombarded Port Hudson, Louisiana, and assisted in its capture in July 1863. She also participated in the Red River expedition. She was decommissioned in July 1865 and renamed *New Era* again. She was commanded by Commander William "Dirty Bill" Porter.

## USS Eastport

Originally built in 1852 in New Albany, Ind., the steamboat was being converted into the *CSS Eastport* at Cerro Gordo on the Tennessee River and half finished when captured by the Phelps raiders on Feb. 8, 1862. She was at least 230 feet long, 43 feet wide, and drafted 6 ft., 3 in. She was towed to Cairo, where she was finished as the *USS Eastport*. She was armed with four 9-inch Dahlgren smoothbores, two 50-pounder and two 100-pounder rifles. She was rebuilt in Oct. 1862-Jan. 1863 and then served on the Lower Mississippi until running into trouble on the Red River in April 1864. She struck a mine and was grounded to prevent sinking. She ran aground eight more times in five days due to low water level. Her captain was ordered to destroy her to prevent capture by the Confederates. Ironically, her captain at that time was none other than Lt. Comm. Phelps.

## The Tinclads

Officially known as light-draughts, these 76 converted steamboats were by far the most numerous class of gunboat on the Mississippi tributaries, replacing the three heavier timberclads. The tinclads were armored with thin layers of iron (despite the name, no tin was involved) and moderately to heavily armed. Most were sternwheelers; the remainder were sidewheelers. No two tinclads were of similar design. The tinclads, introduced in August 1862 and initially headquartered out of Indiana on the Ohio, were used to patrol the rivers against guerrillas and Confederate cavalry/infantry crossings and to escort cargo convoys. The boats came from purchases, seizures, and capture, and were rebuilt at Cairo or Mound City. Generally, a tinclad was about 150 feet long, 200 tons, and drew from two to six feet in draft. The casemates were lightly armored, as was the newly built pilothouse. They could transport up to 200 infantry, although this was not a major function. They were coal-fired but could burn firewood if necessary. They were much faster than the ironclads. Normal armament was two or three 12-pounder or 24-pounder howitzers on each broadside, and two heavier guns, often rifles, in the bow. The tinclads were cheap; the purchase and conversion totaled about $9,000, compared to the $200,000 needed to build an ironclad. The tinclads were each numbered; when one was lost another would be assigned its number.

The tinclads patroled all the rivers. When used as convoy escorts to Nashville they would be dispatched to patrol the Upper Cumberland from Nashville upriver to Carthage, Tenn. while the convoy transports were being unloaded. The tinclads under Lt. Commander LeRoy Fitch's command were also heavily involved in chasing General John Hunt Morgan's cavalry troopers on their famous raid into Ohio in June-July 1863 and preventing them from recrossing the river. In three years of combat, only 13 tinclads were lost, nine of them to Confederate shore batteries.

## USS Neosho River Monitor

The *USS Neosho* was a peculiar-looking ironclad
*(Continued on Page 46)*

| Tinclads on the Tennessee and Cumberland Rivers | | | | |
|---|---|---|---|---|
| Name | No. | Type | Commissioned | Armament |
| Alfred Robb | 21 | Sternwheeler | 6-2-62 | 2 12-pdr rifles, 2 12-pdr smoothbores |
| Brilliant | 18 | Sternwheeler | 10-1-62 | 2 12-pdr rifles, 2 12-pdr smoothbores |
| Elfin | 52 | Sternwheeler | 3-64 | 8 24-pdr smoothbores |
| Fairplay | 17 | Sternwheeler | 9-6-62 | 4 12-pdr smoothbores |
| Fairy | 51 | Sternwheeler | 3-10-64 | 8 24-pdr smoothbores |
| Key West | 32 | Sternwheeler | 5-26-63 | 6 24-pdr smoothbores |
| Linden | 10 | Sidewheeler | 1-3-63 | 6 24-pdr smoothbores |
| Marmora | 2 | Sternwheeler | 10-21-62 | 2 12-pdr rifles, 2 12-pdr smoothbores |
| Moose | 34 | Sternwheeler | 6-15-63 | 6 24-pdr smoothbores |
| New Era | 7 | Sternwheeler | 12-62 | 6 24-pdr smoothbores |
| Paw Paw | 31 | Center | 7-25-63 | 2 30-pdr rifles; 6 24-pdr smoothbores |
| Peosta | 36 | Sidewheeler | 10-2-63 | 3 30-pdr rifles, 3 32-pdr sb, 2 12-pdr sb |
| Reindeer | 35 | Sternwheeler | 7-25-63 | 6 24-pdr smoothbores |
| St. Clair | 19 | Sidewheeler | 9-24-62 | 2 12-pdr rifles, 2 12-pdr smoothbores |
| Signal | 8 | Sternwheeler | 10-62 | 2 30-pdr rifles, 4 12-pdr smoothbores |
| Silver Cloud | 28 | Sternwheeler | 5-4-63 | 6 24-pdr smoothbores |
| Silver Lake | 23 | Sternwheeler | 12-24-62 | 6 24-pdr smoothbores |
| Springfield | 22 | Sidewheeler | 1-12-63 | 6 24-pdr smoothbores |
| Tawah | 29 | Sidewheeler | 6-21-63 | 2 30-pdr rifles, 4 24-pdr sb, 2 12-pdr rifles |
| Undine | 55 | Sternwheeler | 4-64 | 8 24-pdr smoothbores |
| Victory | 33 | Sidewheeler | 7-8-63 | 6 24-pdr smoothbores |

river monitor which sat very low in the water and was equipped with a revolving armored turret at the bow armed with two 11-inch Dahlgren smoothbores. The *Neosho* participated in numerous campaigns on the Lower Mississippi but is noted in this publication for its participation in the Battle of Nashville (Bell's Bend). It was built by James Eads at Carondelet, Mo., launched in February 1863 and commissioned in May. It is named after the river in Indiana and was one of only two in its *Neosho* class (the other was the *Osage*). They were the only paddlewheel monitors; the others were all propeller-driven. During most of her service she was commanded by Acting Volunteer Lt. Samuel Howard. Displacing 523 tons, the *Neosho* was 180 feet long, 45 feet wide, and drafted only four-and-a-half feet. She could make 7.5 knots. The crew numbered 100. The armor measured six inches thick on the turret, 2.5 inches on the sides, and 2 inches on the deck. Coal-fired and steam-powered, it was driven by a single sternwheel protected by a circular enclosure.

The illustration at the left shows the twin Dahlgren guns inside an ironclad monitor, the *USS Passaic,* similar to that of the *USS Neosho.*

The photo below shows the exterior of the *USS Monitor* turret, also similar to the *Neosho,* placement of gunports and indentations caused by projectiles.

# The *USS Cairo*

*The Civil War gunboat, sunk by a mine in 1862, was discovered
and raised a hundred years later and is now on display*

The *USS Cairo*, named for the naval base in Illinois, was one of the seven City Class ironclad casemate gunboats designed by Samuel Pook and built by engineer James Eads in 1861. The *Cairo* was one of three built at Mound City, Illinois, on the Ohio River. The *Cairo* was the first gunboat to reach Nashville, Tennessee, on the Cumberland River, leading a flotilla of troop transports. On Dec. 12, 1862, the *Cairo*, known as the hardluck ironclad, struck an electrically operated Confederate torpedo (submerged mine) and sank into the muck of the Yazoo River in Mississippi. In 1956, historian Edwin Bearss, Don Jacks, and Warren Grabau located the sunken gunboat and launched a lengthy and difficult project to raise her. In 1977 the *USS Cairo* Exhibit and Visitor's Center opened at Vicksburg National Military Park. On display is the partially reconstructed gunboat, which visitors can walk aboard, and a museum housing thousands of artifacts retrieved from the wreck that tell the story of what it was like to be a sailor serving on a river gunboat during the Civil War. The story of the *USS Cairo*, her service and sinking, her rescue and recovery, can be read in Bearss' book, *Hardluck Ironclad: The Sinking and Salvage of the Cairo.*

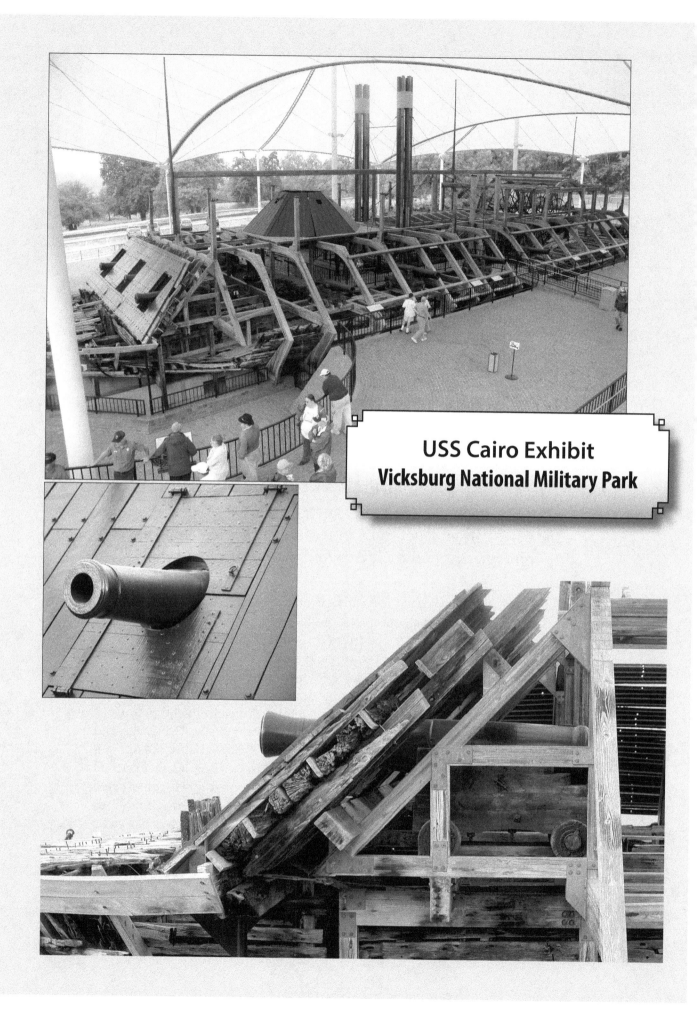

USS Cairo Exhibit
**Vicksburg National Military Park**

The *USS Cairo* carried 13 big guns. The 32-pounder Navy smoothbore, mounted on its original carriage, could fire a solid 32-pound cannon ball about a mile. Each gun required an 12-man crew to load, aim, and fire. Iron plating was mounted as part of the sloping casemate that enclosed the gun deck. The 2½-inch thick charcoal plate iron was backed by a two-foot thickness of white oak timbers. Without the wood to absorb the shock of shot and shell hitting the iron, the metal would have shattered like glass. The pilothouse was originally a tall, wooden, iron-plated structure, later replaced by an octagonal iron-plated structure (shown on opposite page).

The ironclads were 175 feet long and 51 feet wide with a draft of only six feet. They displaced 888 tons. The flat bottom had three keels. The estimated weight of the hull and casemate was 350 tons, plus 122 tons of charcoal iron plating (armor) at 2.5 inches thick. The casemate was sloped 35 degrees on the sides and 45 degrees on the ends. The behemoth was capable of only six knots and consumed one ton of coal per hour. The exterior was painted black and the interior white-washed. The only distinguishing characteristic of each ironclad were colored bands near the top of the 28-foot-high chimneys (smokestacks). The *USS Cairo* bands were gray. The contract cost for each boat was $89,600. The actual cost was $101,808.

In 1990, the *USS Cairo* exhibit at Vicksburg NMP, specifically the engines and boilers, was named a National Historic Mechanical Engineering Landmark. The citation states, in part:

"The propulsion system is the only known early example of the widely used Western Rivers steamboat engine, characterized by multiple fire-tube boilers with shared steam and mud drums, and a two-cylinder, non-condensing engine having a small bore, long stroke, and poppet valves. With a 22-in. bore and 6-ft. stroke, it developed about 600 horsepower and drove a sheltered paddlewheel of 22-ft diameter and 15-ft width.

The engine and boilers were designed by A. Thomas Merritt, a civilian engineer from Cincinnati, Ohio, and built by the Hartupee Company of Pittsburg, Pa. Merritt also served as superintendent of construction of the vessels. James B. Eads, a civilian engineer from St. Louis and an experienced river boat builder, was awarded a contract Aug. 7, 1861, by the U.S. Army to build the gunboats. The *Cairo* was built at the Marine Railway and Ship Yard at Mound City, Ill., and was commissioned Jan. 15, 1862.

"The reciprocating steam engine was the universal prime mover in self-propelled craft during that era. All of these engines were simple, single-expansion, and either condensing or non-condensing. The different types of engines were labelled according to the position of the cylinders — vertical, horizontal, or inclined. The engine position matched the type of paddlewheel used to propel the boat. Vertical or inclined engines were used to drive the sidewheel types. A stern wheel would be driven by a horizontal or an inclined engine, with the latter being more desirable for a gunboat, since the engine would be under the water line. The *Cairo's* recessed paddlewheel was located aft within the protected raceway, between the casemates to protect it from enemy fire. The iron shaft of the paddlewheel was driven at either end by cranks mounted 90 degrees to each other. The two rudders were located aft on each side of the raceway to steer the gunboat. The ironclad was equipped with five fire-tube boilers, each 36 inches in diameter and 25-feet long, with five 7½-inch flues inside each boiler. The sides of the boilers are 5/16-inch thick, with heads 12/16-inch thick. The boilers operated at 140 pounds per square inch steam pressure. Instrumentation installed on each set of boilers was a steam gauge and a water gauge. A cast-iron cap fit on the front of the boiler. The firebox was five feet long. The firebox consumed 18 to 20 bushels — approximately 1,980 pounds — of coal per hour. The bed of the firebox was lined with firebrick and enclosed in good sheet iron. Located under the forward section of each boiler, it supplied hot gases to the boilers by routing the gas aft and under the boilers and into the aft flue mouths of the boilers. The flue gas was drawn forward through the flues and drawn up the tall chimney (44 inches in diameter and 28 feet in height) by natural draft.

"Two mud drums, which supported the boilers and collected sediment of the pumped feed water, were connected to the bottom of the boilers. One was located close to the aft end of the boilers with stop valves for supplying the boilers with water. The other mud drum was located immediately aft of the firebox, but without water supply connections. At one end of this drum was a blow-off valve to drain the boilers. Steam flowed from the boiler to the steam drum. Located in the rear of the boilers, it served as a collector and manifold. Each connection pipe to the drum had a stop valve to cut off steam flow to the drum and, more importantly, to the engine. Connected to the aft side of the center of the steam drum was a pipe carrying steam to the main steam engine, steam-driven capstan, and auxiliary engine. The *Cairo* was equipped with a two-cylinder non-condensing, reciprocating main steam engine. The cylinders, mounted at a 15-degree angle, were made of cast iron with a 22-inch bore and were of a length to accommodate a 72-inch stroke. On one side of the cylinder at each end was a supply nozzle with an opening of 9 inches by 4 inches, with a flange 15-inches square by 1¼-inches thick, for receiving steam. On the other side of the cylinder were two similar nozzles for steam exhaust from the cylinder. The cast-iron piston, with a 4-inch space for packing, was attached to a wrought-iron piston rod which was 4 inches in diameter and 110 inches long. The engine exhaust steam-heated water in the preheater, and then exhausted to the chimney."

**Opposite Page: The five fire-tube boilers with steam drum astern; the port reciprocating steam engine looking astern.**

**This Page: The paddlewheel showing port driveshaft bearing. The other engine and driveshaft were on the starboard side of the wheel;**

**The schematic of the Cairo's steam propulsion system, bow to the left and paddlewheel to the right.**

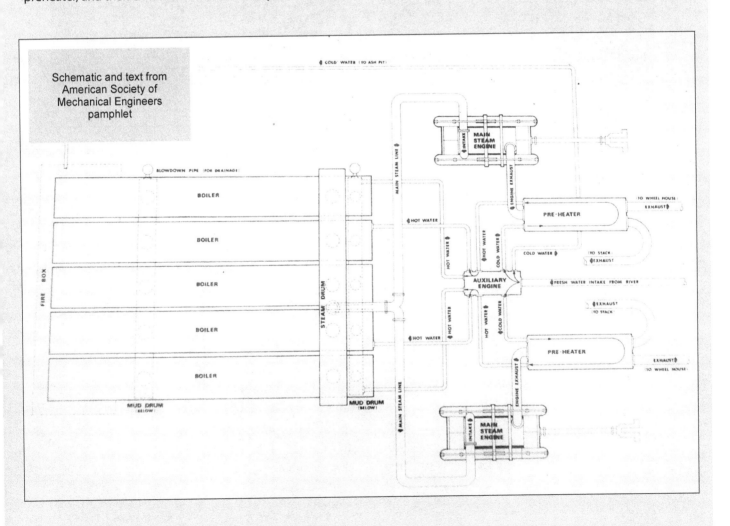

Schematic and text from American Society of Mechanical Engineers pamphlet

Edwin Bearss (USMC ret.), historian, author, and discoverer of the *USS Cairo*

–Chapter Four–

# Canton

*"How long are these murderous, thieving Yankees*
*to be permitted to infest our rivers...?"*

The first encounter between a U.S. gunboat and Confederate cavalry came at Canton, Kentucky, on the east bank of the Cumberland River in November 1861 (the exact date is disputed: Nov. 18, 19 or 20). Opposing forces were led by Lt. Commander Seth Ledyard Phelps of the *USS Conestoga* timberclad and Major David Campbell Kelley of Colonel Nathan Bedford Forrest's cavalry command. This riverside skirmish occurred before Forrest's first acknowledged battle at Sacramento, Ky.

"Don't be surprised if my movements don't correspond with your ideas of military propiety." This warning was issued by Nathanael Greene during the Revolutionary War but one could easily imagine them repeated by Forrest, a self-educated former slave trader and land speculator from Memphis who was one of the richest men in the South. Forrest was a born warrior who disdained West Point Military Academy rules in favor of his own brand of warfare — always taking the offensive, using psychological techniques ("put the skeer into them"), and getting to battle first with the most men. Acclaimed as one of the finest cavalrymen of the war, Forrest was more accurately a leader of mounted infantry (shock troops), moving quickly through the countryside, behind the lines, raiding Union garrisons and wrecking enemy depots and infrastructure. In battle, his men dismounted and fought much like infantry. Normally, three troopers would dismount and fight as infantry while a fourth man held back their mounts. They were supported by horse-drawn field artillery. A man of fierce pride, quick temper, and imposing stature, Forrest was not a man to be trifled with. His men not so much loved him as deeply respected him for leading them into victory.

USS Conestoga

Forrest could burst into a tirade and threaten violence (sometimes more than just a threat), only moments later to show great regret and offer apologies. He was a leader of men and a natural warrior, without any formal military training. He was a great interpreter of terrain. And he meant business — "War is fighting, and fighting means killing." His tactics made him one of the most controversial men of the Civil War. He enlisted as a private when the war began, moved up the ranks, outfitted his men from his own pocket (later they would equip themselves with confiscated Union arms and goods), and ended the war as a lieutenant general. His nemesis, General William T. Sherman, called him the greatest man produced by the war, although during the war, frustrated with Forrest's raids behind the lines, he referred to him as "the Devil himself." At this point in the war, however, Colonel Forrest was barely known.

David Campbell "D.C." Kelley was known as the "Fighting Parson," having served as a Methodist minister before the war. He was born in Leeville, Tennessee on Christmas Day 1833. An 1851 graduate of Cumberland University in Lebanon, Tenn., he became a medical doctor, graduating from the University of Nashville. That same year he traveled to China as a Methodist medical minister for two years. He began his Civil War service at Huntsville, Alabama, as captain of the Kelley Rangers/Kelley Troopers, Co. F, Forrest's Battalion (3rd Tennessee Cavalry). He quickly became one of Forrest's intimates and most trusted associates.

Kelley disdained the position of chaplain, according to biographer Michael R. Bradley, preferring to do the fighting as part of the "church militant." Kelley wrote: "My first acquaintance with the chaplains of the army and navy was when I was in [China in the 1850s]. This acquaintance led me to avoid the chaplaincy in the Confederate army. The chaplain's position needs some more honorable recognition, for neither as officer nor private was he properly recognized. Between the two, he was not honored."

Seth Ledyard Phelps was an old saltwater sailor and a graduate of the U.S. Naval Academy. A native of Ohio, Phelps was "one of the younger generation of naval officers who not only embraced the new technology but did so in an alien environment for a sailor — the western rivers of the United States," wrote his biographer Jay Slagle. Phelps had been instrumental in establishing the Western Gunboat Flotilla and guiding the construction of the three timberclad gunboats. Throughout the fall of 1861 his boats were seen everywhere on the lower reaches of the two rivers, bolstering and assisting

*(Continued on Page 56)*

Colonel Nathan Bedford Forrest

Major David Campbell Kelley

Southern cavalry in Middle Tennessee, specifically in this case the Seventh Confederate Cavalry re-enactors at Stones River National Battlefield.

Union loyalists in Kentucky and keeping a keen eye out for Confederate movements. During this time, the Union gunboats had taken on a reputation of invincibility bolstered by rumors that the gunboats were deliberately manned by felons and reprobates intent on looting, pillage, and rape. Other rumors had the "Lincolnite" boats flying the black pirate flag.

Phelps' boat, the *Conestoga,* was a sidewheeler, converted from an 1859 steamboat, armored with thin iron plate and oak bulwarks, and armed with eight shiny 32-pounder smoothbores. The boat was fast at 12 knots, which was advantageous because it could not withstand heavy fire from field or seige artillery. Although beloved as any captain loves his boat, Phelps called the *Conestoga* "second-rate" due to its lack of iron cladding.

Phelps wrote in his diary: "This vessel has obtained a notoriety along the Cumberland and Tennessee rivers, from which I have taken a number of prizes (boats), and have all along kept seccesh — there rampant and largely in the majority and of the marauding type — quiet and respectful to his Union neighbor. Many of them swear to shoot me on sight but none has yet attempted it."

On Oct. 11, 1861, Phelps and the *Conestoga* ascended the Tennessee River, anchoring just in sight of Fort Henry, then under construction at the Kentucky-Tennessee state line. The next morning, Phelps sat in the pilothouse for hours, watching with a spyglass the progress being made at the fort. At this time, there were rumors gathered by landing parties that powerful new ironclads were being built upriver by the Confederates. But there was no way to definitely confirm or deny those reports.

During the fall of 1861, Commander Phelps led his timberclad flotilla (his flagboat plus the *Tyler* and *Lexington*) on many patrols up both rivers, probing

Lt. Commander Seth Ledyard Phelps

CAVALRY vs. GUNBOAT

CSA Gen. Nathan Bedford Forrest with 6 cavalry companies joined Gen. Charles Clark, Nov. 15, 1861, at Hopkinsville. On reconnaissance learned of USA gunboat Conastoga's intent to destroy CSA supplies at Canton. They met here Nov. 20 in 7 hours of ship-to-shore combat. Conastoga left. Forrest's command had stood ground well, first time under fire. See map other side.

the Confederate defenses and reporting on progress at Fort Henry and Fort Donelson. Near Tobacco Port on one routine patrol, the *Conestoga* took sniping fire. In return, Phelps lobbed a shell into an old barn and scattered an encampment of Confederate soldiers. A messenger was sent into the village to warn that Phelps would burn down the town if such irregular warfare did not cease. He would shoot anyone caught firing upon Union gunboats who was not a Confederate soldier. Such tactics often worked, in specific cases, but the sniping continued throughout the war and consequently a couple of "seccesh" towns were burned to the ground.

Phelps received information that Confederate cavalry had been harassing Unionists at the village of Eddyville, Kentucky, on the Cumberland. He warned the townspeople not to threaten the loyalists, but the reports persisted. On the night of Oct. 26, 1861 Phelps set off up the Cumberland with the *Conestoga* and three companies of the 9th Illinois Volunteer Regiment aboard the transport *Lake*

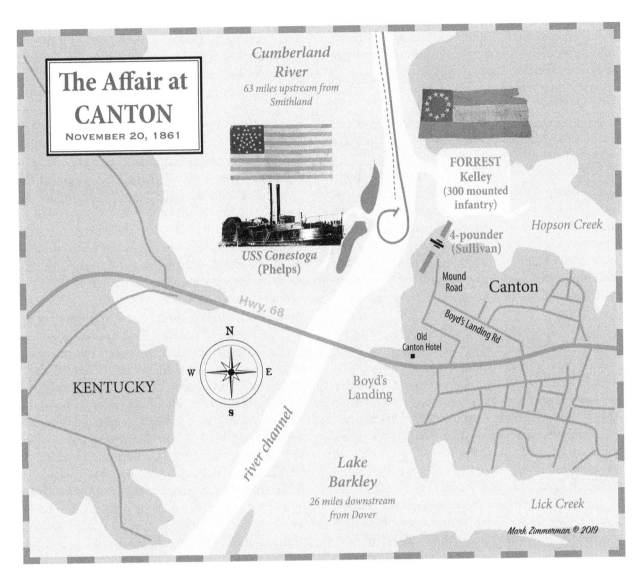

**The Affair at CANTON**

NOVEMBER 20, 1861

*Cumberland River*
63 miles upstream from Smithland

*USS Conestoga* (Phelps)

*Hwy. 68*

KENTUCKY

*river channel*

N
W · E
S

FORREST
Kelley
(300 mounted infantry)

*Hopson Creek*

4-pounder (Sullivan)

Mound Road

Canton

*Boyd's Landing Rd*

Old Canton Hotel

Boyd's Landing

*Lake Barkley*
26 miles downstream from Dover

*Lick Creek*

*Mark Zimmerman © 2019*

*Erie No. 2.* The troops were commanded by Major Jesse Phillips. At the mouth of the Cumberland, the *Conestoga* took the troop transport in tow, with lights out and engines off, to fool the Confederate lookouts at Smithland. The ruse worked. The movement of U.S. troops went unnoticed. At 3:00 am, the troops disembarked at New Forge Landing, around a big bend from Eddyville but only six miles away by land. The boats chugged upriver to Eddyville, with the transport mooring near a wooded landing and the big gunboat anchored at the foot of the main street. Just before dawn, the 9th Illinois crept to within 600 yards of a Confederate encampment at Saratoga Springs, near Eddyville.

The rebel pickets were captured, and at 7:00 am the Federal troops attacked. At 50 yards away, the Federal troops stopped, fired a volley, fixed bayonets, and then charged. "The Confederate commander, Capt. M.D. Wilcox, stood firing two revolvers while his company deserted him. It took nine minié balls to bring him down," according to historian Slagle. Six other Confederates were killed and several wounded. Just before dawn, landing parties from the *Conestoga* surrounded Eddyville; at 10:00 am the infantrymen arrived. Herded aboard the transport were captured horses and mules and 100 rebel prisoners. As they departed, Phelps warned the townspeople that he would hold them and their property responsible for any violence visited upon the Unionist population. The entire Eddyville expedition lasted 29 hours.

Two days later, the editor of the *Louisville Courier* railed, "How long are these murderous, thieving Yankees to be permitted to thus infest our rivers, deprecate upon our property, and murder our people?"

Within a few weeks, Phelps received reports that clothing intended for the Confederate army was stored at a commissary warehouse at Canton and he set out to confiscate the goods. Phelps was familiar with the town and its location on the east bank of the Cumberland 62 miles upstream from the Ohio River. Canton was a thriving river port, loading shipments of iron and tobacco for transport by steamboat.

About this time, Forrest's cavalry troopers rode northward from Memphis to serve with the garrison at Fort Donelson. Forrest was ordered to Hopkinsville, Kentucky, and then to the Ohio River to patrol between the Cumberland and Green rivers. At Princeton, Kentucky, Forrest ordered his second-in-command, Major Kelley, to intercept a transport due the next day on the Ohio. The steamer transport was captured along with its valuable cargo of sugar, coffee, blankets, and other items.

The Phelps excursion to Canton did not remain a secret very long. A civilian from the Smithland area rode 84 miles in 12 hours to Princeton to warn Forrest. Having returned from his foray on the Ohio, Kelley joined Forrest and reached Canton, 32 miles away, after a grueling eight-hour nocturnal march (Forrest himself did not accompany Kelley to Canton). A small four-pounder field artillery piece was masked by the riverside vegetation, just north of Canton, commanded by Lt. Jeremiah Sullivan. In short time, the *Conestoga*, belching black smoke from its tall chimneys, chugged around a river bend into view. But Phelps had been forewarned of the Confederate presence by a Union loyalist of German descent on the riverbank. Crews aboard the sidewheeler loaded their bronze 32-pounders with canister, rendering them giant shotguns, as the drummer beat to quarters. One account states that Kelley's gun opened fire at 50 yards, with the shot

from the Confederate fieldpiece bouncing off the thick oaken sides of the timberclad. Another claims the gunboat laid at the opposite shore and the rebels opened fire when the boat's gunports opened. The *Conestoga* fired her starboard guns, spraying the riverbank with the small shot of canister. The Confederates fired once again from their four-pounder and then pulled back into a gully. Kelley's 300 men, armed with Maynard rifles, aimed at the gunports of the boat. Sgt. Thomas B. Sheridan was given the honor of being the first Forrest man to fire a shot in combat. The *Conestoga* turned in mid-river and exposed her stern gun to the shore. After several hours of exchanging gunfire and artillery shells, the *Conestoga* steamed out of view.

Both sides claimed victory. The Confederates reveled in driving off the gunboat and standing up to its reputed invincibility. The Federals claimed that "the broadsides from the heavy armament on the gunboat made his (Kelley's) position untenable."

One of Kelley's men, Will Corder, wrote, "Our whole battalion rode about 30 miles to fight the thing. We didn't have any artillery except one little four pounder. We hid it in the trees at the bend of the river and waited for the boat. We blew into it and did some damage. The gunboat backed off and opened its gun ports. It had armor and about eight heavy guns. They blew up a lot of dirt, but we were hid in some ravines. We used our Maynard rifles and started pickin' off those sailors right out of those open gun ports. We fought that thing for seven or eight hours, and it withdrew. We learned we didn't have to be afeared of them things. We lost but five or six men and they lost twenty five or so."

One of Forrest's biographers put the Union death toll at 17. Phelps' biographer stated, "Besides a large quantity of lead embedded in her side, the only damage to the *Conestoga* consisted of a broken guy wire, numerous holes in her chimneys, and a flesh wound to Phelps' dog, Sancho."

As the *USS Conestoga* steamed downriver to Paducah following the Canton skirmish, Lt. Commander Phelps must have enjoyed the satisfaction of having sparred successfully with the Confederate cavalry, but it's doubtful he would ever forgive them for wounding his dog.

–Chapter Five–

# Fort Henry

*The ironclads snatch a victory from the army*
*against a determined but poorly situated foe*

On Jan. 27, 1862, President Lincoln issued General War Order No. 1, which required all of his generals to show movement against the enemy by February 22. General U.S. Grant had already been pressing his superior, General Henry "Old Brains" Halleck, to allow him to move up the twin rivers. Flag Officer Andrew H. Foote assured Halleck that his ironclad gunboats could defeat any Confederate river fort. Then it was learned that Confederate General P.T.G. Beauregard had been ordered to Kentucky with 15 regiments to reinforce the Western Theater army of General Albert Sidney Johnston. Although this rumor was false (Beauregard brought no men with him), on January 30, Halleck wired Grant: "Make your preparations to take and hold Fort Henry."

On the last day of January 1862, the timberclads *Conestoga* and *Lexington* moved up the Tennessee River ever closer to Fort Henry, trying to get one last look before the upcoming attack. Accompanying Lt. Commander Seth Ledyard Phelps was landlubber Brigadier General Lew Wallace, the future author of the bestselling novel *Ben Hur*, who took notes of his fascinating trip. The boats had anchored for the night in mid-channel, planning to conduct their reconnaissance first thing in the morning. Then the baying of hounds was heard on the shore, getting louder and ever closer. Emerging from a riverside cornfield was their target, an escaped slave. The black man was running toward the boats. A landing party was sent. The Union men used their paddles to drive away the hounds and rescued the fugitive slave, a contraband. He was taken back to the gunboat.

*Battle of Fort Henry* by Andy Thomas, artist.

At the crack of dawn, the gunboats paddled slowly upstream, with two men in the bow on either side, staring intently into the waters ahead. They were searching for torpedoes, as submerged naval mines were called in those days. At least a dozen underwater mines had been anchored in the western chute of the river around Panther Island, which was located about two miles downstream from Fort Henry. The torpedoes were sheet-metal cylinders about six feet long, a foot in diameter, filled with 70 pounds of black powder, and sporting a protruding prong, which would trigger an explosion if tripped by the bottom of a passing boat. It was flood season and the river level was rising, the currents strong. As it turned out, due to the floodwaters, most of the torpedoes had been swept away and sank or rendered inert due to damage or seepage.

The flagboat *Conestoga* cleared Panther Island and boldly moved into the main channel, in full view of the fort's occupants, who were ready and waiting. What Phelps and Wallace saw was a bastioned fort "built squat on low ground" and covering ten acres, with one of its bastions extending out into the river

and holding three heavy guns. They counted 17 guns in all, 11 trained on the river. A water-filled ditch circled the fort, as did rifle pits. Behind the fort on slightly higher ground were trees bearing watermarks, indicating that at flood stage the fortification would be underwater. On the opposite side of the river, further upstream and in Kentucky, was the unfinished fortification known as Fort Heiman, much higher in elevation than Fort Henry. Engineers had been ordered to build Fort Heiman back in November 1861, but it remained unfinished.

Fort Henry (named for Confederate Senator Gustavus Henry) had been poorly sited, as noted by several engineers, but it was built at Kirkman's Landing nonetheless. In June 1861, at the time of the fort's construction, Kentucky was still neutral, so the fort had to be situated on Tennessee soil. The water level was low during the summer 1861 and nearly everybody assumed the war would be a short and decisive one. One factor in Fort Henry's favor was that it was only 12 miles west of Fort Donelson on the Cumberland River. The forts could reinforce

*(Continued on Page 62)*

**FOOTE**

*USS Lexington*
(Shirk)

*USS Tyler*
(Gwin)

*USS Conestoga*
(Phelps)

*USS Essex*
(Porter)
(disabled)

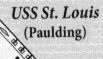

*USS St. Louis*
(Paulding)

*USS Carondelet*
(Walke)

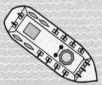

*USS Cincinnati*
(Stembel)

# The Capture of
# FORT HENRY
## FEBRUARY 6, 1862

N
W   E
S

A—32-lb. smoothbore
B—24-lb. rifle
C—10-in. Columbiad
D—12-lb. smoothbore
E—42-lb. rifle
F —24-lb. smoothbore

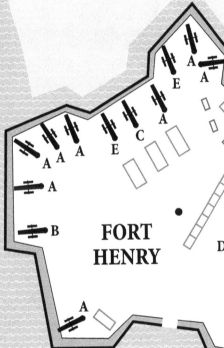

*ditch*

**FORT
HENRY**

**TENNESSEE RIVER**

**CSA Hospital Boat**
*Patton*

**TILGHMAN**
Taylor's Battery
Lt. Col. Milton Haynes
100 men

*Mark Zimmerman © 2019*

**Not Drawn to Scale**

USS Essex

each other, as it was correctly assumed that both forts would not be attacked at the same time.

Fort Henry's commander, Brigadier General Lloyd Tilghman, a native of Paducah, knew that the location of Fort Henry at Kirkman's Landing was unfortunate. In his after-action report, he wrote, "The history of military engineering records no parallel to this case." Historian Kendall Gott argues that the mouth of Standing Rock Creek or Boswell Landing would have been a much better site.

Fort Henry bristled with 17 heavy guns, ten of them 32-pounders, with eleven trained on the river, including a 10-inch Columbiad, a 42-pounder rifle, and two 42-pounder smoothbores (these were inoperable due to lack of suitable ammunition). During training, the Confederate gunners were having trouble with the recoil of the big Columbiad, as the length of the chassis was too short and the massive tube threatened to dislodge itself.

Where did the Confederates obtain such large siege artillery pieces? The Columbiads were cast at the famous Tredegar ironworks in Richmond, Va., but the other guns came from the 1,200 heavy artillery pieces confiscated by Virginia state troops

when they captured the Federal naval yard at Gosport/Norfolk in April 1861. The Confederates certainly would have been ill-equipped without the bounty seized from that early raid.

Fort Henry was garrisoned by 1,885 men and Fort Heiman by 1,100 men, although sickness had reduced the effective total strength to 2,600. Many were not properly trained or equipped, the exceptions being the 10th Tennessee and the 4th Mississippi regiments.

In a classic case of too little too late, Fort Heiman was built on the high west banks of the river, overlooking Fort Henry. This bastion was named for its commander, Colonel Adolphus Heiman, a Prussian architect who had emigrated to America in 1834. A hero of the Mexican War, Heiman was the colonel of the 10th Tennessee Infantry Regiment. "Construction began in December 1861 with the arrival of the Twenty-seventh Alabama and Fifteenth Arkansas infantry regiments who, along with some 500 slaves, were tasked with building the works," stated National Park Service (NPS) Historian Timothy Parsons. "Its suitable defensive position—protected by 150-foot bluffs

The 24-pound rifle bursts inside Fort Henry, killing several gunners.

in front and impassible roads and rough terrain in the rear—stood in marked contrast to the poor placement of Fort Henry. On the morning of February 3, General Tilghman made an inspection of the incomplete works at Fort Heiman."

Onboard the *Conestoga*, Phelps had seen enough, satisfied with his observations. Before the gunboats withdrew, however, a solitary figure "stepped out on the parapet by the big gun of the lower bastion of the fort, and entertained himself returning our bravado like for like." The naval men later learned that the bold belligerent rebel had been General Tilghman himself.

On Feb. 3, 1862, a convoy of steam transports carrying Federal troops left the Ohio River port of Paducah and made its way up the Tennessee River. The transports were escorted by the ironclad gunboats *Essex* and *St. Louis*. A few hours later, the remainder of the gunboats, the City Class ironclads *Cincinnati* and *Carondelet*, and the three timberclads, *Conestoga*, *Lexington*, and *Tyler*, departed, all under the command of Flag Officer Foote. Their target

was Fort Henry. The army troops, under the overall command of Grant, disembarked on the east bank of the river several miles below the fort, planning to advance upon the Confederates in a joint attack with the naval forces. Another small Federal force put ashore on the west bank and advanced upon Fort Heiman, the small unfinished bastion on high ground overlooking Fort Henry directly across the river. The weather had been rainy and the river was swollen, making advancement by the infantry difficult due to the muddy conditions.

Reports were reaching the Confederate fort's commander that transports were landing thousands of U.S. soldiers below the fort, and the gunboats were shelling the riverbanks as Confederate cavalry patrols skirmished with the advancing forces. On February 4 at noon, three gunboats moved to within two miles of the fort and began shelling it. The boats were out of range of the 32-pounders so the rebel gunners discharged the Columbiad and 24-pounder rifle. Several shots from the Columbiad threatened to dismount it, so it was abandoned.

Soon the range had closed to a point where the 32-pounders were ordered to open fire. After half an hour, with none of the gunboat blasts landing in the fort, the gunboats withdrew.

The next day the Confederate garrison at Fort Heiman was ferried across the river to bolster Fort Henry. Tilghman's chief of artillery, Lt. Col. Milton Haynes, thought Fort Henry should be abandoned due to the rising level of the river and his estimation that the Confederate forces were vastly outnumbered. They agreed that the fight at Fort Henry would be a holding action. Tilghman ordered Heiman to remove all the remaining troops from Fort Henry except for Taylor's Battery, which would remain to man the guns.

On the morning of Thurs., Feb. 6, 1862, the Federal gunboat flotilla pulled away from Bailey's Landing at 10:50 am and headed for the fort. The four ironclads lined up abreast with their bows to the enemy (the *St. Louis* positioned closest to the east bank, then the *Carondelet*, *Cincinnati*, and *Essex*). The vulnerable timberclads (*Conestoga*, *Lexington*, and *Tyler*) would stay behind the ironclads and provide artillery support. When the

A torpedo (underwater mine) made from a gunpowder cask. The torpedos at Panther Island were of a different design, however.

range had closed to 1,700 yards, Flag Officer Foote ordered the captain of the *Cincinnati*, Commander Roger Stembel, to open fire. This was the signal for all of the gunboats to commence firing. At 12:34 pm, the bottle-shaped 8-inch Dahlgren in the bow of the *Cincinnati* roared to life. The commander of the *Essex*, William "Dirty Bill" Porter, cautioned his gunners to watch the flight of the shells from the *Cincinnati* before firing. As the first shells fell short, the gunners raised the elevation of the guns. The No. 2 port bow gun of the *Essex* spoke with authority and landed the first hit on the fort's earthworks, exploding "handsomely" with a scattering of dirt and evoking a cheer from the sailors. The percussive pounding of the big guns, accompanied by the flames and bursts of gray smoke, lighter in color than the black sooty discharges of the chimneys, echoed back and forth from the riverbanks. It seemed as if all hell had broken loose. "The gunboat-men enjoyed the terror they inspired," Wallace duly noted.

Despite all this, the Confederate gunners held their fire. Then the Columbiad opened the ball, followed by the 24-pounders, and finally the 32-pounder smoothbores. All this time Tilghman was receiving reports that troops were moving upon Fort Heiman and the outer rifle pits of Fort Henry itself, which was now about one-third underwater.

10-inch Columbiad on seige carriage

US ironclad gunboats shell Fort Henry

As the officers aboard the *Essex*, including Commander Porter, prepared to go below, a solid shot hit the pilothouse, sending deadly wooden splinters through the air. The pilot was killed instantly while his assistant fell to the deck below and died within minutes. On the gundeck, Porter ordered the changing of gun crews, one in relief of the other, and at that time another solid shot hit a porthole and tore its way through the iron plating and oak backing and struck the middle boiler, causing a terrific blast of scalding steam to escape. The resulting scene was "almost indescribable," stated Second Master James Laning. One of the gunners was kneeling while handing a new shell to the gunner and caught the scaulding steam right in the face. The steam blast forced many gunners to leap out the gunports and into the river, some managing to cling to the casemate. Others weren't so lucky. The acting master's mate was killed instantly and Porter was scalded badly. He tried to jump into the river, but a crewman caught him and carried him

astern. The first master took over the commander's duties as the *Essex* drifted downriver, away from the fort, "a number of her officers and crew dead at their posts, whilst many others were writhing in their last agony." Porter managed to stay conscious until a crewman told him that the fort had surrendered. He called for three cheers but by the second cheer he collapsed, exhausted. He would survive his injuries and eventually report back for duty.

Ten crewmen on the *Essex* died, 23 were wounded, and five went missing. The gunboat had taken 15 hits while discharging 72 shells from her three 9-inch Dahlgrens.

All in all, the Confederate gunners at Fort Henry hit the gunboats 59 times, with more than half aimed at the *Cincinnati*, in an attempt to disable Foote's flagboat. The gunners also remarked that the *Cincinnati* seemed to be dispensing more accurate fire than the other gunboats. The rebel gunners managed to shred the spar-deck, chimneys, after-cabin, and small boats, while a direct strike on the pilothouse dented it but bounced away. On the gundeck one round tore through the seam between the front and port side of the casemate, decapitating a gunner. Another shell crashed through and splintered the woodwork and hit the paddlewheel. One 8-inch Dahlgren was hit and one 32-pounder smoothbore disabled. Nine casualties were suffered in all. The *Cincinnati* fired 112 rounds at the fort.

Elsewhere, the *Carondelet* and the *St. Louis* collided, interlocked, and remained mated for a large portion of the battle. The *Carondelet*, commanded by Henry Walke, fired 107 projectiles and was struck nine or ten times. One shot from the *Carondelet* went through the upper deck of the *Patton*, a Confederate hospital boat trying to escape upriver. The Federal gunners realized their mistake when they finally were able to see the boat's yellow flag. Nobody on the hospital ship was injured.

The *St. Louis* fired 116 times, the most of any gunboat, and was hit seven times but suffered little damage and no casualties.

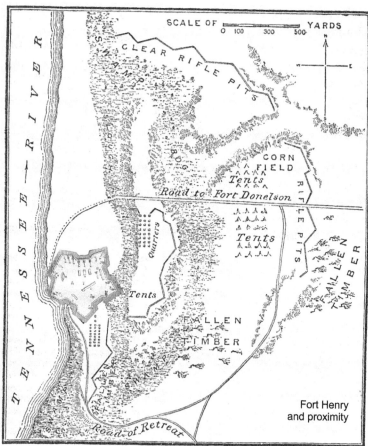

Fort Henry and proximity

Inside the fort, Captain Jesse Taylor was directing the gunners, telling each crew to concentrate on one gunboat. Then he took charge of the big 24-pounder rifle, while Capt. Charles Hayden manned the 10-inch Columbiad. Shortly after the *Essex* was disabled, the 24-pounder burst, killing a sergeant and disabling the crew. Then, the priming wire got stuck in the breech of the Columbiad and could not be cleared, rendering the big gun unusable. As the gunboats plowed to within a thousand yards of the fort, two of the 32-pounder guns in the fort were struck and put out of action. A premature discharge at another 32-pounder killed two of its gunners. By the time the gunboats were within 600 yards, the fort had only seven functioning guns. A few minutes later, only four guns remained serviceable. The cannoneers were exhausted from an hour's worth of tremendous effort loading and firing the heavy guns.

Colonel Heiman, who had led the majority of the fort's defenders on the march to Fort Donelson 12 miles away, returned to Fort Henry and asked Tilghman how to proceed. Heiman agreed with Col. Gilmer that the time had come to surrender, but Tilghman refused. The general threw off his coat and manned one of the 32-pounders himself. Heiman was ordered to fetch 50 men back to the fort to man the guns. By this time, the three ironclads had closed to within 600 yards of the fort, which was now being ripped apart. Finally, Tilghman agreed to surrender but not right away. He tied a white flag to a staff and waved it atop a parapet but the smoke was too dense for the flag to be seen. After another conference with his officers, Tilghman ordered the colors struck. While Taylor struck the colors at the fort, Haynes, who had not been consulted, ordered the Confederate flag raised again and directed that any man who tried to interfere be shot. Haynes

*USS St. Louis*

sought out Tilghman and became indignant when told of the pending surrender. Haynes wanted no part of it and left the fort, headed to Fort Donelson.

The battle lasted 75 minutes. Two Confederate officers rowed a small boat to the *Cincinnati*. Stembel and Phelps were ordered by Foote to take possession of the fort. After raising the Union flag over the half-submerged fortification, Stembel accompanied Tilghman back to the *Cincinnati*. The Federal sailors went crazy with jubilant emotion, so much so that Foote "had to run among the men and knock them on the head to restore order."

Fort Henry's garrison suffered 99 casualties (five dead, 11 wounded, five missing, and 78 captured) during the holding action. Seventeen pieces of heavy ordnance were captured or destroyed. The hospital boat *Patton* was captured. General Grant reached the fort about an hour after its capture. Entering the fort, Union officers described what they saw. "The effect of the fire on the fortifications here was terrible — guns dismounted — earthworks torn up and the evidences of carnage meet the eye on every hand." Another remarked that "the devastation astonished me all the more when I recalled the short time in which it had been accomplished." One sailor noted, "On every side lay the lifeless bodies of the victims, in reckless confusion, intermingled with

shattered implements of war."

Flag Officer Foote worried about the damage to his fleet. He vowed "never again will I go into a fight half-prepared." He also thought that "we have made the narrowest escape possible with our boats and our lives." The gunboats were ordered back to Paducah and Cairo for repairs.

The fall of Fort Henry to the Federal gunboats made a heavy impression upon Confederate theater commander Albert Sidney Johnston, who noted that the battle "indicates that the best open earth works are not reliable to meet successfully a vigorous attack of iron clad gun boats." Johnston began to intimate that he might pull his entire army out of Kentucky and southward into Tennessee.

On Fort Henry, the Union's first significant victory of the war, historian Gott wrote: "One of the poorest lessons the Confederate troops learned from their officers was that surrender or fleeing the battlefield was somehow tolerable. Colonel Heiman, Lt. Col. Haynes, and Major Gilmer fled from the scene even though they were inside the fort at the time of surrender...the precedent had been set that a fortified position was not necessarily defended to the bitter end."

Grant telegraphed headquarters, "Fort Henry is ours." Halleck wired Washington: "The flag of the

Union is re-established on the soil of Tennessee. It will never be removed." Grant also told Halleck, "I shall take and destroy Fort Donelson on the 8th and return to Fort Henry."

Foote took his victorious yet heavily damaged fleet back downriver to its headquarters at Cairo for needed repairs, flying the captured rebel flag of Fort Henry upside-down from his flagboat's stern staff. Phelps' three timberclads remained on the scene and were ordered by Foote up the Tennessee River on a bold and daring raid. On February 11, after days of delay, the first of Grant's troops began heading eastward toward Fort Donelson on the Cumberland River.

Ironically, two days later, Fort Henry would disappear altogether under the rising waters of the Tennessee River.

Historian Benjamin F. Cooling wrote, "Fort Henry demonstrated that the Civil War in the West would be fought largely for control of the rivers—antebellum commercial arteries that became wartime barriers to effective Confederate unity and Union avenues for military, political, and economic reconstruction."

The significance of the capture of Fort Henry was stated plainly by *New York Times* correspondent Franc B. Wilkie, who wrote: "The value of the victory at Fort Henry will, in view of the shortness of the battle and the small number of prisoners, be very generally regarded as of no great consequence. In truth, the result is quite the contrary ... The surrender of the fort breaks up the rebel line of fortification, which extended from Columbus on the west to Bowling Green on the east, and opens to our forces a highway easy to be traversed and along which operations can be carried nearly to the Gulf without opposition. By its taking, our troops can reach the very heart of the South without formidable hindrance—indeed there are no works of any kind between Fort Henry and any point further north than Tuscumbia, in Alabama."

–Chapter Six–

# The Phelps Raid

*A daring raid deep into the heart of the Confederacy*
*deals a psychological blow to secessionists*

Immediately following the surrender of Fort Henry on Feb. 6, 1862, Lieutenant Commander Seth L. Phelps led his flotilla of three timberclad gunboats up the Tennessee River on a daring raid deep into the heartland of the Confederacy. The excursion had been ordered beforehand by Flag Officer Andrew H. Foote. Their first and main objective was the destruction of the Memphis, Clarksville & Louisville Railroad bridge at Danville, 25 miles upriver (south) of the fort. If the raid went well, the flotilla might also threaten the Memphis & Charleston Railroad bridge at Big Bear Creek in northwestern Alabama.

Phelps' flagboat was the *USS Conestoga*, the smallest and fastest of the timberclads, armed with four 32-pounder smoothbores. The *Conestoga* was one of the "racier breed of boats and walked the water like a thing of life," according to a newspaper correspondent. The *USS Tyler*, the slowest of the three and commanded by Lieutenant William Gwin, was armed with a 32-pounder smoothbore and six 8-inch Dahlgrens. A native of Indiana, Gwin had transferred to the western rivers from duty on the seagoing *USS Susquehanna*. In early 1862 he would succeed Phelps as leader of the timberclad flotilla. He was then transferred to the flagboat *USS Benton* and was wounded in action at Haines Bluff, Miss. on Dec. 27, 1862. He died a week later. The *USS Lexington* was armed with two 32-pounder smoothbores and four 8-inch Dahlgrens. It was commanded by Lt. James W. Shirk. A native of Pennsylvania, Shirk had been a midshipman aboard Commodore Matthew C. Perry's ship *Mississippi* during the opening of trade with Japan in the 1850s.

Shirk was constantly at sea prior to his posting with the western rivers assignment. Later, he would skipper the ironclad *Chillicothe* and serve as commander of the Tennessee River District, eventually becoming the longest-serving junior officer in the Mississippi Squadron. Commissioned a commander in 1866, Shirk died in 1873.

Responding to Foote's Special Order Three, the timberclad flotilla cast off at 5:00 pm, immediately following the fall of Fort Henry. The Confederate steamer *Dunbar,* commanded by Captain Gus Fowler, had watched the battle from upstream and had an hour's headstart on the gunboats. The flotilla's first task, however, came at Paris Landing, near the mouth of the Big Sandy River, where a landing party from the *Conestoga* torched the abandoned camps of the 48th and 51st Tennessee Regiments. As the flotilla approached the 1,200-foot-long Danville swingbridge at 7:30 pm, the *Conestoga* caught up with the other two gunboats. They were fired upon by Confederate riflemen. A shelling from the *Lexington* ended that threat. The bridge was closed shut after the machinery to open the bridge had been jammed by the retreating Confederates.

Smoke upriver about one-and-a-half miles indicated several fleeing steamboats (the *Dunbar, Appleton Belle, Lynn Boyd, Samuel Orr,* and *Time*) laden with goods from the bridge encampments. According to one newspaperman, the *Dunbar* "flew like a deer before a pack of hounds, giving warning to all boats and all points along the river." Capt. Fowler informed all ashore that the advancing Yankees were "firebrands, burning, destroying, ravishing, and pillaging." By 9:00 pm, when the bridge mechanism was fixed, the Confederate boats had a good lead. The *Tyler,* commanded by Gwin, was ordered to destroy the railroad approaches on both sides of the bridge and to secure all military stores. Second Master Jacob Goudy's men were assigned to the task. Also, back at Fort Henry, General Grant dispatched Missouri troops aboard the steamer *Illinois* to paddle upriver and assist in the bridge's

The swingbridge over the Tennessee River at Danville

destruction. In destroying the bridge trestlework and the adjacent Confederate encampment, the *Tyler* landing party seized papers belonging to Isaac Newton Brown, a former U.S. Navy lieutenant, which detailed plans for the building of Confederate ironclad gunboats. Mississippi cavalry from Paris, Tennessee, under Lt. Col. John H. Miller, seized the bridge after the *Tyler* departed and prevented the work detail on the *Illinois* from landing.

Meanwhile, the *Conestoga* and *Lexington* steamed in pursuit and caught up to the *Samuel Orr* in the next two hours, ten miles from the bridge. The steamer's paddlewheel had been damaged, and realizing their fate was doomed, the rebel captain grounded his steamboat (loaded with 1,700 pounds of black powder and 27 submarine mines), set it on fire, and abandoned ship. The cargo exploded with great fury, and fire consumed the vessel.

Now the swift *Conestoga* took the lead, with the *Lexington* bringing up the rear. By 2:00 am on February 7, they had almost caught up with the *Appleton Belle* and the *Lynn Boyd*. The captains of those steamers realized that they could not escape and grounded their transport boats on the riverbank near the house of Judge Creavatt, a well-known Union sympathizer, and torched them. One of the boats, the *Appleton Belle,* loaded with 3,000 pounds

*(Continued on Page 72)*

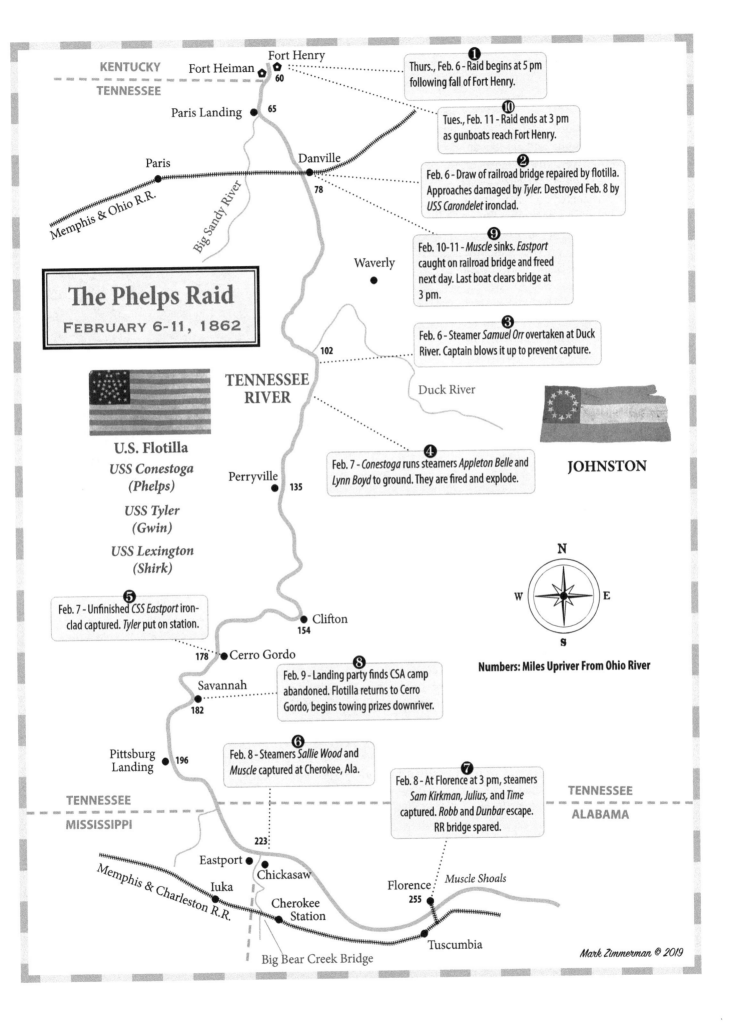

# The Phelps Raid
## FEBRUARY 6-11, 1862

KENTUCKY
TENNESSEE

Fort Heiman ⬡ ⬠ Fort Henry
60

Paris Landing ● 65

Paris ●
Danville ●
78

Memphis & Ohio R.R.

Big Sandy River

Waverly ●

TENNESSEE RIVER

Duck River

**U.S. Flotilla**

*USS Conestoga*
(Phelps)

*USS Tyler*
(Gwin)

*USS Lexington*
(Shirk)

**JOHNSTON**

Perryville ● 135

102

Clifton ●
154

178 ● Cerro Gordo

Savannah ●
182

Pittsburg Landing ● 196

TENNESSEE
MISSISSIPPI

223

Eastport ●
Chickasaw ●

Iuka ●

Cherokee Station ●

Memphis & Charleston R.R.

Big Bear Creek Bridge

Florence ● 255  *Muscle Shoals*

Tuscumbia ●

TENNESSEE
ALABAMA

**N** / **S** / **E** / **W**

**Numbers: Miles Upriver From Ohio River**

**❶** Thurs., Feb. 6 - Raid begins at 5 pm following fall of Fort Henry.

**❿** Tues., Feb. 11 - Raid ends at 3 pm as gunboats reach Fort Henry.

**❷** Feb. 6 - Draw of railroad bridge repaired by flotilla. Approaches damaged by *Tyler*. Destroyed Feb. 8 by *USS Carondelet* ironclad.

**❾** Feb. 10-11 - *Muscle* sinks. *Eastport* caught on railroad bridge and freed next day. Last boat clears bridge at 3 pm.

**❸** Feb. 6 - Steamer *Samuel Orr* overtaken at Duck River. Captain blows it up to prevent capture.

**❹** Feb. 7 - *Conestoga* runs steamers *Appleton Belle* and *Lynn Boyd* to ground. They are fired and explode.

**❺** Feb. 7 - Unfinished *CSS Eastport* ironclad captured. *Tyler* put on station.

**❽** Feb. 9 - Landing party finds CSA camp abandoned. Flotilla returns to Cerro Gordo, begins towing prizes downriver.

**❻** Feb. 8 - Steamers *Sallie Wood* and *Muscle* captured at Cherokee, Ala.

**❼** Feb. 8 - At Florence at 3 pm, steamers *Sam Kirkman, Julius,* and *Time* captured. *Robb* and *Dunbar* escape. RR bridge spared.

*Mark Zimmerman © 2019*

of black powder, exploded with a terrific roar which lit up the night and rained debris for a half-mile down the river. The skylights on the *Conestoga*, 1,000 yards away, were shattered and her upper deck lifted and damaged. Doors were forced open, and fasteners shaken loose on the boat. The house on the bank, unoccupied at the time, was blown to smithereens. "The whole river for half a mile around about was completely beaten up by the falling fragments and the shower of shot, grape, balls, etc.," Phelps wrote in his after-report.

Lt. Commander James Shirk (above) and Lt. Commander William Gwin (right).

At this point, Phelps decided to anchor and wait for the other timberclads to catch up. The *Lexington* arrived within the hour and the *Tyler* appeared at daybreak on Feb. 7. The raid resumed at 6:00 am southward up the Tennessee River. At 9:00 am, a Confederate flag was cut down at Hawesport and at 10:50 am the Union flotilla touched shore briefly at Perry Landing to the cheers of a small group of Unionists waving handkerchieves and U.S. flags. By dusk on the second day of the raid the timberclads reached Cerro Gordo, a landing in Hardin County, where they claimed an exciting prize. On the east bank of the river sat the *CSS Eastport*, a 230-foot-long sidewheeler steamboat being converted into a Confederate ironclad. Sharpshooters fired upon the Union gunboats and the landing party from the *Conestoga*, but shelling from the gunboats drove them off. The flotilla spent the night at Cerro Gordo (named for a battle in the Mexican War). It was quickly learned that the Confederates had broken pipes on the unfinished vessel to scuttle her, but the damage was fixed before she sank. The gunboat was half-finished and in excellent condition, with her iron plating stacked on the riverbank along with lumber and other materials. She had been built in 1852 in New Albany, Ind., for $45,000; plied the Mississippi River on the New Orleans route for nearly ten years; and purchased for conversion by Major General Leonidas Polk in November 1861 for $9,689. The sidewheeler was powered by two steam engines and five boilers. More papers authored by Lt. Isaac Brown were seized, reporting to Confederate authorities that submarine mines were impractical against enemy boats in the swift western rivers. Again, the *Tyler* was assigned to stay behind and guard the prize.

On February 8, the *USS Carondelet* ironclad, commanded by Lt. Commander Henry Walke, was ordered to the Danville bridge with the 32nd Illinois Regiment aboard. The detachment ripped up bridge trestles and caused major damage to a bridge pier. No more trains would be crossing the Tennessee River at that site.

Also that day, the Union timberclad flotilla seized the steamers *Sallie Wood* and *Muscle* at Waterloo Landing near Chickasaw, Alabama. The *Muscle* was caught hauling a load of pig iron bound for Confederate foundries in Richmond, Virginia. At 8:30 am, a message was received at

Florence from Gen. Albert S. Johnston to destroy the railroad bridge over the Tennessee River. The city on the north bank of the river was connected to the south bank and the main railroad line by a railroad spur and bridge. It was here that navigation on the Tennessee River ended due to Muscle Shoals. Despite the general's orders, the local populace refused to damage their beloved bridge.

Leaving a prize crew behind with the captured steamboats, the Union flotilla steamed to Florence at 3:30 pm, only to be met by two steamers afire on the shore (the *Time* and *Samuel Kirkman*) and a third steamer, the *Julian H. Smith,* torched and set adrift in reverse with engines at full throttle. The timberclads maneuvered hastily to avoid the inferno. The blazing steamboat eventually was blown into the riverbank by the wind. The timberclads took fire from sharpshooters and responded with round shot. The gunboats tied up near the railroad bridge and landed a party, which confiscated more than $100,000 in Confederate stores destined for Fort Henry. The cargo from the two scuttled transports was more than the Yankees could load onto their gunboats. The remainder on shore was destroyed, including ten tons of salted pork (that which wasn't consumed at the scene).

Two Confederate boats, the *CSS Robb* and *Dunbar,* had been notified of the Yankee advance and escaped up the shallow Big Cypress Creek near Eastport. Now, on the entire lower Tennessee River, only four of the 13 steamboats operating at the time of Fort Henry remained in operation.

A delegation of Florence citizens met with Lt. Phelps, concerned that the Yankees would harm the women and children, their fears motivated by wild rumors that the Yankee gunboats were manned by convicts and reprobates yearning for pillage and rape. The citizens also asked that the railroad bridge be spared. Phelps agreed, believing that the bridge was of little military importance and might block Union navigation if destroyed. Phelps came to regret his decision as the Confederate army used the bridge later in the war to move men and supplies quickly across the Tennessee River. The bridge was eventually destroyed by the Confederates in 1863.

In his after-action report, Phelps stated, "A deputation of citizens of Florence waited upon me, first desiring that they might be made able to quiet the fears of their wives and daughters with assurances from me that they would not be molested; and, secondly, praying that I would not destroy their railroad bridge. As for the first, I told them we were neither ruffians nor savages, and that we were there to protect from violence and to enforce the law; and with reference to the second, that if the bridge were away we could ascend no higher, and that it could possess, so far as I saw, no military importance, as it simply connected Florence itself with the railroad on the south bank of the river."

The procession of the three Yankee timberclads, heavily armed but lightly armored, motivated the citizens of Huntsville, Alabama, several miles to the east, into forming a militia armed with one brass 6-pounder and a Parrott rifle. Confederate President Jefferson Davis informed them that the 9th Mississippi Regiment and two artillery batteries had been ordered to nearby Tuscumbia. He urged the civilians to arm themselves and "go to meet the enemy," hoping that they would capture the gunboats. His message reached Huntsville the day after the gunboats had left Florence and headed back downriver.

Confederate authorities also were concerned about the vulnerability of the railroad bridge at Big Bear Creek in Alabama. CSA Major General Polk, commander of West Tennessee, ordered six companies of the 38th Tennessee, Deshler's Arkansas artillery battery, and another section of artillery to move from Corinth, Miss. to the bridge at the creek. The commander at Corinth, Major General Benjamin Franklin Cheatham, already had dispatched Colonel James R. Chalmers and his 9th Mississippi infantry to guard the bridge. As it turned out, the flotilla did not attempt to capture or destroy the Big Bear Creek bridge.

While the rest of the flotilla had steamed to Florence, Lt. Gwin on the *Tyler* enrolled 25 Tennesseans into Federal service at Cerro Gordo and learned about a large Confederate winter encampment several miles upstream at Savannah, Tenn., composed of the 700 men of Lt. Col. James M. Crew. It was said that a large portion of those men had been impressed against their will and that they were inadequately armed.

After spending three hours at Florence, the *Conestoga* and the *Lexington* started back downriver (northward) at dusk. They reunited with Gwin and the *Tyler* at Cerro Gordo the morning of February 9, having brought along the two captured steamboats. The captured *Eastport* had been loaded with 50,000 feet of lumber, in addition to machinery, iron plates, spikes, and nails. Meanwhile, the commanders consulted and decided to attack the encampment a few miles upstream at Savannah. This time the *Lexington* was left behind to protect the *Eastport* at Cerro Gordo while the *Conestoga* and *Tyler* cast off for the raid. On board the *Conestoga* were *Lexington* commander Shirk and 30 of his best men. A landing party of 130 men was organized enroute with Lt. Gwin in charge. The landing party, armed with a 12-pounder rifled howitzer, swarmed ashore and found to their immense disappointment and "mortification" that the Confederates had abandoned their log huts and burned them. However, a large quantity of arms, clothing, shoes, utensils, provisions and implements were confiscated or destroyed. Also, a cache of about 70 rifles was secured by another landing party at a point downstream from the camp.

The *Conestoga* and *Tyler* returned downstream to the *Lexington* at Cerro Gordo and each timberclad took a prize in tow — the *CSS Eastport*, the *Muscle*, and the *Sallie Wood*. Before departing, the Yankees burned down the lumber mill that had processed the timber. The flotilla reached the bridge at Danville at 11:00 am on February 10, but not before the *Muscle* sprang a leak and had to be abandoned. It sank, along with 5,000 feet of prime sawed wood. In passing through the gap in the bridge, the *Eastport* got hung up on a bridge pier. The men of the 14th Missouri infantry, who had arrived at the site aboard the *Illinois*, struggled to free the vessel. It was mid-morning on February 11 before the *Eastport* could be cleared and the flotilla journey resumed. The Phelps raid ended at 3:00 pm on February 11 as the gunboats arrived back at Fort Henry.

During the six-day raid, the three timberclads had wrecked a vital Confederate railroad bridge,

## Cedar Grove Iron Furnace

Tennessee's iron industry was strategically important to both North and South. Numerous furnaces supplied iron to foundries to manufacture munitions as well as armor for ironclad vessels. The fall of Forts Henry and Donelson in February 1862 opened the Tennessee River to Union gunboats. That month, one such flotilla (*USS Conestoga, Tyler,* and *Lexington*) shelled this ironworks, where the ironmaster's house, office, company store, workers' houses, barns, smokehouse, and other buildings surrounded the furnace. At least 100 people, black and white, worked here.

*Historical marker located at 6554 Buckfork Rd., Linden, TN 37096*

forced the scuttling of six transports and their cargoes, caused a seventh vessel to be destroyed trying to escape, and captured the *CSS Eastport* ironclad and two other vessels. The raid had rattled the Confederate authorities and frightened Southern civilians while encouraging those who remained loyal to the Union.

The panic which later gripped the citizens of Nashville and Clarksville, up the Cumberland River from Fort Donelson, and the abandonment of three forts on that river upon the approach of the gunboats attests to the apprehension that these floating batteries generated. Much of that fear was due to wild rumors and imagination, but no small part was due to the successful raid by Lt. Phelps deep into the heart of the Confederacy meeting minimal resistance. Forays much later in the war, such as Sherman's March to the Sea, would be noted for their effect on Southern morale. The Phelps raid early in the war had the same effect.

"The Union could move up the river as it chose," wrote historian Jack Smith. The Charleston *Mercury* had to admit that the raid was "an audacious and hazardous thing." It was the only time that all three timberclads acted together under one commander.

Lt. Phelps was much impressed with the greetings of loyalists during the raid. In his report, he stated: "We have met with the most gratifying proofs of loyalty everywhere across Tennessee, and in the portions of Mississippi and Alabama we visited most affecting instances greeted us almost hourly. Men, women, and children several times gathered in crowds of hundreds, shouted their welcome and hailed their national flag with an enthusiasm there was no mistaking. It was genuine and heartfelt. Those people braved everything to go to the river bank, where a sight of their flag might once more be enjoyed, and they have experienced, as they related,

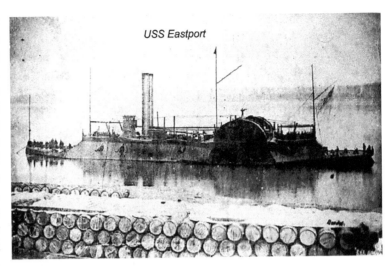

*USS Eastport*

every possible form of persecution. Tears flowed freely down the cheeks of men as well as of women, and there were those who had fought under the stars and stripes at Moultrie, who, in this manner testified to their joy.

"This display of feeling and sense of gladness at our success, and the hopes it created in the breasts of so many people in the heart of the Confederacy astonished us not a little, and I assure you, sir, I would not have failed to witness it for any consideration. I trust it has given us all a higher sense of the sacred character of our present duties. I was assured at Savannah that of the several hundred troops there, more than one-half, had we gone to the attack in time, would have hailed us as deliverers and gladly enlisted with the national force.

"In Tennessee the people generally in their enthusiasm braved secessionists and spoke their views freely; but in Mississippi and Alabama what was said was guarded. If we dared express ourselves freely you would hear such a shout greeting your coming as you never heard. We know there are many Unionists among us, but a reign of terror makes us afraid of our shadows. We were told, too, Bring us a small organized force with arms and ammunition for us, and we can maintain our position and put down rebellion in our midst. There were, it is true, whole communities who, on our approach, fled to the woods, but these were where there was less of the loyal element and where the fleeing steamers in advance had spread tales of our coming with

firebrands, burning, destroying, ravishing, and plundering."

An interesting footnote to the Phelps raid is the fate of Lt. Phelps and the *CSS Eastport*. Finished and outfitted at Mound City as the *USS Eastport*, she was extended to 280 feet long and 43 feet wide, and heavily armed. Her bow was outfitted with a three-ton wrought-iron ram designed to literally tear into enemy boats. The newly converted *USS Eastport*, which bore no resemblence to the old steamer it had once been, was to be the pride of the flotilla and serve as its flagboat. She went into action in August 1862 with Phelps as her commander, serving on the Mississippi River, one of the largest ironclads afloat. However, within a year's time the ironclad had seen no action but had to be outfitted with two new bottoms due to wear and tear. On the river, she proved to be much slower and troublesome than expected, and began to inherit a hardluck reputation.

The *Eastport* steamed from Cairo to join her squadron at Vicksburg, Miss., but struck bottom on Feb. 2, 1863 and returned to Cairo for repairs. She stood down the river on June 19 for Helena, Arkansas, and served the rest of her career on the Mississippi River and its tributaries as a convoy and patrol vessel, helping capture more than 14,000 bales of cotton. On March 5, 1864, she dropped down to the mouth of the Red River for a joint Army-Navy expedition. She passed through the obstructions below Fort De Russy, in whose capture she joined, then continued up the Red River above Grand Ecore. On April 15, 1864, she suffered a torpedo (naval mine) explosion. Numerous times, the *Eastport* grounded and had to be put back afloat. Despite every effort to bring her out, she had to be destroyed to prevent her from falling into Confederate hands.

Phelps wrote to his superior Admiral Porter: "[Destroying the *Eastport*] has been the most painful one experienced by me in my official career. She was the finest vessel of your squadron and one of the best possessed by the Government." Even to the last, the *Eastport* struggled. The first attempt to detonate gunpowder charges put aboard the gunboat failed. Then an additional 3,000 pounds of gunpowder were placed aboard. The after-casemate blew up, followed by the stern magazine, which threw great chunks of casemate into the sky. A few minutes later the forward casemate blew up. There followed seven explosions, and then the gunboat was consumed by fire. A year later, after the war, the steamer Ed. F. Dix sank on top of the submerged wreck of the gunboat. In 1989-93, archaeologists with the U.S. Army Corps of Engineers found the remains of both boats buried under 30 feet of sand about one mile below Montgomery, Louisiana. The boats were excavated and examined, the hull of the *Eastport* being largely intact and in good condition. The wrecks were then reburied, where they still remain.

"The *Eastport* was among the largest vessels lost by the U.S. Navy during the Civil War," according to historian Charles E. Pearson. "Plagued by bad luck and misfortune throughout her military career, she never lived up to the Navy's expectations as a fighting vessel."

The fate of Phelps' flagboat, the *USS Conestoga* timberclad, was also a sad one. During the rest of her service, the *Conestoga* continued to operate along the rivers. She took part in the bombardment of Saint Charles, Arkansas, in June 1862 and was formally transferred to the navy in October of that year. In April and July 1863, she was involved in expeditions to Palmyra, Tenn., and up the Red River in Louisiana. The following March, she went up Louisiana's Black and Ouachita rivers. Soon after, on March 8, 1864, the *Conestoga* was sunk in an accidental collision with the *USS General Price*.

Phelps wrote: "The pilot of the *Price* managed to run into the *Conestoga* and to injure her so badly that she sank in 30 feet of water within five minutes time. Few people escaped except two — the hospital steward and a seaman — but with nothing save the clothes they stood in. Poor old *Conestoga!* A vessel whose good fortune had been a marvel for years has at length met a tragic end. It is a great pity, for there are few vessels whose history is so full of adventure in this war."

– Chapter Seven –

# Fort Donelson, Clarksville, and Nashville

*The Cumberland River is conquered despite the defeat
of the ironclads by Confederate gunners*

General Grant's troops spent Feb. 11-13, 1862 investing the sprawling 554-acre Fort Donelson, their 12-mile march from Fort Henry having been hotly contested by Colonel Forrest's troopers. Flag Officer Foote tended to his damaged fleet at the Cairo dockyards and prepared for another naval expedition. This time the attacking fleet would consist of the City Class ironclads *Carondelet* and *St. Louis,* plus the *Louisville* (Commander Benjamin Dove) and the *Pittsburg* (Egbert Thompson), and two of the timberclads, the *Conestoga* and the *Tyler.* Meanwhile, General Albert S. Johnston, commander of Confederate forces in the Western Theater, began to withdraw from his base at Bowling Green, Kentucky, and headed to Murfreesboro, Tennessee, declining to reinforce the troops at Fort Donelson or defend Nashville. Due to several factors, he reacted to the fall of Fort Henry by professing apprehension of the Federal gunboat fleet. He did not believe that Fort Donelson could withstand a naval assault. He became alarmed at the thought of being caught between Grant's army and that of Union General Don Carlos Buell, moving southward from Louisville, Kentucky.

Unlike Fort Henry, the river batteries at Fort Donelson, located between the earthen fort itself and the river and just downstream from the village of Dover, were located significantly above the surface of the Cumberland River. The elevated site would allow plunging fire from the Confederate guns to hit the sloped sides of the ironclads at right angles, with much more force, instead of glancing off.

*Exchanging Iron Valentines* by Andy Thomas, artist

Also, the ironclads were more lightly armored on the top deck and around the rear of the casemate. The rudders in the stern were also vulnerable. The pilothouses, thinly armored, were easy targets and prone to damage (later, the pilothouses would be converted to the heavily clad octagonal structures, as seen on the recovered *USS Cairo*).

Fort Donelson's lower battery, the one furthest downstream and closest to the advancing gunboats, was 20 feet above the river's surface and featured a 10-inch Columbiad that fired a 128-lb. shell, and eight 32-pounder smoothbores. The upper battery was 150 feet upstream and 50 feet above the river and featured a 10-inch Columbiad rifle that fired a 68-lb. shell and two 32-pounder naval carronades, which had a much more limited range. Both batteries were commanded by Colonel Milton Haynes and directed by Lieutenant Joseph Dixon, with 200 men of Captain Reuben Ross' Maury Artillery (part of the 1st Tennessee Artillery) manning the guns. Lt. Hugh Bedford directed the Columbiad in the lower battery, while Capt. Ross commanded the rifled Columbiad in the upper battery.

Around noon on Wed., Feb. 12, 1862, the U.S. ironclad *Carondelet,* commanded by Henry Walke, arrived in the fort's vicinity under tow from the steamer *Alps.* Approaching the fort alone, the *Carondelet* opened fire to provoke a response and signal to Grant that the gunboat flotilla had arrived. The Confederates held their fire. The gunboat retreated.

At 10:00 am the next morning, the *Carondelet* again pushed upstream alone into position about a mile from the imposing river batteries and opened fire from her three bow guns. This time, Dixon ordered the two Columbiads to return fire. Their third shot zeroed in on the gunboat but caused little damage. At the end of the 90-minute duel, however, disaster struck, as a projectile from the 6.5-inch rifled Columbiad hit the corner where the port side of the *Carondelet's* casemate joined the bow protection. "Tearing through the exterior," wrote historian Jack Smith, "it ricocheted over the temporary log barricade Walke had placed around the boilers, jumped over the steam-drum, hit upper

*(Continued on Page 80)*

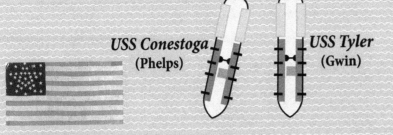

USS *Conestoga*
(Phelps)

USS *Tyler*
(Gwin)

**FOOTE**

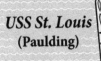

USS *St. Louis*
(Paulding)

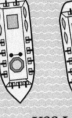

USS *Louisville*
(Dove)

USS *Pittsburg*
(Thompson)

USS *Carondelet*
(Walke)

## The Battle at FORT DONELSON
### FEBRUARY 14, 1862

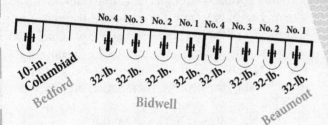

No. 4  No. 3  No. 2  No. 1  No. 4  No. 3  No. 2  No. 1

10-in.
Columbiad
Bedford

32-lb.  32-lb.  32-lb.  32-lb.  32-lb.  32-lb.  32-lb.  32-lb.

Bidwell

Beaumont

**Lower Battery**

■
magazine

**CUMBERLAND RIVER**

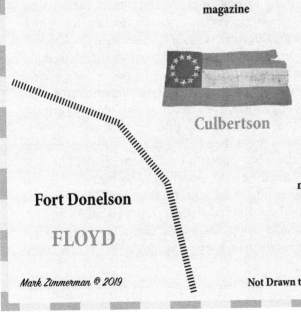

Culbertson

No. 1      No. 2      No. 3

32-lb.      6.5-in. rifle      32-lb.
carronade                      carronade

■
magazine

**Upper Battery**

Ross

**Fort Donelson**

**FLOYD**

Dover
↓

*Mark Zimmerman © 2019*          **Not Drawn to Scale**

The lower battery at Fort Donelson National Battlefield looking downstream on the Cumberland River. The view is slightly distorted by the wide-angle lens of the camera. Shown are 32-pounder cannons on seige carriages.

deck beams, carried away the railing around the engine room, and burst the steam-heater before bouncing back to rest in the engine room." One of the assistant engineers later remarked that the shot seemed to "bound after the men like a wild beast pursuing its prey." Twelve sailors were wounded, seven severely, mostly by flying wooden splinters of various sizes.

On the other hand, one of the 139 shells launched by the *Carondelet* that morning hit the carriage of a 32-pounder and dismounted it, wounding four and killing two men, including Capt. Dixon, who was struck in the side of the head by a dislodged piece of hardware and killed instantly. Replacing him was Captain Jacob Culbertson.

The Yankee ironclad withdrew from the skirmish only to return in the afternoon to play a cat-and-mouse game with the gunners. She nearly depleted her magazine by expending 45 more shells, causing more damage to the fort that day than the following day's major naval battle involving six gunboats.

Friday, Feb. 14, 1862 found Foote's gunboat fleet exchanging "iron valentines" with the two river batteries at Fort Donelson. At dawn the temperature was ten degrees and there was two inches of snow on the ground. At 2:38 pm, the rifled Columbiad opened fire on the four ironclads a mile-and-a-half away, the two timberclads a thousand yards further back. At 2:50 pm, the guns of the flagboat *St. Louis*

opened fire within range of the fort's 32-pounders. During the exchange, the *Carondelet* began firing so rapidly that the methodical Foote hailed Walke with his speaking trumpet and told him to slow down. The smoke from the guns and the belching chimneys plus the thunderous explosions of the guns, the paddling of the wheels against the strong current, and the clanking of shells against iron cladding thrilled the shorebound audience of blueclad Federal troops, the Confederates in the fort, and the villagers of Dover. Within 45 minutes, the gunboats had approached to 400 yards of the lower battery.

The behavior of Colonel Nathan Bedford Forrest and his second-in-command Major D.C. Kelley, the "Fighting Parson," was particulary interesting during this battle. Capt. J.C. Blanton of Co. C noted: "During this bombardment and when it looked like the furies of hell were turned loose on us, I looked down the line and saw Kelley sitting on a camp stool leaning on a tent pole reading his Bible. My curiosity was at once excited, and wondering if it were possible for a man to be interested even in reading God's word under such circumstances, I walked to where he was, stood close to him until I was satisfied that he was deeply interested in the Book. I went back and called some comrades' attention to it, and after going close to him they returned in perfect amazement that any man could be so composed amid such roaring of cannon shots, and screaming shells. Why, the very earth was quivering under us."

Forrest, on the other hand, was definitely concerned about the shelling. He watched the shot of the 32-pounders "roll off the boats like water off a duck's back." The heaviest gun in the rebel battery was knocked off its carriage, leaving only a single heavy gun (the 32-pounders remained in service). Not a man to be easily alarmed or intimidated, Forrest asked Kelley pointedly, "Are you praying? Pray, Major, only God almighty can save us. We have no power to look to but God and one gun."

At this point, however, many of the shells from the gunboats were flying over the river batteries and into the ranks of Federal troops beyond, those who had invested the earthen fort.

Then a Confederate gunner at the rifled Columbiad exclaimed to his fellows that he was going to take away a chimney. He pulled the lanyard and his shot did exactly that — one of the chimneys on the *Carondelet* was carried away. "Come on, you cowardly scoundrels; you are not at Fort Henry!" the gunner bellowed at the sailors. The *Carondelet* was being literally shot to pieces. One of the shells hit the metal pilothouse and an iron splinter mortally wounded the civilian pilot. Another shell wounded the second pilot. Planking and plating were being ripped away "as lightning tears the bark from a tree," according to one witness.

At one point in the frenzy, the premature firing of the *Carondelet's* port-bow 42-pounder resulted in an explosion that rocked the boat, wounding more than a dozen men. The big gun burst into four large pieces, one of which tumbled through the port and into the river. Amazingly, no one was killed — the crew had recognized the impending danger and had time to back away before the explosion.

The flagboat *St. Louis* was hit 59 times and had her rudder chains severed. The pilot was killed in his house and Flag Officer Foote himself wounded,

The stern rudders and tiller linkage on the gunboats proved vulnerable to gunfire.

in the foot. The *Louisville* was hit numerous times, one shot decapitating three sailors and splattering Commander Dove with their brains.

The *Pittsburg* sustained 30 hits and was hit below the hull and took on water. She turned and crashed into the stern of the *Carondelet*, disabling her starboard rudder.

The gunboats were all drifting downriver away from the fort, the *Carondelet* exposing only her bow. The Confederate gunners began skipping their shots across the water like flat stones. One rattled into and through a bow port but caused no damage. Another shot glanced off a bow gun and decapitated two sailors who refused to follow the "Down!" command. Signal Quartermaster Matthew Arther of the *Carondelet* later received the Navy Medal of Honor for carrying out his duties as signal master and captain of the rifled bow gun.

Shells from the timberclads back in the rear of the formation began to hit the ironclads. An 8-inch shell from the *Tyler* hit the stern of the *Carondelet*; a piece of shrapnel was later dug out of the wood and kept by Commander Walke, no fan of the timberclads, as a souvenir. All in all the *Carondelet* was hit 54 times, with four killed and 29 injured.

The battle ended as the disabled Union ironclads were carried downriver by the current. During the

*(Continued on Page 83)*

FLAG-SHIP ST. LOUIS,
Near Fort Donelson, Cumberland River, February 15, 1862
Major-General HALLECK,
Commanding Army of the West, Saint Louis, Mo.

SIR: I have the honor to report that, as you regarded the movement as a military necessity, although not in my judgment properly prepared, I made an attack on Fort Donelson yesterday, the 14th instant, at 3 o'clock pm with four iron clad and two wooden gunboats, the St. Louis, Carondelet, Louisville, and Pittsburg, with the Tyler and Conestoga, and after a severe fight of an hour and a half, being in the latter part of the action less than 400 yards from the fort, the wheel of this vessel, by a shot through her pilot-house, was carried away, and the tiller-ropes of the Louisville also disabled by a shot, which rendered the two boats wholly unmanageable. They then drifted down the river, the relieving tackles not being able to steer or control them in the rapid current. The two remaining boats, the Pittsburg and Carondelet, were also greatly damaged between wind and water, and soon followed us, as the enemy rapidly renewed the fire as we drifted helplessly down the river. This vessel, the St. Louis, alone received 59 shots, 4 between wind and water and one in the pilot-house, mortally wounding the pilot and others, requiring some time to put her in repair. There were 54 killed and wounded in this attack, which, notwithstanding our disadvantages, we have every reason to suppose would in fifteen minutes more, could the action have been continued, have resulted in the capture of the two forts bearing upon us, as the enemy's fire materially slackened and he was running from his batteries when the two gunboats helplessly drifted down the river from disabled steering apparatus, as the relieving tackles could not control the helm in the strong current, when the fleeing enemy returned to their guns and again boldly reopened fire upon us from the river battery, which we had silenced.

The enemy must have brought over twenty heavy guns to bear upon our boats from the water batteries and the main fort on the side of the hill, while we could only return the fire with twelve bow guns from the four boats. One rifled gun aboard the Carondelet burst during the action. The officers and men in this hotly-contested but unequal fight behaved with the greatest gallantry and determination, all deploring the accident rendering two gunboats suddenly helpless in the narrow river and swift current.

On consultation with General Grant and my own officers, as my services here, until we can repair damages by bringing up a competent force from Cairo to attack the fort, are much less required than they are at Cairo, I shall proceed to that point with two of the disabled boats, leaving the two others here to protect the transports, and with all dispatch prepare the mortar boats and Benton, with other boats, to make an effectual attack upon Fort Donelson. I have sent the Tyler to the Tennessee River to render impassable the bridge, so as to prevent the rebels at Columbus re-enforcing their army at Fort Donelson.

I transmit herewith a list of casualties. I am informed that the rebels were served by the best gunners from Columbus.

Very respectfully, your obedient servant,
A. H. FOOTE,
Flag-Officer, Comdg. U. S. Naval Forces on the Western Waters.

70-minute shootout, the ironclads were hit 180 times, resulting in nine dead and 45 wounded.

The Confederate gunners had fired 370 shot and shells and did not sustain a single casualty. The gunners in the batteries and soldiers in the rifle pits put up a great celebration, shouting until they were hoarse. "That cheer was the most direful sound," said one soldier from Iowa. The dreaded gunboats, once thought invincible, had been beaten back. One Confederate colonel ordered that the victorious gunners receive a round of good Tennessee whiskey.

During the next two days, the Confederates in the fort pushed the surrounding Federal forces aside in an attempted break-out which was eventually thwarted by indecision within the Confederate high command. The two highest-ranking officers voted to surrender the fort and then fled for their lives; Grant was accorded his demand for unconditional surrender; and 13,000 Confederate soldiers became prisoners of war. Only Colonel Forrest and his cavalry managed to escape the enclosement, fording icy streams, and finding their way to Nashville to fight another day. Many of the Confederates taken prisoner would die in Northern POW camps, while those who survived were pardoned late in 1862. The surrender of so many soldiers was unprecedented, and the Federal officials were woefully unprepared to take care of them.

Grant was hailed throughout the North for his victory and his demand for unconditional surrender, but it wasn't originally his idea. The demand had been suggested previously by Flag Officer Foote and General Charles Ferguson Smith.

Although Grant was a pipe smoker, a newspaper correspondent saw him chewing on a cigar stub and publicized him as a cigar smoker. Celebrated as the victor in the North's first great victory, admirers sent Grant dozens of boxes of cigars which he enjoyed throughout the war. (In 1885 Grant would die of

One of the 32-pounder smoothbores mounted on carriages in the lower Confederate battery at Fort Donelson. (Below) A 32-pounder carronade, one of two mounted in the upper battery.

throat cancer.)

Fort Donelson National Battlefield Historian Jim Jobe speculates that one major reason for the Federal naval defeat on February 14 was that the gunboats needlessly approached too close to the rebel batteries. The gunboats could have stopped at 1,600 yards and shelled the batteries and fort almost with impunity, he noted.

General Johnston was wrong about his fear of the gunboats. Historian Kendall Gott wrote: "When Fort Henry fell to a purely gunboat attack in but two hours, General Johnston himself became convinced that Fort Donelson had no hope of standing up to them. From that point, it seems that Johnston lost his will to put up a determined resistance. Had Johnston seen for himself just how poorly Fort Henry was constructed, he would have realized that its fall was not due simply to the ironclads, and that though they were powerful, they were not invincible."

Church services were suspended in Nashville the morning of Sun., Feb. 16, 1862 when the shocking and unexpected news of the surrender of Fort Donelson arrived. Unsure what to do, and certain that the dreaded gunboats would reduce the city to rubble, the citizens launched into what has been described as the "Great Panic." Depositers rushed the banks, crowds mobbed the warehouses, and southbound trains were filled to overflowing, all while the retreating Confederate army of General Johnston tramped through the city on their journey from Bowling Green to Murfreesboro. Johnston subsequently announced that the army would not defend the city.

"A perfect panic reigned throughout the whole city," said a local Union loyalist. "The streets were thronged with people wild with excitement."

Johnston abandoned Nashville much to the chagrin of the citizenry and moved southward to Columbia. (The Confederate forces would eventually converge at Corinth, Mississippi.)

Nashville Mayor R.B. Cheatham, after consulting with Johnston, addressed a crowd at the courthouse, begging for calm and asking his citizens not to burn the city. He said he would surrender the city to General Buell when he arrived. The First Missouri Regiment was assigned to guard the city against vandalism and looting.

On Feb. 18, 1862, the *St. Louis* destroyed the Cumberland Iron Works, just upstream from Dover, which was partially owned by former U.S. Senator John Bell. Two of Bell's partners were taken prisoner. Bellwood Furnace was also destroyed.

Three days after the fort's surrender, on Feb. 19, 1862, Flag Officer Foote proceeded from Fort Donelson up the Cumberland River toward Clarksville (pop. 5,000) with the timberclad *Conestoga* and the ironclad *USS Cairo* (captained by Lt. Commander Nathaniel Bryant). At mid-afternoon they reached Linwood Landing, a mile below Clarksville, and under the high bluff occupied by Fort Sevier (later called Fort Bruce and Fort Defiance). The fort displayed a white flag, having been abandoned the day before. Although formidably gunned, the fort had been sited too high on the hillside (by CSA engineer Edward Sayers) and at a bad angle to the river. Shortly thereafter, the gunboat crew sighted Fort Clark, housing three guns, at the confluence of the Red River. Apparently a storm had blown down the white flag there; a muddy and dirty white flag was raised up the standard, only to be quickly replaced by the Stars and Stripes of a landing party. Much like Fort Henry, Fort Clark had been sited on a flood plain and was partly underwater.

The dirty flag brings up the curious notion offered by some citizens of Clarksville who feared the intentions of the Lincoln gunboat men since they supposedly had been seen flying the black flag of the pirates. Apparently the U.S. sailors had allowed the Union flag on the gunboats to be sooted to the extent that it resembled from a distance a "dark" flag. Exaggerated rumors then took over.

Three prominent Clarksville citizens, including the mayor, met with Flag Officer Foote and advised that the Confederates had abandoned the city after hearing of the gunboats' approach but not before torching the railroad bridge over the Cumberland River (it was saved) and the road bridge over the Red River. Two-thirds of the panic-striken population had fled the town. Foote assured the delegation that "we came not to destroy anything but forts, military stores, and army equipment."

Landing parties at Clarksville found a message in the telegraph office that the Confederate commander in the town had sent ahead to Nashville advising that the gunboats were coming. The Union officers were thus convinced that Nashville was in a panic and would surrender to the gunboats without firing a shot, which is what eventually did happen.

Clarksville was left with a small garrison of Federal troops, consisting of two regiments commanded by Col. Rodney Mason.

The subsequent history of Clarksville during the early years of the war was a turbulent one. During

*(Continued on Page 88)*

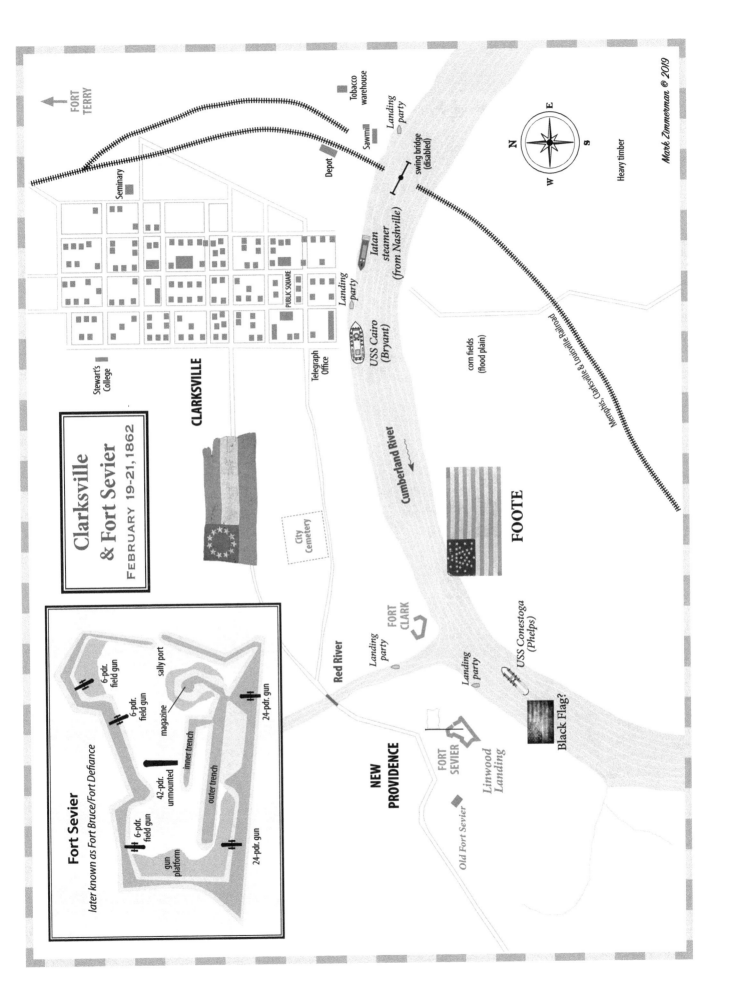

# Clarksville & Fort Sevier
## FEBRUARY 19-21, 1862

### Fort Sevier
*later known as Fort Bruce/Fort Defiance*

- 6-pdr. field gun
- 6-pdr. field gun
- magazine
- sally port
- inner trench
- outer trench
- 24-pdr. gun
- 42-pdr. unmounted
- 6-pdr. field gun
- gun platform
- 24-pdr. gun

**CLARKSVILLE**

Stewart's College

Seminary

FORT TERRY

Depot

Tobacco warehouse

Sawmill

*Landing party*

PUBLIC SQUARE

*Landing party*

Telegraph Office

Iatan steamer (from Nashville)

swing bridge (disabled)

USS Cairo (Bryant)

corn fields (flood plain)

Memphis, Clarksville & Louisville Railroad

Cumberland River

City Cemetery

FOOTE

FORT CLARK

*Landing party*

Red River

*Landing party*

USS Conestoga (Phelps)

Black Flag?

NEW PROVIDENCE

FORT SEVIER

Linwood Landing

Old Fort Sevier

Heavy timber

N E S W

Mark Zimmerman © 2019

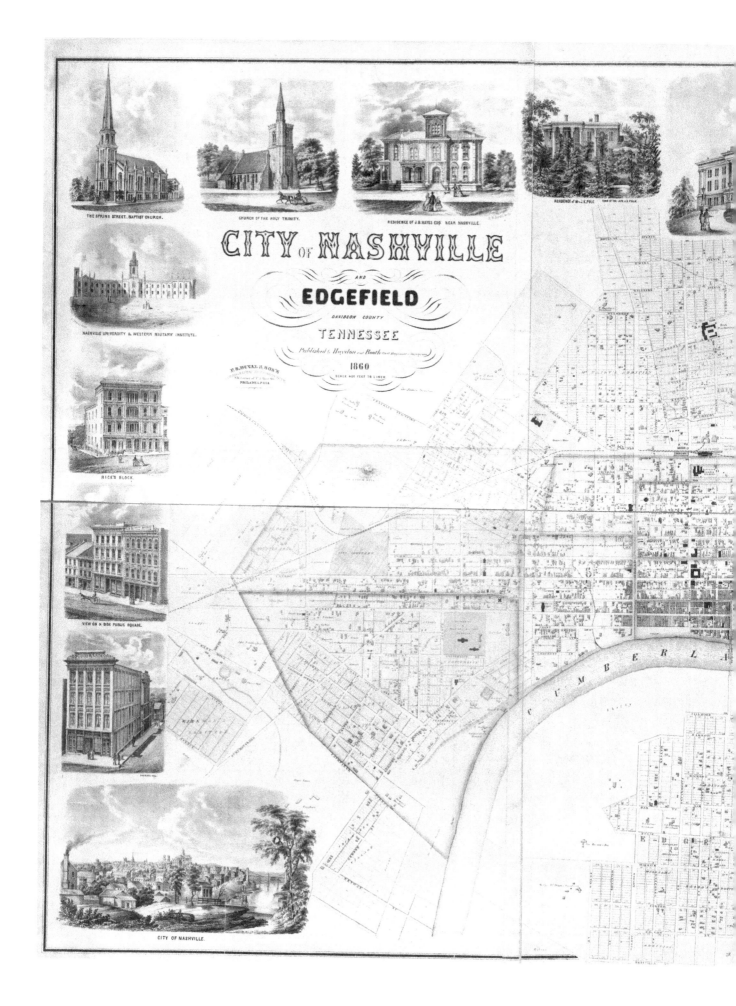

THE SPRING STREET. BAPTIST CHURCH.

CHURCH OF THE HOLY TRINITY.

RESIDENCE OF J.B.HAYES ESQ. NEAR NASHVILLE.

RESIDENCE OF Mrs. J. K. POLK.

TOMB OF THE LATE J.K. POLK.

NASHVILLE UNIVERSITY & WESTERN MILITARY INSTITUTE.

# CITY OF NASHVILLE
### AND
## EDGEFIELD
#### DAVIDSON COUNTY
### TENNESSEE

Published & Engraved and Sold

**1860**

SCALE 400 FEET TO 1 INCH

P. S. DUVAL & SON'S

PHILADELPHIA

RICK'S BLOCK

VIEW ON N. SIDE PUBLIC SQUARE.

CITY OF NASHVILLE.

CUMBERLAND

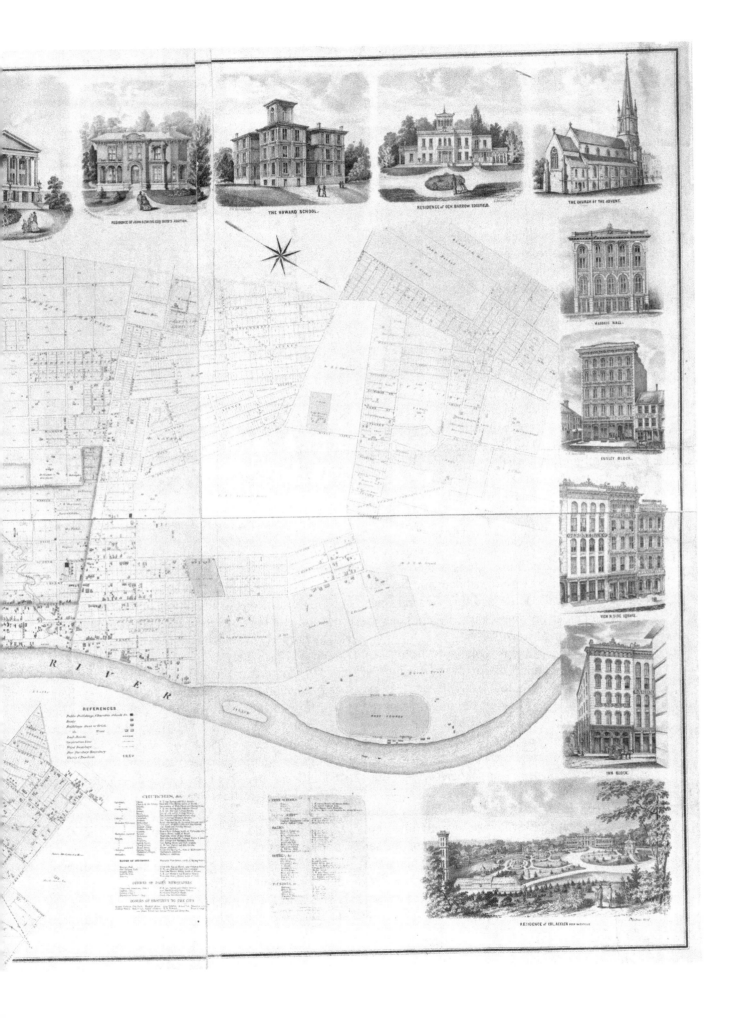

RESIDENCE OF JOHN O.EWING ESQ BOYD'S ADDITION.

THE HOWARD SCHOOL.

RESIDENCE of GEN. BARROW, EDGEFIELD.

THE CHURCH OF THE ADVENT.

MASONIC HALL.

ENSLEY BLOCK.

VIEW IN SIDE SQUARE.

INN BLOCK.

RESIDENCE of COL. ACKLEN NEAR NASHVILLE.

REFERENCES

RIVER

July-August 1862, there was an increase in guerrilla activity around Clarksville. On August 18, Clarksville was re-captured by Confederate cavalry. Col. Mason was cashiered for surrendering Clarksville without much of a fight. In September, Federal troops were sent from Fort Donelson to retake Clarksville. Skirmishes were fought at New Providence and Riggins Hill on September 7. The town and forts were reoccupied by Federal troops, who remained for the rest of the war. Col. Sanders D. Bruce was placed in command at Clarksville, and Fort Sevier was renamed Fort Bruce (it is now called Fort Defiance).

On February 20, Foote returned to Dover to assemble a task force to move on Nashville only to learn that General Halleck had ordered that the gunboats go no further than Clarksville. Many of the gunboats in the task force would be used instead to assault the

*Fortified railroad bridge over the Cumberland River at Nashville.*

Confederate works at Columbus, Kentucky, on the Mississippi River. Halleck was paranoid about Grant's accomplishments overshadowing his own contributions. Halleck decided that General Buell, then stationed at Bowling Green, should have the honor of capturing Nashville.

On February 21, four regiments from Gen. Charles Ferguson Smith's division were transported up the river from Dover to Clarksville, under cover of the *USS Cairo*. Landing parties found flour and bacon in the city's warehouses and coal reserves at the steamboat landing. They dismantled the batteries at the forts and completed the destruction of the railroad bridge. The soldiers set up their camps at Fort Sevier and Fort Clark.

Private John King of the 92nd Illinois noted in his diary that Clarksville was a pretty town but notorious for "making the world nastier and filthier by raising and shipping large quantities of that weed called tobacco" which "boys love to eat, chew, and smoke and they learn to swear and become lazy, filthy loafers."

A delegation of Nashville citizens chartered the steamer *Iatan* on February 23 and met with Union officials at Clarksville under a white flag. They brought surgeons to attend to Confederate soldiers wounded at Fort Donelson and asked for assurances that property would be protected once the army reached Nashville.

The *Iatan* was accompanied by the *Cairo* back to Nashville. At this time, two hours behind them, 16 steamers were carrying the troops of Brigadier General William "Bull" Nelson up the river. They had boarded the boats at West Point, Ky. five days earlier, originally intending to fortify the army at Fort Donelson. Buell had dispatched Brigadier General O.M. Mitchel and his 9,000 men from Bowling Green to march on Nashville. They would reach Edgefield on the east bank of the river opposite Nashville and would need to be ferried across. The retreating Confederates had burned both bridges over the river at Nashville. At this time, the Cumberland River was in full flood. En route to Nashville, the transports would leave the main channel and pass directly over farms and cruise by houses with families living on the second floor, the ground floor inundated with water.

A five-gun battery was spotted on an island at Harpeth Shoals but the troop transports did not stop, Nelson knowing that the *Cairo* had already passed. At 9:30 pm, 15 river miles downstream from Nashville, the gunboats and transports tied up to the bank for the night.

Earlier that month, Confederate soldiers had erected Fort Zollicoffer six miles below Nashville on a high bluff 130 feet above the river and boasting 13 heavy guns. One was a 6-inch rifle weighing 9,490 pounds and made at Tredegar Iron Works in Richmond. One of the others was a six-pounder made by Ellis & Co. of Nashville. The fort was named for General Felix Zollicoffer, a Nashville newspaper editor who had been killed at the Battle of Mill Springs (Fishing Creek) far up the Cumberland River in Kentucky on Jan. 19, 1862.

On the sunny morning of Feb. 25, 1862, the boats sighted the guns of Fort Zollicoffer at the top of a high cliff. A landing party of Col. Jacob Ammen's 36th Indiana found the fort in shambles. According to historian Ed Bearss: "Several of the oak barbette carriages were still smouldering. Thirteen guns, ranging in size from 32-pounder smoothbores to 6.5-inch rifles, had been dismounted or spiked. Scattered about the stronghold's interior were thousands of bars of railroad iron, many of them badly twisted by the terrific explosion that had shattered the magazine that they were intended to shield. Cotton bales used to reinforce the parapets had been burned."

Reboarding and getting underway, the convoy came around a bend and saw the taller buildings and spires of the capital city, several white flags flying but no Stars and Stripes, and none atop the capitol building. Aboard the *Diana*, Gen. Nelson ordered the transport ahead at full speed. At 9:00 am blueclad soldiers walked ashore at the wharf under the watchful guns of the *Cairo* ironclad. Even then, small patrols of Confederate cavalry were just leaving the city and lurking on the outskirts. Nelson met with Mitchel and Buell on the east bank at Edgefield. Soon Buell's men were across the river and marching up Cedar Street to the magnificent stone capitol building with its Greek choragic tower. The 6th Ohio Volunteer Regiment assisted retired sea captain William Driver, a noted resident of Nashville, in hoisting his old ship's Union flag up the mast over the main portico, a flag he called Old Glory.

That afternoon, Mayor Cheatham and ten citizens crossed the river by steamer to Edgefield and officially surrendered the city to General Buell as regimental bands from Indiana and Ohio entertained the curious crowd by playing "Dixie." A Northern newspaper correspondent stated "there is but little Union sentiment expressed here; in fact, far less than I had anticipated. All hands appear to hate us cordially."

The next day, as the Federals continued to occupy the city, a dozen of John Hunt Morgan's troopers brashly snuck into the city and set fire to a steamer moored near the city waterworks well within sight of Federal troops.

In time, Buell's army would be marching southwestward to meet up with Grant's army, which had been transported up the Tennessee River from Fort Henry to Pittsburg Landing. In April, there would be a mass reckoning there near the old Shiloh meetinghouse.

-Chapter Eight-

# Shiloh

*The timberclads sparred with rebel cavalry at the landing;*
*a month later they covered Grant's left wing at Shiloh*

The famous Battle of Shiloh, fought at Pittsburg Landing on April 6-7, 1862, shocked the nation with its astounding number of casualties. Naval activity on the Tennessee River proved to be a major factor in the Union victory. But most people don't know that a battle was fought there a full month earlier, between two Union timberclads and Confederate infantry and cavalry. If that confrontation of March 1, 1862 had not taken place, the Confederates might have developed Pittsburg Landing into a formidable riverbank artillery battery. The subsequent establishment of Federal camps there might have been difficult if not impossible. § Following the conquest of the river forts and the capture of Nashville, the timberclads began patroling the Tennessee River (particularly between the Danville bridge and Savannah) and U.S. planners focused their attention on the small village of Corinth in northeastern Mississippi, the point where the tracks of the strategically vital Memphis & Charleston Railroad and the Ohio & Mobile Railroad intersected. The railways literally linked the Ohio River to the Gulf of Mexico and the Mississippi River to the Atlantic Coast. By controlling Corinth, the U.S. army could control both railroads at the same time. The closest significant moorage on the Tennessee River was Pittsburg Landing about 22 miles northeast of Corinth and nine miles upstream and south of Savannah.

All of this was known to the Confederates, of course, and in late February, the 18th Louisiana Regiment left their camp at Corinth and marched two dozen miles northeastward to guard the northern end of the Corinth Road at Pittsburg Landing. The Confederate force commanded by Colonel Alfred Mouton comprised nine companies (1,000 men) along with 500 cavalrymen of the 2nd Mississippi. When they arrived, they noticed that the landing, the best moorage between Savannah and Eastport, Miss., was about 200 yards wide for about half-a-mile along the Tennessee River, marked by several small log cabins and bordered by dense woods. The river was about 600 yards wide. The landing had been named for Pittser "Pitt" Tucker, who established a frontier trading post there in 1848, selling mostly whiskey. Not far inland sat a Methodist meetinghouse known as Shiloh. In addition to Mouton's Confederate command, the rebels stationed two batteries of Miles Light Artillery (Gibson's Battery of Capt.

Statue of Colonel Alfred Mouton

Claude Gibson) at the landing — four 6-pounder rifles of 1st Lieutenant E.D. Terrebonne 300 yards upstream (south) and two 12-pounder howitzers of 2nd Lieutenant Charles A. Montaldo 100 yards downstream (north) near a log cabin.

That same day, late at night, the *Izetta* troop transport, guarded by the timberclad gunboats *Tyler* and *Lexington*, landed at Savannah, nine miles north of the landing. The *Tyler* sported six 8-inch smoothbores and a 32-pounder cannon while the *Lexington* carried four 8-inch guns and two 32-pounders. Detailed aboard the two gunboats as marines were 120 to 150 riflemen of the 32nd Illinois Regiment — 67 from Company C of Capt. Thaddeus Phillips and the remainder from Company K of 1st Lt. John J. Rider. The Union expedition's target was the railroad bridge near Iuka, just east of Corinth (the Memphis & Charleston Railroad bridge over Big Bear Creek).

At noon on Sat., March 1, 1862, the Confederate pickets just north of Pittsburg Landing detected the gunboats approaching by their engine noise — "a series of staccato cracking reports." A little after 1:00 pm, Terrebonne's rifled cannon opened fire at 1,200 yards. The *Tyler* closed to 1,000 yards and opened fire, with the *Lexington* joining two minutes later. Mouton's sharpshooters fired at the gunports from exposed rifle pits on the bluff but withdrew under heavy fire. After 40 minutes of sustained fire, Terrebonne withdrew his guns. Montaldo's guns did not engage due to lack of adequate manpower. At

his courtmartial later in April, Montaldo testified his battery was not prepared to fire, a neglect of duty that reflected upon Capt. Gibson. (Gibson's battery was consolidated with a Missouri battery in June 1862). Mouton pulled his troops from their exposed positions and reformed eight companies in a ravine between the bluffs, out of sight of the enemy. The gunboats continued to fire canister into the shore for another hour and, receiving no response, the commanders decided to land a party. The gunboat commanders reported that the timberclads had "silenced" the enemy batteries. The Union reports claimed that the log cabin, which had been set afire by the cannons, and the rifle pits were a "fortified" position.

Confederate Major Silas Grisamore later wrote in his diary: "Having never seen but our company and the battery, it is presumed that they imagined the force on land to be small and to have retreated."

At 3:00 pm, a force of 100 marines of the 32nd Illinois disembarked from the gunboats in five skiffs and landed uncontested. Second Master Jason Goudy commanded Rider's company from the *Tyler* and Second Master Martin Dunn commanded Phillips' company from the *Lexington*. The Federals, who believed they had just run off a small Confederate force, came under fire at the top of the slope and learned the real strength of their enemy, who had remained hidden. Outnumbered ten-to-one, the landing party fell back under the protection of cannon fire from the gunboats. The Confederates

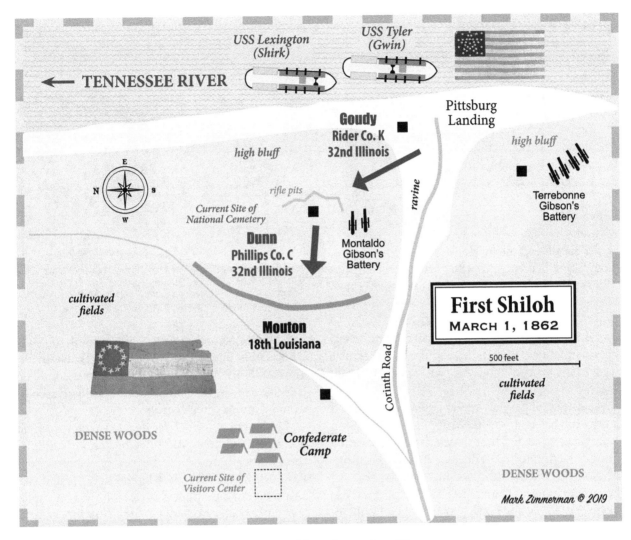

Mark Zimmerman © 2019

claimed the Yankees fell into a "precipitious rush" back to the landing boats. The small riverside cabin, said to be "fortified," was in flames. The drummer boy of the 18th Louisiana climbed a tree to beat the charge. Having pushed the rebels back, the landing party returned to their boats, receiving a hail of lead on their way to the timberclads. Commander William Gwin of the *Tyler* hailed the gunboats' civilian pilots for their coolness "under such a tremendous fire of musketry, our vessel being perfectly riddled with balls." Gwin later claimed that "the small force actually drove back the rebels and held them in check until they accomplished their difficult object, which was to discover their real strength and purpose, and to destroy a house in close proximity to the place where the batteries had been placed."

As was often the case, both sides claimed victory. After the three-hour battle, which would become known as the First Battle of Shiloh, casualty estimates varied. Col. Mouton counted 21 casualties of his own while Gwin reported 20 Confederates killed and 100 wounded. The Federal commander reported two killed, six wounded, and three missing of his own men. The rebel commander counted 13 Union casualties.

The timberclads fired a multitude and variety of projectiles. The *Tyler* expended 95 shells, 30 grapeshot, 10 canister, and 67 shrapnel (total of 202), and the *Lexington* fired 86 shells (45 8-in. shells, 25 6-in. shells, and 16 grapeshot).

Col. Mouton and the 18th Louisiana were

hailed and congratulated by Confederate Brig. Gen. Daniel Ruggles for "their brilliant success on their first encounter with the enemy."

Then Colonel Mouton withdrew three miles inland to a log Methodist meetinghouse known as Shiloh (Hebrew for "place of peace"). Five weeks later, Mouton would be wounded at the Battle of Shiloh. He would be killed in April 1864 leading a charge at Mansfield in his native Louisiana. Subsequent Union landing parties would find two 32-pounder cannons unmounted near the so-called fortified house at Pittsburg Landing, according to naval historian Chuck Veit, indicating the Confederates were in the process of building a heavy fortification there.

Southeast of Corinth was the village of Iuka and a little further east was the Memphis & Charleston R.R. bridge over Big Bear Creek, a tributary which flowed north into the Tennessee River at Eastport, Mississippi. This 110-foot-long bridge was to become an object of fascination for Lt. Commander Gwin of the *Tyler* and for U.S. Army General William Tecumseh Sherman during February and March of 1862. If the Federals could destroy the bridge over Big Bear Creek, they could shut down the major railway between Memphis and Chattanooga.

On February 20, Gwin and the *Tyler* steamed upriver to Eastport on a mission to land troops which would then march southward to capture the railroad bridge. Local civilians warned Gwin, however, that the Confederates had 4,000 men guarding the bridge. Since he commanded only 60 marines, Gwin called off the attack. Later he would learn that he had been misinformed by the civilians.

On March 10, 1862, the *Tyler* escorted 82 steam transports in the task of landing thousands of blue-clad troops at Pittsburg Landing, where Sherman set up his headquarters. By the end of the month, the Union camps boasted 34,000 troops. Sherman

The *Lexington* and *Tyler* stream upriver and bombard Confederate troops south of Pittsburg Landing during the Battle of Shiloh on April 6, 1862. An inaccuracy shows the chimneys of the *Lexington* amidships instead of near the bow.

and Grant planned to wait at the landing for Gen. Don Carlos Buell's army to arrive from Nashville. The combined forces would then move south on Corinth. For the time being, however, the riverboats would continue their patrols.

On March 12, the *Tyler* and *Lexington* steamed upstream (southward) to Chickasaw Landing, across the mouth of Big Bear Creek from Eastport, where the Confederates had situated two 24-pounder smoothbores on a bluff. For one hour, the timberclads exchanged fire with the battery, expending 275 shells between the two of them. The fire was so fierce that Commander Gwin thought there were at least five 32-pounders facing the Union boats instead of just two. The Union gunboats disengaged and steamed back to their ports.

On March 14, it was Sherman's turn to try to take the bridge. By noon, elements of his Fifth Infantry Division, along with the 5th Ohio Cavalry, had loaded onto 19 transports escorted by the *Tyler*. At a landing near Yellow Creek, the cavalry disembarked at 7:00 pm in a heavy rain. Four hours later, the rain ceased and the troopers began their march. The rain resumed, and it was 3:00 am on March 15 before Sherman could land his infantry. Sherman's men marched four miles until they came to an impassable bayou. Word was received that

*(Continued on Page 96)*

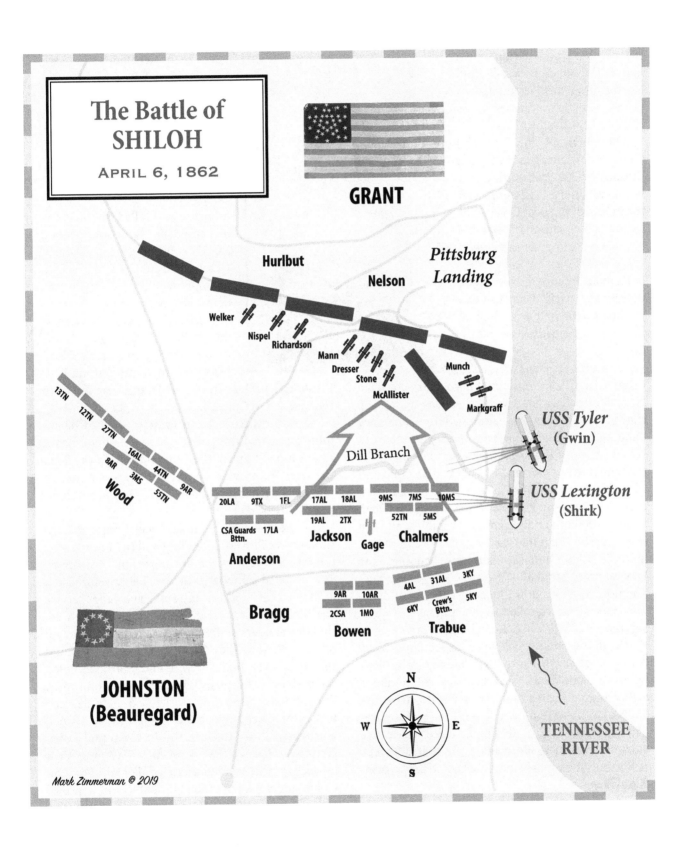

The Battle of
SHILOH

APRIL 6, 1862

GRANT

Hurlbut

Pittsburg
Landing

Nelson

Welker

Nispel

Richardson

Mann

Dresser

Stone

McAllister

Munch

Markgraff

USS Tyler
(Gwin)

USS Lexington
(Shirk)

13TN

12TN

27TN

16AL

44TN

8AR

3MS

55TN

9AR

Wood

Dill Branch

20LA    9TX    1FL    17AL    18AL    9MS    7MS    10MS

19AL    2TX    52TN    5MS

CSA Guards    17LA    Jackson    Gage    Chalmers
Bttn.

Anderson

4AL    31AL    3KY

9AR    10AR    6KY    Crew's    5KY
Bttn.

2CSA    1MO

Bragg

Bowen    Trabue

N

W    E

S

JOHNSTON
(Beauregard)

TENNESSEE
RIVER

Mark Zimmerman © 2019

the cavalry wasn't faring much better. The attack was called off. By the time the Federal troops reimbarked their transports, the river had swollen by 15 feet.

On March 24, the *Tyler* and *Lexington* exchanged fire at a distance of 200 yards with a new two-gun battery at Eastport near the mouth of Big Bear Creek. One of the *Tyler*'s chimneys was hit. The *Tyler* fired four shells with 20-second fuses but they failed to explode because the fuses were defective. A week later, the two gunboats returned and fired at the batteries but drew no return fire.

On April 1, 1862, the *USS Cairo* City-Class ironclad gunboat arrived from Nashville to lead the two timberclads and troop transports *Empress* and *Tecumseh* to Chickasaw Landing. At one point, the *Lexington* had to actually tow the cumbersome ironclad. Aboard the transports were two battalions of the 57th Ohio and 77th Ohio and 150 men of the 5th Ohio Cavalry, plus two 12-pound howitzers. The *Lexington* began firing at 1:00 pm and expended 45 rounds, all with no reply. The 77th Ohio was dropped off at Eastport and the 57th Ohio at Chickasaw Landing. The Federal men found all the earthworks abandoned. The flotilla returned to Pittsburg Landing at dusk. The ironclad was recalled to its namesake city and was moored there when the fighting began.

The thunderbolt struck on the Sabbath morning, April 6, 1862, when Albert Sidney Johnston's waves of Confederates attacked the Union camps at Pittsburg Landing and threatened to drive the Yankees into the Tennessee River. The Confederates had converged at Corinth and managed to advance along the muddy roads to attack the Federal camps at Pittsburg Landing before Buell could arrive from Nashville.

The *Tyler* and *Lexington* timberclad gunboats would have a role to play in the bloody battle of Shiloh, the significance and importance of which

Brigadier General U.S. Grant

have been debated ever since. Toward the end of the day, the gunboats assisted Grant's artillery in turning back the Confederate assault at the Dill Branch ravine. During the ensuing night they continuously shelled the Confederates in their makeshift camps as it rained relentlessly. Johnston was killed that first day of battle; his successor, General P.G.T. Beauregard, claimed victory, thinking the final triumph would come easily the next day. Meanwhile, elements of Buell's army began arriving at the battlefield. On April 7, the Federal troops fought hard and reclaimed their campgrounds at Pittsburg Landing. The Confederates were forced to retreat back to Corinth.

There is evidence that prior to the battle General Johnston feared the power of the Union gunboats, and planned to push the Federal troops away from the river "to prevent unnecessary exposure of our men to the enemy gunboats," and pin the bluecoats against Owl Creek.

At the time of the attack, the *Tyler* had been stationed at Pittsburg Landing and the *Lexington* at Crump's Landing, six miles north and downriver. The ironclad gunboat fleet was being refurbished at Mound City and was thus unavailable for service at Shiloh. Unfortunately, as the battle commenced, the commanders of the timberclad gunboats had no orders to follow. They could not see inland, beyond the high river bluffs. Gwin and Shirk occupied themselves with guarding the river transports. Three times during the day, the *Lexington* steamed to Crump's Landing, found no service to render, and returned to Pittsburg Landing. Around noon, Gunman Herman Peters of the *Tyler* was sent ashore to the headquarters of Fourth Division Commander Gen. Stephen Hurlbut to seek approval to open fire, which was wholeheartedly granted. Hurlbut provided Peters with precise and elaborate instructions on siting the *Tyler*'s guns. At 2:50 pm the *Tyler* opened fire for one hour, concentrating on Confederate artillery positions and the Reserve Corps of Gen. John C. Breckenridge. The cannon fire silenced several Confederate batteries. Later, Peters would be sent ashore again, this time to the temporary headquarters of Gen. Grant, who sent word to the captain to use his own discretion. At 4:15 pm, the gunboats stationed themselves about three-quarters of a mile south of the landing. Fifteen minutes later, they opened fire on Confederate Gen. Ruggles' inland battery of 53 field artillery pieces.

A newspaperman from Cincinnati witnessed the shelling, which "went tearing and crashing through the woods, felling trees in their course, and spreading terror wherever they fell."

At 5:30 pm, five brigades of Confederate Gen. Braxton Bragg's men attacked the Dill Branch ravine northward, the last obstacle between Confederate forces and the Federals who had retreated to the river landing. The 80-foot-deep ravine was swollen with water, which allowed the gunboats to converge closer than usual (the river was ten feet above flood stage). They opened with shot and shell for about ten minutes (the shelling was "thick and fast with telling effect") before the riflemen of the Tenth Mississippi briefly forced the gunboats to the opposite shore. After Bragg's attack was forced back, Stanford's Confederate battery lowered their field artillery down into the ravine, intending to engage the gunboats. Confronting the floating batteries, the graycoats wisely reconsidered and withdrew their guns. The gunboats returned to the near shore and fired at targets of opportunity. A single shell from the timberclads killed three horses and disabled seven more. The Confederate attack was called off after 20 minutes of intensive combat.

At 9:00 pm, at the direction of newly arrived Gen. William "Bull" Nelson, a former U.S. Navy officer, the *Tyler* began lobbing shells at 10-minute intervals, each shell fitted with a different-length fuse and at incremental elevations of one-half degree, creating a "creeping" effect.

*Cincinnati Daily Gazette* reporter Whitlaw Reid wrote about the gunboat shelling that night: "But presently there came a flash that spread like sheet-lightning over the ripples of the river current, and

the roar of a heavy naval gun went echoing up and down the bluffs, through the unnatural stillness of the night. Others speedily followed. By the flash you could just discern the black outline of the piratical-looking hull, and see how the gunboat gracefully settled into the water at the recoil; the smoke soon cast up a thin veil that seemed only to soften and sweeten the scene; from the woods away inland you caught faintly the muffled explosion of the shell, like the knell of the spirit that was taking its flight."

Confederate Brig. Gen. Patrick Cleburne, one of the hardest fighting officers of the war, recalled bitterly that "every fifteen minutes the enemy threw two shells from his gunboats, some of which burst close around my men, banishing sleep from the eyes of a few, but falling chiefly among their own wounded, who were strewn thickly between my camp and the river. History records few instances of more reckless inhumanity than this."

At 10:00 pm, it began raining hard. At 1:00 am, the *Lexington* took over for the *Tyler*. The shelling stopped at 5:30 am as the newly arrived forces of Gen. Buell advanced. The timberclads had little role to play the second day of battle except for guarding the Union boats on the river and carrying the wounded to hospital boats.

Confederate commanders mentioned the U.S. gunboats 51 times in their after-action reports; eight mentioned moving troops out of the range of the gunboats. Beauregard told his men, referring to the Yankee enemy: "You drove him from his camps to the shelter of his iron-clad gunboats, which alone saved him from complete disaster."

In recent years, Spencer Tucker, historian at the Virginia Military Institute, contended that the two gunboats played an important role in the battle. He stated that the shelling of the gunboats helped persuade Beauregard (the commander following the death of Johnston) to call off the attacks at dusk. Also, he said that control of the river was vital to the arrival of Buell's troops. "That these troops could cross the river, bring in supplies, and evacuate wounded was owing to the U.S. Navy, an important fact often overlooked..."

Naval historian Veit goes so far as to say that Shiloh "was one of two instances when Yankee gunboats intervened to literally save a Union army from utter destruction." (The other was Malvern Hill.)

In his after-battle report, Commander Gwin told Flag Officer Foote: "Your old wooden boats, I feel confident, rendered invaluable service on the 6th instant to the land forces. Gunner Herman Peters deserves great credit for the prompt and courageous manner in which he traversed our lines, conveying communications from this vessel to the commanding generals."

President Lincoln's close aide Leonard Swett wrote to his boss: "I went to Pittsburg Landing immediately after the battle there and spent three days riding over the field. From all I could learn I believe the gunboats *Lexington* and *Tyler*, commanded by Lieutenants Gwin and Shirk, saved our army from defeat. At least it is within bounds to say they rendered us invaluable services."

Historian Gary Joiner wrote: "The periodic firing by the timberclads had psychological effects on both armies during that night, and this may be the most important contribution of the gunboats at Shiloh. The vessels provided a morale boost to the dispirited Federal soldiers all through that night."

A Federal soldier of the 70th Ohio stated: "The terrible shrieking of the large navy shells had a demoralizing effect on the enemy, causing him to change his position several times during the night, besides robbing him of much needed sleep and rest; while it was soul-stirring music to our ears."

Five days later, on the evening of Sat., April 12, 1862, a small task force led by General Sherman headed upriver from Pittsburg Landing to destroy the railroad bridges at Big Bear Creek and at Florence, Alabama (the bridge spared by the Phelps raiders in February). Guarded by the *Tyler* and the *Lexington*, the flotilla consisted of the transports *Tecumseh* and *White Cloud* bearing 100 men of the 4th Illinois Cavalry under Major S.M. Bowman and 1,900 men of the 2nd Brigade, 6th Division, under

**Report of Lieutenant Gwin, U.S. Navy, commanding *U.S.S. Tyler*
Pittsburg, Tenn., April 14, 1862**

Sir: I have the honor to inform you that the *Tyler* and *Lexington* convoyed two transports, containing 2,000 troops, infantry and cavalry, under the command of General Sherman, to Chickasaw, Ala., where they disembarked and proceeded rapidly to Bear Creek Bridge, the crossing of Memphis and Charleston Railroad, for the purpose of destroying it and as much of trestlework as they could find. I am happy to state that the expedition was entirely successful.

The bridge, consisting of two spans, 110 feet each, was completely destroyed (i.e., superstructure), together with some 510 feet of trestlework and half mile of telegraph line. The rebels made a feeble resistance to our cavalry, 120 in number, but soon made a hasty retreat, losing 4 killed; our loss none.

I regret to state that in firing a salute on the 12th, John D. Seymore, boatswain's mate, was so much injured by the premature discharge of a gun as to cause his death yesterday morning.

Brig. Gen. James B. Fry, Buell's chief of staff.

Reaching Chickasaw Landing by 7:00 am the next morning, the cavalry disembarked and headed directly to the Bear Creek Bridge. The superstructures of the two 110-foot spans and 500 feet of trestle on the Memphis & Charleston Railroad were destroyed, with the men returning to the boats by 9:00 pm. Next the flotilla headed toward Florence, but it was forced to abandon its mission due to shallows at Beetree Shoals and Colbert Shoals. Sherman deferred to the extensive river knowledge of the steamboat pilots. Ironically, one week later, the Florence railroad bridge was destroyed by Confederate forces under orders of General Beauregard.

–Chapter Nine–

# Dover

*The Mosquito Squadron rescues a Union garrison
under attack from Confederate cavalry — or not*

The beginning of 1863 witnessed a bloody battle at Stones River near Murfreesboro, Tennessee. The three-day battle was a tactical draw but a Union strategic victory when Confederate General Braxton Bragg left Union General William Rosecrans holding the field. At the same time, Confederate cavalry leader Nathan Bedford Forrest was concluding his West Tennessee raid with a messy affair at Parker's Crossroads. One of the few Confederate heroes of Stones River was a young cavalry commander, Brig. Gen. Joseph Wheeler, who had harassed the Union army as it advanced from Nashville toward Murfreesboro. Following the battle, Bragg decided to place Wheeler in command of Forrest's men along with those of Colonel John Wharton.

Almost immediately following Stones River, Lincoln and the Union officials in Washington called on Rosecrans to mount an offensive through Tennessee to Chattanooga. An energetic yet flighty man, Rosecrans vowed he would not move until his Army of the Cumberland was properly supplied. To handle the matériel, his men began building a massive supply depot between the Stones River battlefield and Murfreesboro which would be named Fortress Rosecrans. Back in the fall of 1862, the command of the Western Gunboat Flotilla had been formally handed over from the War Department to the U.S. Navy and the emphasis had moved from river invasion to the protection of steamer-transport convoys moving from Louisville and Cincinnati to Nashville. But there weren't enough gunboats to guard the convoys against Confederate cavalry, irregulars, and guerrillas.

Rosecrans constantly hounded his superiors and the naval officials at Cairo for more gunboats. The army commander even suggested that the army outfit, crew, and command its own gunboats to patrol the rivers. Lincoln quickly put that ungainly idea to rest. Frustrated, Ole Rosey complained of "the perils by land and water, negroism and abolitionism, worthless quartermasters, and vexation of every kind and description."

In response, one of the new naval commanders, Lieutenant Commander LeRoy Fitch, a native of

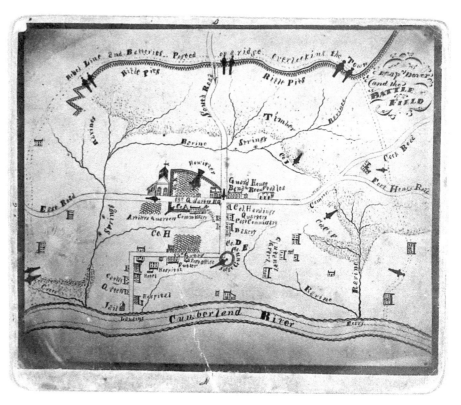

Logansport, Indiana, supervised the construction of a fleet of tinclad gunboats that would be used to guard the supply convoys and patrol the rivers. These gunboats were converted from steamers, lightly clad with iron plating, and armed with shiny bronze Dahlgren howitzers. They were much faster than the timberclads or City Class ironclads and could maneuver in shallow waters. They would be known as the Mosquito Squadron.

On Jan. 27, 1863, a convoy of 31 freighters and ten barges reached Clarksville enroute to Nashville. At Betsytown, 20 miles upstream beyond Clarksville, a steamer was fired upon from the riverbank by Wheeler's cavalry forces. The *USS Lexington* timberclad was dispatched, and a landing party burned down the warehouses at Betsytown in reprisal. On its way back to Clarksville, the *Lexington* was hit three times by a Parrott rifle masked on shore. The convoy successfully arrived at Nashville the next day. At this point in time, the rebel cavalry was stranded on the south side of the Cumberland River because all of the ferryboats and conveyances upriver from Dover had been destroyed.

In late January, the 12,000 men of Major General Gordon Granger's Army of Kentucky began assembling at Louisville, preparing to travel to Middle Tennessee to bolster Rosecrans at Nashville. (Stones River had proven to be the bloodiest battle of the entire war for the Union, based on casualties as a percentage of men engaged.) Twenty-eight steamer transports were made ready at Louisville to accommodate Granger's 20 infantry regiments, four cavalry regiments, and four artillery batteries. The steamer fleet consisted of *Robert B. Hamilton, James Thompson, Capitola, Poland, Empire City, Horizon, Ella Faber, Hazel Dell, Diadem, John A. Fisher, May Duke, Dove, Ollie Sullivan, Freestone, Huntress, Shenango, St. Cloud, Adelaide, Arizona, Lady Franklin, Science, Golden Era,* and *Tempest.*

Aboard the *Tempest,* John M. King of the 92nd Illinois Volunteer Infantry wrote: "We were to have a long boat ride down the Ohio and up the Cumberland Rivers, where we would ride by day and night, view all the beautiful scenery and catch a glimpse of four or five states … We could watch the sunbeams, stars and moonlight sparkle, glitter, and dance on the waves of those beautiful rivers."

By Feb. 1, 1863, the weather had turned much colder. The next day at 2:00 am, the convoy shoved off under cold, clear skies lit by a bright moon. The convoy reached Smithland at the mouth of the Cumberland River before dawn on the third of the month and picked up its escort, consisting of the tinclads Fairplay, *Robb*, Brilliant, *St. Clair*, and *Silver Lake* and the timberclad Lexington. The next stop would be Dover.

A replica of the swivel gun in the Dover town square.

In the months following the February 1862 fall of Fort Donelson on the Cumberland River, the occupying Union forces abandoned the old rebel works and fortified the nearby riverfront village of Dover. The Union garrison of 600 men was composed of the 83rd Illinois infantry, commanded by Colonel Abner C. Harding, a banker by occupation, and the 5th Iowa Cavalry. Stationed at the town square was the impressive swivel gun, a 32-pounder confiscated from the former Confederate river battery, and four 12-pounders under the supervision of Capt. James H. Flood's Battery C, 2nd Illinois Artillery. The seige gun was almost certainly commanded by Virgil Earp of the 83rd Illinois. Earp would become famous in 1881 when he, as marshal of Tombstone, Arizona, along with his three younger brothers and friend Doc Holliday, fought at the O.K. Corral. Half of the 83rd Illinois, commanded by Lt. Col. A.A. Smith, and two field pieces, were positioned at fortifications behind the old village graveyard several hundred yards west of the town square.

Believing erroneously that the Federals had shut down shipping on the Cumberland River, Wheeler decided to attack the garrison at Dover. Capturing the village would, in effect, place a blockade on the river. On February 1, the hearty cavalrymen of Gen. Forrest reached Palmyra, between Dover and Clarksville, and joined with Wheeler's mounted men, which included those of Wharton. Forrest's command was down to 15 rounds of small arms ammunition per man. Wheeler was anxious to hit and disrupt shipping on the Cumberland but there was a lack of suitable targets. The Confederates were unaware of the approaching Union convoy transporting Granger's troops. Wheeler wanted to attack Dover, but Forrest disagreed, noting that the village was too heavily defended and that they couldn't hold the village long even if they captured it. Wheeler decided to attack anyway. Forrest asked his aide-de-camp, Capt. C.W. Anderson, and brigade medical officer Dr. Ben Wood, "If I am killed in this fight, will you see justice is done by me by officially stating that I protested against the attack, and that I am not willing to be held responsible for any disaster that might result?"

Eight miles east of Dover all but four men of Company G, 5th Iowa cavalry, were captured by the rebels at the Cumberland Iron Works. The four who escaped alerted the garrison at Dover. Colonel Harding herded all the women and children of the village onto two steamboats and sent them downriver out of harm's way. Major Elijah C. Brott and two companies of the 83rd Illinois were ordered aboard the *Wildcat* and sent downriver to seek out gunboats and direct them to Dover. Harding telegraphed his commander, Col. William Lowe, at Fort Henry a dozen miles away, asking for reinforcements.

On February 3rd at 1:00 pm, Wheeler and his 3,000 men with six field guns reached the eastern outskirts of Dover. The 8th Texas Cavalry (Terry's Texas Rangers) was sent off to guard Fort Henry

Road and watch for possible Federal reinforcements. Wheeler (who was likely confusing fortified Dover with nearby Fort Donelson) sent a note to Harding: "Having invested Fort Donelson with a force sufficient to take it, and desiring to prevent the effusion of blood, we have the honor to demand an immediate and unconditional surrender, of the fort, with all the forces, stores, etc. If you surrender, you will be treated as prisoners of war; if not, you must abide the consequences."

Harding replied, "I decline to surrender the forces under my command or my post, without an effort to defend them."

Wheeler ordered the attack to begin at 2:30 pm. A movement of Union forces was mistakenly interpreted by Forrest as an effort by them to escape; Forrest prematurely attacked the Federal left flank (which consisted of 300 riflemen and a 32-pounder cannon) and his men suffered severe blasts of cannon fire for his efforts. "In an instant the 32-pounder was double-shotted with canister, and turned upon them and discharged, tearing one man to atoms and two horses, within 10 feet of the muzzle," said Harding in his after-battle report. Forrest's troops withdrew and dismounted. He positioned his artillery in a commanding position, which drove the Federals back to the town-square redoubt. Forrest attacked again and had his second horse shot out from under him and was severely injured.

Meanwhile, on the rebel left flank, Wharton drove Smith from the graveyard location, captured one gun, and occupied the western half of Dover, but then his troopers ran out of ammunition. Wharton was forced to pull back under terrific counterfire. Soon dusk turned to night under a bright moon. Meanwhile, the Texas cavalry harassed the relief force from Fort Henry, the 13th Wisconsin under Col. W.P. Lyon, five miles west of Dover.

The rebel commanders held a council of war and decided that the garrison was too strongly entrenched. To a man, they were running out of ammo; Federal gunboats and steamers were approaching. Confronted again, Harding rightly refused a second time to surrender.

Earlier in the afternoon, the Union convoy could hear the fighting upstream. The *Wildcat* located the convoy 24 miles from Dover. Fitch's gunboats pressed on "at all possible speed," but it took five hours to reach the village, at about 8:00 pm. With the moon shining bright, a Union officer from Dover went aboard the *Fairplay* and pinpointed both the Federal and Confederate positions. The rebels were 800 yards west of Harding's men in a ravine extending north almost to the river. They were not expecting to face gunboats. All six of the gunboats opened fire into the ravine, the graveyard, and the valley beyond. The naval guns ceased fire at 10:00 pm. Fitch reported, "The rebels were so much taken by surprise that they did not even fire a shot, but immediately commenced retreating." Fitch claimed his gunboats turned the tide of battle and his men "had the gratification of knowing that scarcely a projectile went amiss, and out of the four hundred and odd reported killed and wounded the gunboats could claim their share."

Eugene Marshall of the 5th Iowa Cavalry agreed with Fitch's assessment, stating that the Confederates would have prevailed except for the Federal gunboats. "The enemy force was too strong," he claimed.

Wheeler reported: "The gunboats commenced a heavy fire, without any effect whatever and without causing a man to increase his gait from a slow walk." He said that his grayclad soldiers withdrew for the lack of ammunition.

Historian Terry Wilson stated: "If the naval gunfire did not force the Confederates off the field, it did solidify Harding's somewhat tenuous position."

Author and historian Robert Mackey stated, "The effectiveness of the gunboats should not be underestimated … Fitch's vessels demolished the attacking Confederates, pouring shot and shell into the massed Confederate ranks as they prepared for a final assault on the works."

During the Battle of Dover, in which the gunboats came to the rescue and fought the cavalry, the Federal forces lost 13 killed, 51 wounded, and 46 missing. Wharton lost 17 killed, 60 wounded, and eight missing. Forrest suffered 200 casualties.

The three Confederate commanders spent the

*(Continued on Page 104)*

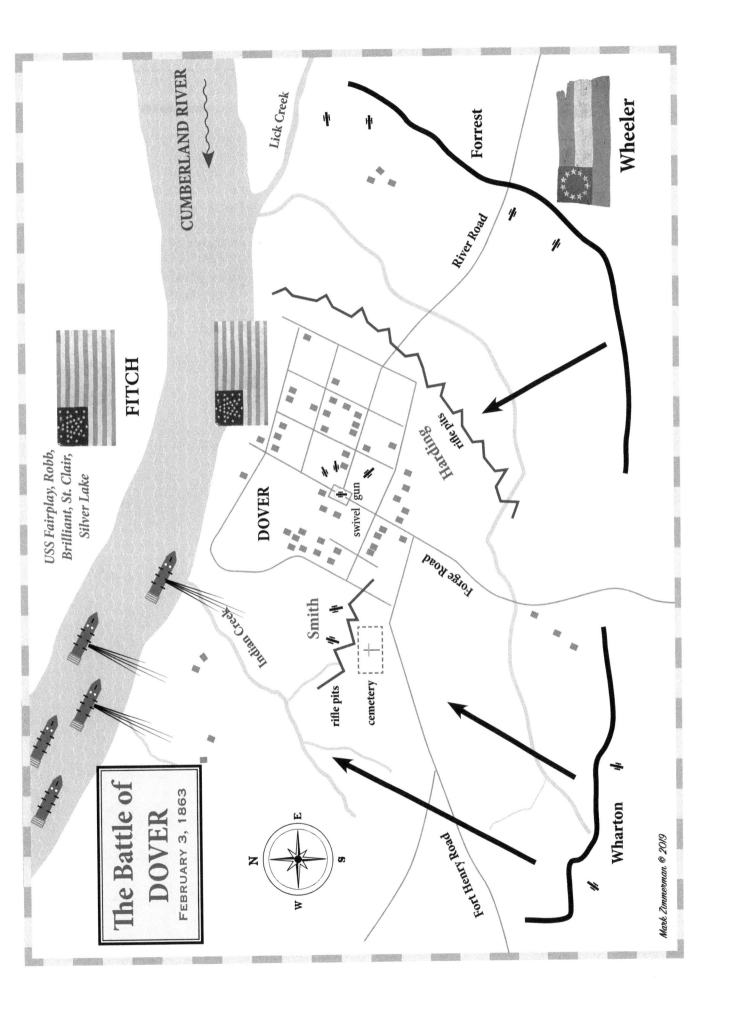

# The Battle of DOVER
### FEBRUARY 3, 1863

CUMBERLAND RIVER

Lick Creek

Forrest

Wheeler

River Road

FITCH

USS Fairplay, Robb,
Brilliant, St. Clair,
Silver Lake

DOVER

Harding

rifle pits

swivel gun

Forge Road

Indian Creek

Smith

rifle pits

cemetery

Fort Henry Road

Wharton

Mark Zimmerman © 2019

night in a house four miles south of Dover. A dejected and despondent Forrest told his commander, "General Wheeler, you know I was against this attack…nothing will bring back my brave fellows lying dead or wounded and freezing around that fort tonight. You know I mean no disrespect; you know the personal friendship I feel for you. But you've got to put one thing in that report to Bragg: tell him I'll be in my coffin before I'll fight again under your command. And if you want it, you can have my sword." Wheeler rejected Forrest's request and said he would take the blame himself. The next day the Confederate cavalry made its way back to Columbia, Tenn.

The Union convoy arrived at Dover the next day at noon. Federal soldiers came ashore to help clean up, bury the dead, and collect souvenirs. An eyewitness said of the Federal soldiers, "They all express themselves surprised to think how in the world we sustained against such powerful odds and held the post so successfully."

The convoy moved out from Dover on the morning of February 6, having been joined by an additional 17 transports the previous day, and reached Nashville on February 7 at 4:00 pm. Two days later, the convoy returned to Smithland, Kentucky.

– Chapter Ten –

# The Duck River Affair

*U.S. horse marines chase Texas Rangers*
*after escorting the Federal 'Jackass Brigade'*

The April 26, 1863 combat on the Tennessee River between U.S. naval forces and Confederate cavalry qualifies not only as one of the strangest encounters on the Western rivers but also as one of the most successful counter-insurgency operations, albeit a minor one, of the entire war. The spirited skirmish occurred on the east bank of the Tennessee River just upstream (south) of the confluence of the Duck River. The combatants were the Mississippi Marine Brigade, a Federal counter-insurgency and escort force, facing a Texas cavalry battalion under Major Robert M. White.

The Mississippi Marine Brigade (MMB) was named for the river (its main area of operations) and not the state; it had no connection to the U.S. Marine Corps; and it was not technically a brigade. Led by Brigadier General Alfred Washington Ellet, the MMB consisted of the 1st Battalion MMB Infantry, the 1st Battalion MMB Cavalry, and Walling's Light Artillery Battery. The three gunboats in the flotilla at the time of the battle were the *Autocrat*, the *Diana*, and the *Adams*. The Mississippi Marine Brigade ranked "among the most unorthodox and controversial fighting units" of the Civil War, according to Ellet's biographer, Chester Hearn.

The story of the Mississippi Marine Brigade dates back to the beginning of the war and an energetic and enterprising 51-year-old engineer from New York named Charles Ellet Jr. (Alfred's older brother), who petitioned the Navy and War departments to adopt his unique scheme for defeating the Confederacy on the rivers, much in the same manner as James Eads had approached the administration about ironclads. Instead of ironclads, however, Ellet proposed the building of lightly armed but swift-moving rams. These converted civilian steamboats would be designed with reinforced hulls, extra timber in the bows, and a powerful prow that could smash the hulls of enemy boats and sink them. The usage of rams dates back all the way to the ancient Greeks and the battle of Salamis. Ellet came up with the idea after serving as an observer in the Crimean War in Russia during the 1850s. The concept was reinforced in his mind during his trans-Atlantic voyage on the liner *Arctic,* which sank after a collision with a much smaller vessel. Ellet's name carried some weight in Washington; he could boast of being the engineer of the world's longest suspension bridge, over the Ohio River at Wheeling. Ellet pestered officials with the Navy Department about his proposal and left empty-handed. But, somehow, Ellet did gain the attention of War Secretary Edwin Stanton, who approved funds for the ram boats.

Ellet scoured the Ohio River ports and purchased nine sidewheeler steamers that could be converted into rams. Although Ellet did not personally desire to wear a military uniform, he did intend to lead his newly formed Ram Fleet into battle. So he was appointed to the Army as a colonel in April 1862. He then recruited 15 family members into the fleet, including his two sons and his younger brother, Alfred, who served as his chief of staff. Alfred began the war as the lieutenant colonel of the 59th Illinois Infantry. The Ram Fleet was manned by men from the 59th Illinois and also from the 63rd Illinois Infantry. In essence, the Ram Fleet was a riverine force commanded by an Army officer who answered directly to the Secretary of War and not the regional commander. This unwieldy command structure would cause many problems for the Ram Fleet and its eventual successor, the Mississippi

Brigadier General Alfred Washington Ellet

U.S. Secretary of War Edwin Stanton

Marine Brigade, during the course of the war.

In June 1862, however, Charles Ellet's Ram Fleet performed well at the Battle of Memphis, defeating and helping to destroy the Confederate River Defense Fleet. During the battle, fought entirely on the Mississippi River, Charles Ellet was fatally wounded, and died shortly thereafter. The command of the Ram Fleet defaulted to Alfred, who eventually was promoted to brigadier general in the army.

At this point in the war, there was little use for the Ram Fleet, as it was effective only

Ellet's Mississippi Marine Brigade attacks Confederate cavalry on the Tennessee River.

against enemy vessels and not against enemy shore batteries. Few Confederate gunboats remained on the rivers after the summer of 1862, so Ellet and his commander, Lt. Commander David D. Porter (Stanton had directed Ellet to work with the Navy commander), decided to develop a river-based counter-insurgency force, the Mississippi Marine Brigade. The swift-moving MMB would be used to conduct amphibious operations against Confederate guerrillas and partisans harassing Union shipping on the Mississippi River.

Several new steamboats were acquired and converted expressly for MMB operations at a total cost of $350,000. According to historian Thomas E. Walker, the boats required extensive refitting. The boilers were protected with heavy, thick timbers. Two inches of solid oak along the bulwarks provided protection for the Federal riflemen, who would shoot through loopholes. The pilothouses had large sheets of boilerplate iron installed along the walls. Pulleys hanging from the forecastle were used to raise and lower a large, railed gangway, which allowed two horses to embark or disembark at the same time. This ramp facilitated the on-loading and off-loading of troops and equipment. By the start of 1863, according to Walker, the Mississippi

Marine Brigade had a fleet that consisted of three sternwheelers and four sidewheelers, with three steam-powered tugs used for courier and resupply duties. Six coal barges were used to re-supply the fleet. Each of the five transports could carry 125 cavalry horses and riders and 250 infantrymen. Thus, the total strength of the MMB came to 625 cavalry and 1,250 infantrymen.

Manpower for the boat crews, again, was lacking. Recruiters were sent to convalescent hospitals in the Midwest to entice potential signees with an appeal to their creature comforts: "No long hard marches, camping without tents or food or carrying heavy knapsacks, but good, comfortable quarters and good facilities for cooking at all times." Nevertheless, as with most riverine operations, obtaining adequate manpower was troublesome. Despite the inducements, recruitments fell short. The MMB could muster only 527 infantrymen, 368 cavalrymen, and 140 artillerymen manning six light field guns. The recruits would be known as Ellet's Scouts. Throughout the war, the MMB would be plagued with morale and disciplinary problems, the commanders having trouble controlling their men.

The brigade was mustered into service in November 1862 and participated in Sherman's assault on the Chickasaw Bluffs near Vicksburg and other operations during that campaign. Records of the MMB were lost or destroyed after the war, so details of its service are sketchy, but there was at least one occasion that the Mississippi Marine Brigade was used on the Tennessee River, as an escort for Streight's raiders.

Some background is in order. During the long hiatus following the Battle of Stones River (Murfreesboro), U.S. commanding General William Rosecrans directed one of his more ambitious subordinates, Colonel Abel Streight, to conduct a raid across northern Alabama into Georgia to destroy and disrupt the Western & Atlantic Railroad, used by Confederate forces near Chattanooga. Due to a scarcity of horses, Streight decided to mount his troopers on mules gathered from West Tennessee. Not surprisingly, the mules behaved badly, often breaking loose and forcing soldiers to scurry about the countryside and round them up. One story had Confederates tossing a beehive into the mule corral in a successful effort to create havoc among the ornery beasts. The raiders thus became known, not affectionately, as the Jackass Brigade. The Mississippi Marine Brigade under Ellet was directed to the Tennessee River to haul the mules, escort Streight's troop transports, and conduct counter-insurgency operations.

On April 17, 1863, the Mississippi Marine Brigade, along with numerous transports, shoved off from Fort Henry destined for Eastport, Mississippi, with a cargo of 1,250 mules. The flotilla consisted of the flagboat *Autocrat*, *Diana*, *Adams*, and the tug *Cleveland*. It should be noted that the U.S. Navy's Mosquito Fleet of tinclad gunboats under Lt. Commander LeRoy Fitch also participated in the operation. Fitch's fleet consisted of the tinclads *Argosy*, *Covington*, and *Queen City*, and the timberclad *Lexington*.

Ellet reached Eastport on April 19, and joined Fitch, who had been waiting impatiently. The mules mutinied while being unloaded, stampeding away in all directions and delaying the start of the raid by several days. By that time, Confederate Brigadier General Nathan Bedford Forrest and his cavalry command had arrived in the vicinity and

given chase to Streight's raiders. Forrest caught up to Streight by May 3 before the Yankees could reach the railroad. Streight surrendered to Forrest after being hoodwinked into believing that Forrest outnumbered him. The raid by the Jackass Brigade turned out to be a disaster for the Federals.

Back at Eastport, the Mississippi Marine Brigade, minus the mules, began its secondary mission, that of counter-insurgency, with great zeal. During its departure, the village of Eastport burned to the ground. Ellet reported no cause for the destruction, the village having somehow mysteriously burst into flames. Beginning April 23 and moving northward (downstream) toward Clifton, the brigade set ashore at several places, burning mills and stores and confiscating cotton, mules, and horses. Not surprisingly, the MMB earned the hatred of local residents and rebel partisans alike.

During the river operations, *Diana* accidentally ran into the tugboat *Cleveland* and sank it (perhaps evoking memories of the defunct ram fleet). The flotilla managed to raise the tug the next day. Ellet later reported inaccurately that *Diana* had run aground and that *Cleveland* had struck it.

Although the main attack occurred on April 26th between Ellet's MMB and Confederate cavalry, it was actually Navy Lt. Commander Fitch and his tinclad gunboats who first paddled into the sights of the Texas cavalry battalion led by Major Robert M. White, in a rare night fight at 2:00 am on April 24, north of the Duck River. The riverboats were easy targets, even at night, while the naval gunners could fire only at the muzzle flashes of White's four field artillery pieces. First fired upon was the tinclad *Emma Duncan*, commanded by Acting Master William N. Griswold and manned by inexperienced sailors. One of the sailors noted that the rebels were "peppering it into us hot and heavy." One rebel shell struck the No. 1 Parrott gun portside, exploded, and mangled the arms of three sailors so badly that the three arms had to be amputated on the spot. The nighttime exchange lasted about 45 minutes before the Texans stopped firing and withdrew. The *Emma Duncan* had been hulled seven times, and suffered extensive but mostly minor damage.

Two days later, on the foggy morning of April

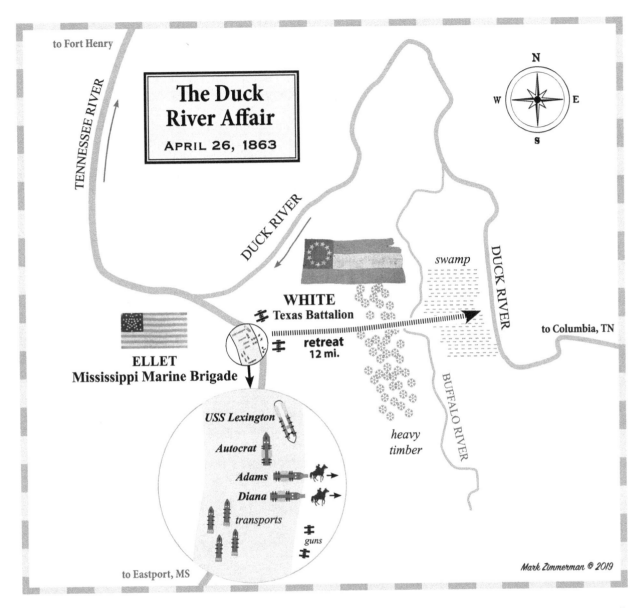

26th, Ellet and the Mississippi Marine Brigade steamed northward on the Tennessee River toward the dangerous shoals near the confluence of the Duck River. The river was narrow at this point (the channel less than 50 yards from the east bank) and allowed for no maneuvering. At 8:30 am at the shoals, Ellet's squadron finally tangled with the Texas Rangers.

Robert M. White knew the terrain and the river well. He had been born and raised in Tennessee near the river. By the 1850s, he and his wife had moved to Bell County, Texas, where he prospered as a grocer. He served as 1st lieutenant in the Bell County Rovers, later commanding the 25 men of Bob White's Ranging Company, defending the local settlers against hostile Comanche Indians. An ardent supporter of secession, White raised a company of cavalry, which was incorporated into the Sixth Texas Cavalry, at Dallas in September 1861. The next year he was promoted to major. He and his men served in Arkansas, the Choctaw Indian Nation, Georgia, Mississippi, and Alabama. By 1865 only 18 men of the original Bell County cavalry company had survived the war.

Major White's special battalion consisted of one company from each regiment of Sullivan Ross' brigade — the 3rd, 6th, and 9th Texas cavalry and Waul's Texas Legion. White's 600 to 700 men stationed their four masked guns on the east bank opposite the shoals, where he knew the boats could not maneuver. They were expecting cargo-laden freighters and perhaps a tinclad or two.

On April 26, 1863, Ellet's flagboat, the *Autocrat*, under sailing master Samuel Henecks, led the flotilla into the narrow chute at the Duck River Shoals, unaware of any pending trouble. "The channel at this point is narrow and torturous, and the current swift, making it necessary for a steamer, when once she has entered the passage of these rapids, to go through without stopping," according to the recollections of the sailors.

The *Autocrat* was suddenly pounded with a barrage from the four-gun battery on the eastern shore, along with a flurry of lead bullets from dozens, if not hundreds, of rifles. The U.S. gunboat returned fire, as did the *Diana* and *Adams*. According to one sailor "…the river itself was quickly overhung with a dense cloud of sulpherous smoke."

Fired upon at point-blank range, eight shells penetrated the *Autocrat*, one hitting the upper casemate and passing through the officers' mess-room, another passing entirely through the upper structure and exploding on the other side. Many brigade members on the gunboats were wounded by wooden splinters. The pilothouse was struck with 80 rounds of bullets and canister, all the glass shattered, and only the boilerplate cladding saving the lives of the pilots. The *Diana* was struck six times and easily penetrated with cannon shells, while the grape, canister, and minié balls were stopped by the heavy oak planking of the gunboat's gunwales.

As soon as the *Autocrat* cleared the shoals, about two miles downriver, she came about and sounded her landing whistle, plowing into the riverbank, lowering her ramp, and dispensing her complement of cavalrymen. Lt. William F. Warren, the signalman atop the gunboat, worked his wigwams (signal flags), ordering the other gunboats to follow suit. Lt. Col. George Currie commanded the landing party, with Major James M. Hubbard in charge of

**Report of Brig. Gen. Alfred W. Ellet, U. S. Army, commanding Mississippi Marine Brigade, with itinerary of the command for April, 1863**
**Cairo, Ill., April 30, 1863**

I have the honor to report that, in compliance with instructions received from Admiral Porter, I proceeded with my command up Tennessee River to Eastport, Miss., without interruption from the enemy. Returning in consequence of low water, I made several raids into the country, and destroyed a number of important mills and considerable amount of subsistence and supplies belonging to the enemy. At the mouth of Duck River my boats were attacked by 700 cavalry, with two pieces of artillery, commanded by Major (R.M.) White, of Sixth Texas Rangers. The fight was spirited for a few moments only. The enemy were driven back and pursued some 12 miles in the interior, with the loss of Major White, mortally wounded and left near the field, and 1 lieutenant and 8 men killed. They carried off a large number of wounded in wagons and on horses. We buried their dead. Our loss was 2 men killed and 1 wounded. The west bank of the Tennessee River was lined with refugees, who have been driven from their homes for love to the old Union. I exhausted my supplies in providing for their necessities. The Tennessee River is too low for my boats to operate in with safety. My orders from Admiral Porter do not provide for this emergency. I shall hope to receive instructions from the Department.

the cavalry and Captain Daniel P. Walling in charge of the artillery units.

Major White's men, expecting to confront only transports, could hardly believe what they were witnessing — the enemy was putting ashore armed horsemen to do battle with them on land. About that time, the timberclad *Lexington*, part of Fitch's downstream force, hove into view and let loose with her big guns. That's all the persuasion the Texans needed. They quickly limbered their guns and headed eastward away from the river at a brisk pace.

Federal pursuit was slow and deliberate. According to historian Walker: "The terrain favored a defending force — a marshy, soft ground covered with thick, patchy woods and winding roads—which provided a topography with many opportunities for a defending force to ambush pursuing troops. The rapid deployment of the Mississippi Marine Brigade forced the Confederate troops to withdraw, and the only further contact came from the rebel rearguard."

Several times the Federal cavalrymen pushed far enough ahead to engage the Confederate rearguard, but they could not induce the Texans into making a stand. Eventually the chase was called off, about 12 miles inland. Casualties were light. Four Confederates were found dead on the riverbank, and four more, including a lieutenant, were killed during the pursuit. One was taken prisoner. The biggest casualty of the skirmish was the Confederate leader himself. Two to four miles inland, Major White was discovered in an abandoned house, dying of a rifle wound to the breast. He would later be taken back to Texas for burial.

The marine brigade suffered two killed (a sergeant in the infantry and a private in the cavalry) and several wounded, most from wooden splinters. Six horses were killed while aboard the gunboats. The cavalryman was killed by a shell hitting the *Autocrat* which then took off the foot of another marine, and sliced off the bayonet and scabbard of a third soldier onboard.

Of the combat, historian Hearn noted, "This marked the first time that Ellet's brigade operated exactly the way (Naval commander) Porter envisioned by landing fifteen hundred troops, with field artillery, at a moment's notice."

Accounts vary as to whether Confederate Lt. Colonel Thomas G. Woodward (White's commander) participated in the skirmish. Woodward's Brigade consisted of White's battalion, the 2nd Kentucky Cavalry, and King's Missouri Battery. Based at nearby Cumberland Furnace, Woodward had been harassing Federal communications in the Dover area,

Colonel Thomas G. Woodward

attacking Palmyra and Harpeth Shoals. His men were often seen in the region. Colonel Woodward had a colorful and eventful career, to say the least. He was a native of Connecticut and attended West Point and Yale but was dismissed from both institutions due to drunkeness. He practiced law in Hopkinsville, Kentucky, and entered service as the captain of the Oak Grove Rangers. He obtained the rank of colonel and led the 2nd Kentucky Cavalry, assisting in the re-capture of Clarksville in 1862. He fought at Fort Donelson, Parker's Crossroads, and Perryville. Few details are known of his experiences because he failed to file after-combat reports with the War Department. In 1864 he was suspended from command for insubordination. Woodward was court-martialed four times, suspended from command once, and reprimanded once. On a drunken spree in August 1864, he rode into Hopkinsville, armed with a pistol in each hand, exclaiming that he was going to single-handedly take the town. He was shot off his horse and killed by a sharpshooter. He was buried at Clarksville.

According to some reports, Woodward's 2nd Kentucky Cavalry took up positions on the east bank of the Tennessee River downstream of the Duck River Shoals, armed with two light field artillery pieces. Their targets were steam transports moving down the river which they intended to plunder. Back at a plantation serving as Woodward's headquarters, a feast was prepared to celebrate a bountiful Confederate victory. Some accounts state that on April 26th the MMB pursued 12 miles inland and stopped when they reached Woodward's plantation. The plantation had been abandoned by the rebels, so the marines stopped and helped themselves to the unattended feast and emptied the estate's pantry and smokehouse.

Again, Woodward's involvement is suspect. General Ellet did not mention Woodward in his report; Major White did not file a report (he was killed that day); and Woodward himself did not submit after-action reports to his superiors. Records of the MMB are incomplete, having been destroyed or lost at the end of the war, according to researcher and author Hearn.

The April 26, 1863 skirmish was the only combat the MMB would experience on the Tennessee River. Following the skirmish at the Duck River Shoals, the Mississippi Marine Brigade was withdrawn and spent the next year operating along the Mississippi River, creating even more controversy, until the brigade was disbanded in late 1864.

Secretary of the Navy Gideon Welles noted in his diary that the Ellets were "brave, venturous, intelligent engineers, not always discreet or wise, but with many daring and excellent qualities. They had under them a set of courageous and picked men."

Perhaps the final word on the Mississippi Marine Brigade comes from *U.S. Army Counterinsurgency and Contingency Operations Doctrine 1860-1941—*

"Perhaps the most remarkable counter-guerrilla unit was the Mississippi Marine Brigade, an amphibious organization created in November 1862 in response to guerrilla attacks on federal shipping along the Mississippi River. Over the course of the next two years the 'marines' led an active life, skirmishing with rebel guerrillas, conducting raids, and participating in conventional operations. Although effective, the unit was troubled by morale and discipline problems and soon developed a reputation for robbery and arson as it steamed up and down the Mississippi burning towns, destroying plantations, and carting off loot. Some of the destruction was authorized in line with the Army's tough retaliatory policies, but the brigade exercised little discretion in picking its targets. Moreover, the unit's special boats were costly to maintain and considerations of economy and reputation eventually led the Army to disband the marine brigade in 1864."

–Chapter Eleven–

# Convoys, Guerrillas, and Bushwhackers

*"There is no impropriety in destroying houses affording shelter to rebels; it is the only way to stop guerrilla warfare"*

Military historian Antoine-Henri Jomini noted that wars are not just fought by massed armies: "The partisans, or irregular corps, which act by their own impulse, able to move in all directions, escape all pursuits, cut the communications upon a thousand points without ever being cut off themselves, are as valuable to those making use of them, as they are disastrous to those whom they harass."

Once Nashville had been secured in February 1862, the capital of Tennessee became an occupied city, eventually ringed by a line of fortifications from the Cumberland River in the east running in a wide arc back to the river west of the city. The crowning structure was Fort Negley, the largest inland stone fortification built during the war. Raw recruits passed through the town headed southward as the wounded and dead and the captured prisoners of war moved northward. Many of the city's sturdiest structures were converted into military hospitals. The railroad lines, terminals, and bridges were fortified and huge warehouses built to hold the massive amount of war ordnance and materiél moving through the city. In 1863 the huge Fortress Rosecrans depot was built near Murfreesboro, southeast of Nashville. As John Hunt Morgan and Nathan Bedford Forrest hit the main railroad links, the importance of Cumberland River cargo transport became more important. In the single-most destructive act against a railroad during the war, Morgan disabled the 1,000-foot-long Big South Tunnel north of Nashville in August 1862 by running a train of burning flatcars into it.

During a church service in Shelbyville, Tennessee, a pro-Southern preacher prayed: "O, Lord, let the rain descend to fructify the earth and to swell the rivers, but O Lord, do not raise the Cumberland sufficient to bring upon us those damn Yankee gunboats."

Because the water level of the Cumberland River greatly fluctuated with the seasons, the low water preventing the passage of large freighters, the Nashville & Northwestern Railroad was extended west of Nashville to the Tennessee River, where a huge fort and depot named Johnsonville was built, offering an alternative route of supply.

During most of the war, Forrest and Wheeler and a host of partisan rangers and guerrillas operated against the Union supply lines, causing many headaches for Federal officials, general officers, and quartermasters. "To the west of the city, Confederate units seemed to move at their own pleasure," stated historian Walter Durham.

Getting ready to launch the Atlanta campaign in 1864, Gen. William Tecumseh Sherman stated: "The great question of the campaign was one of supplies. Nashville, our chief depot, was itself partially in hostile country, and even the routes of supply from Louisville to Nashville, by rail and by way of the Cumberland River, had to be guarded." He admitted, "I am never easy with a railroad which takes an whole army to guard, each foot of rail being essential to the whole; whereas they can't stop the Tennessee (River)…"

Steamboats carried a lot of freight. One steamer transport could carry 500 tons of cargo, enough rations and forage for a 40,000-man army and 18,000 animals. The same amount of cargo would require 250 wagons or 125 rail flatcars. As the war progressed, Sherman became frustrated and angered by the rebel resistance: In December 1863, he wrote to a military friend: "For every bullet shot at a steamboat, I would shoot a thousand 30-pounder Parrotts into even helpless towns."

Brigadier General Philip Sheridan stated: "The feeding of our army from the base at Louisville was attended with many difficulties, as the enemy's cavalry was constantly breaking the railroad and intercepting our communications on the Cumberland River at different points that were easily accessible to his then superior force. The accumulation of reserve stores was therefore not an easy task."

Southern civilians thrilled to the exploits of their partisan warriors, but one Federal soldier spoke for many of his comrades when he called Southern guerrillas "thieves and murderers by occupation, rebels by pretense, soldiers only in name, and cowards by nature."

Lawlessness and atrocities were committed by both sides. U.S. General George Crook recalled that when his command landed in Carthage, Tennessee, in 1863, the Unionists disembarked the riverboats and immediately began looting the town. The general sighed: "I had my hands full, what with looking out for the enemy and restraining the lawlessness of our own people."

"Immediately after the fall of Nashville in 1862, a strict embargo was placed on all shipments of freight and high charges collected for its transportation," according to steamboat historian Byrd Douglas. "Before commercial freight could be shipped during the war, it was necessary to obtain a priority permit, which carried a high tax. The surveyor of Customs Office in Nashville collected these taxes and issued the permits. It soon became one of the busiest places in the city. Old records at this office prove that the merchants of Nashville, despite the intervention of war, continued to do a relatively good business during the occupation of the city by the Federal government."

Rear Admiral David Dixon Porter, commander of the Mississippi Squadron at Cairo, declared: "You can never go wrong in doing a rebel all the harm you can. I am no advocate for the milk and water policy."

On Oct. 18, 1862, Porter issued General Order No. 4 from his Cairo headquarters directing that Federal gunboats never tie up at riverbanks, keep deck guns loaded and aimed at the banks, and keep small arms loaded and ready to repel boarders. The gunboats were ordered to shell and destroy any houses near sharpshooter attacks regardless of civilian casualties.

"When any of our vessels are fired on, it will be

*(Continued on Page 116)*

# CONVOY
## with Escort

one mile

N / E / S / W (compass)

**Transport steamer fleet:**
Robert B. Hamilton
James Thompson
Capitola
Poland
Empire City
Horizon
Ella Faber
Hazel Dell
Diadem
John A. Fisher
May Duke
Dove
Ollie Sullivan
Freestone
Huntress
Shenango
St. Cloud
Adelaide
Arizona
Lady Franklin
Science
Golden Era
Tempest

*USS Fairplay*

**U.S. Navy Gunboat Flotilla:**
USS Fairplay (flagship)
USS Robb
USS Brilliant
USS St. Clair
USS Silver Lake
USS Lexington (timberclad)

Convoy originated at Louisville, Ky, destined for Nashville, Tenn, picking up gunboat escort at Smithland, Ky. Twenty-three steamer transports guarded by six gunboats (five tinclads and one timberclad).

TENNESSEE

To Dover

CUMBERLAND RIVER

USS Silver Lake
USS Robb

Union troops unloading to outflank Confederates while they're held by gunboat fire.

USS St. Clair

USS Fairplay

**Palmyra**

tunnel

←26 miles upstream from Dover
11 miles downstream from Clarksville→
38 miles east to Harpeth Shoals→
27 miles south to Charlotte →

*This map is a composite of various aspects of convoy operations and does not depict any one specific wartime event.*

On April 4, 1863, in retribution for serving as a gathering spot for guerillas and bushwhackers, the village of Palmyra was burned to the ground by Union forces.

USS Brilliant

USS Lexington

To Clarksville

**Confederate Partisan Rangers**
Woodward
2nd KY Cavalry
White's TX Battalion
King's MO Battery
*elevated terrain*

*Mark Zimmerman. © 2019*

the duty of the commander to fire back with spirit, and to destroy everything in that neighborhood within reach of his guns. There is no impropriety in destroying houses supposed to be affording shelter to rebels, and it is the only way to stop guerrilla warfare. Should innocent persons suffer it will be their own fault, and teach others that it will be to their advantage to inform the Government authorities when guerrillas are about certain localities."

Naval officer and historian Alfred T. Mahan stated: "The feeling in the country favored the Confederate cause, so that every hamlet and farmhouse gave refuge to these marauders, while at the same time the known existence of some Union feeling made it hard for officers to judge, in all cases, whether punishment should fall on the places where the attacks were made."

As noted previously, immediately following the Northern victory at Stones River (Murfreesboro), on Jan. 3, 1863, the commanding general, William Rosecrans, began a campaign of cajoling Federal officials in Cairo and Washington for more gunboats on the Cumberland River. The hearty cooperation promised him was compromised by a lack of crews and armament for new gunboats, periods of low water, lack of coordination between the army and navy, and faulty lines of communication, all tempered by constant rumors of Confederate armies on the move. It reached the point where Rosecrans implored the Washington authorities to allow him to purchase steam transports, convert them into army gunboats, and crew them with infantry. Fortunately, the powers in charge did not agree to this proposal.

The U.S. Army operated a small fleet nevertheless. "The U.S. Army Quartermaster Department operated a fleet of ersatz gunboats on the Western rivers," wrote brown-water navy historian Jack Smith. "The majority of these were very small, were manned by civilian crews with military gun crews for the usual two or three cannon, and were protected by cotton bales or planking. The most famous of these were the *Silver Lake No. 2* and *Newsboy*, which operated on the Cumberland River, and the *Stone River*, which steamed on the Tennessee. In March 1864, the *Newsboy* rescued three transports under attack on the upper Cumberland, while in October,

the *Stone River* participated in the defense of Decatur, Alabama, from the army of General John Bell Hood."

Confederate Major J. R. "Dick" McCann was known as the Guerrilla Chieftain. He was captured in August 1863 at Weems Springs, Tennessee, and imprisoned at Johnson's Island in Ohio. A veteran of the Mexican War, he formed the Cheatham Rifles, later Company B of the 11th Tennessee. After the war he was court clerk of Nashville until his death in 1880. One of his captors wrote of McCann: "His name has been an epitome of the seven deadly sins, and if a dastardly act were committed by a Hottentot between Knoxville and Nashville, 'Dick McCann did it.' We assure our readers that he is not the fiend he has been written and painted. He is about five feet eight inches high, 140 pounds weight, fair complexion, bright blue eyes, brilliant, polished and humorous in conversation. He was born of Irish parents at Petersburgh, Va., and came to Tennessee with his family when a mere child. He is married, having four children now in Nashville, his wife being in East Tennessee. He is not now, nor ever was for a disruption of the American Republic. He never has had but two disunionists in his command." Against secession before the war, McCann nonetheless went with his adopted state. He claimed that if Lincoln offered general amnesty to the Southerners the war could be ended quickly.

Despite their assignment to the 9th Tennessee Cavalry, McCann's Squadron continued to do independent partisan service for much of the fall and winter of 1862-63. After the war, a writer for the *Confederate Veteran* magazine stated: "It would be impossible to relate all of his numerous adventures. He was busy prowling around night and day, and rarely permitted the enemy to venture beyond the fortifications of Nashville without some evidence of his thoughtful attention."

On Jan. 13, 1863, the transport *Charter* was attacked by McCann's guerrillas at Ashland, five miles upstream from Harpeth Shoals on the Cumberland. The cargo of hay, corn, and commissary stores was destroyed and the boat burned. The crew was paroled except for six captured

*(Continued on Page 118)*

# Field Artillery of the Civil War

## 12-Pounder Napoleon smoothbore

Bronze smoothbore developed in France in 1850s for Emperor Napoleon III. Fired shot, shell, case shot, and canister. Federal version had muzzle swell; Confederate type had straight tube. The 12-pound shot was 4.5 in. dia. Tube was 66 in., weighed 1227 lbs. Bore was 4.62 inches. Powder charge was 2.5 lbs. Range at 5 degree elevation was 1619 yds.

## 6-Pounder Smoothbore

Nearly obsolete by start of war, gun was used by both sides in the early years. It fired solid shot, round shell, canister, and case. Later, in the South, they were melted down; in the North they were rifled for James projectiles. Bronze tube was 60 in., weighed 884 lbs. Bore was 3.67 in. Range at 5 degrees elevation was 1523 yds.

## 10-Pounder Parrott Rifle

Patented in 1861 by Robert P. Parrott and produced at West Point Foundry. Identified by cast-iron band around the breech. Model 1863 shown; 1861 Model had muzzle swell. Fired shell and case, sometimes a solid iron bolt. Three-in. bore dia.; 78-in. cast-iron tube weighing 890 lbs. One pound powder charge.

## 12-Pounder Howitzer

Confederate gun was made in 1862 at the Tredegar Iron Works in Richmond, Va. This short-barreled cannon fired at a higher trajectory than the Napoleon. Bronze tube is 53 in., weighs 788 lbs., and the bore is 4.62 in. Used a one-pound powder charge. Range at 5 degrees elevation was 1072 yds.

## 12-Pounder Rifled James

Bronze gun converted from six-pound smoothbore to 12-pound rifle. Charles T. James of Rhode Island militia developed projectile that could be used in any cannon specifically rifled for it (15 lands and grooves). Other ammunition was often substituted. The range at 5 degrees elevation was 1700 yds. It used solid shot, shell, and canister. Tube weighed 886 lbs.

## 3-Inch Ordnance Rifle

Accurate wrought-iron gun could shoot great distances. Developed by John Griffen in 1855. Considered superior to the Parrott, 1,000 were bought by the North, and prized as captured weapons by the South. Usually shot Hotchkiss Schenkl patented shells or case shot. Tube is 73 in. and weighs 816 lbs. Powder charge is one pound. Range at 5 degrees was 1835 yds.

contraband deckhands (former slaves), who were led ashore and each executed with a shot to the head. In September 1862, McCann's unit vandalised the Louisville & Nashville Railroad between those two cities. In January 1863, in retribution, General Mitchell, commander of the Nashville garrison, ordered the houses and barns owned by McCann and an associate burned to the ground by the 85th Illinois Infantry. Up to a dozen other houses in that neighborhood were also torched that night.

On Jan. 13, 1863, the same morning as McCann's attack, three boats carrying wounded Federal soldiers, *Hastings*, *Parthenia*, and *Clio*, left Nashville flying hospital flags. Waiting for them at Harpeth Shoals was the brigade of Wheeler's troopers under Colonel William B. Wade. The lead boat, *Hastings*, was ordered to halt by Wade's men, but the civilian pilot turned the boat over to Chaplain Maxwell P. Gaddis of the 2nd Ohio Infantry, the military's senior representative aboard. Gaddis responded that the boat could not stop, and was fired upon by muskets. Gaddis decided to pull over to the bank, but his maneuvers were viewed by the rebels as an attempt to escape. Two artillery rounds hit the hospital boat. When the boat finally grounded, Wade's men, many of them drunk, boarded and began to loot the passengers. The captains of the other two boats went to shore, believing the flotilla had stopped to refuel. Unknown to Gaddis and Wade, the boats also contained cotton cargo. Wade ordered all of the wounded soldiers ashore so the boats could be fired. Gaddis demanded an official order from Wade's superior, Wheeler, and a courier was sent off to retrieve it. Wheeler ordered all of the 260 Federal soldiers paroled but only if Gaddis agreed to burn the cotton upon reaching Louisville. In the meantime, the U.S. Army steamer *W.H. Slidell,* armed with two or three field pieces and commanded by Lt. William Van Dorn, arrived upon the scene. The army gunboat ran aground on the opposite bank and surrendered. The rebels managed to cross the river with the boat, and its cannon were thrown into the water. All of the Union men were put aboard the *Hastings* except for three contrabands, who were summarily executed. The three other boats were torched and soon the full

blast of the heat was so intense it set the grass aflame on the opposite shore.

News of the capture and destruction of the boats spread quickly, the civilian population rejoicing and the Union authorities reacting with great trepidation. The gruesome murder of the contrabands was further sensationalized by the Northern press.

On Jan. 18, 1863, a partisan ranger battalion led by Capt. D.W. Holman captured the transport *Mary Crane* as she was loading firewood at Betsy's Landing near Harpeth Shoals. She had been en route from Evansville, Indiana to Nashville loaded with beans, sugar, flour, corn, soap, and candles. The transport had been escorted by the tinclads *Brilliant* and *St. Clair,* but they had dropped out of formation to refuel. The partisans shot and killed the pilot, destroyed the cargo, and burned the *Mary Crane* to the waterline.

General Rosecrans complained that the partisan attacks at Harpeth Shoals and elsewhere represented "inhuman violations of the rules of civilized warfare by the rebel authorities" that revealed the "barbarism of these rebel leaders." Meanwhile, Confederate General Bragg recommended a promotion for Wheeler as a "just reward to distinguished merit."

On Feb. 20, 1863, following the battle at Dover, Federal tinclad gunboats led by Lt. Commander LeRoy Fitch began a reconnaissance up the Tennessee River all the way to Muscle Shoals. Along the way, the gunboats ran into a small battle at Clifton, where 60 troopers of the 3rd Michigan Cavalry under Capt. Cicero Newell had surrounded and attacked the infamous guerrilla leader Col. John F. Newsom and his men at dawn. Newell was wounded and succeeded by Capt. Frederick C. Adamson. Newsom was shot in the left arm and captured along with 53 of his men, who were described as a "ragamuffin collection." The remainder of the guerrillas fled and the town was torched. The gunboats saw the smoke and responded. Fitch agreed to ferry the Wolverines and their captured prisoners and horses across the river. The surgeon aboard the *USS Brilliant* remarked about the Confederates, "They are good marksmen and if they fire from planted guns, we stand a chance to be well pounded as a ball from a 12-pounder would go through us like so much paper."

More than anyone else, Lt. Commander LeRoy Fitch devised the counterinsurgency techniques and convoy maneuvers that ensured that the needed supplies would reach Nashville and the armies in the Western Theater. A native of Logansport, Ind., and a graduate of the U.S. Naval Academy, Fitch was appointed by Flag Officer Charles Davis to head up a fleet of light-draught tinclads known as the Mosquito Fleet to escort convoys and patrol the Ohio, Tennessee, and Cumberland rivers. His biographer, Jack Smith, stated that Fitch "gained a reputation for his prosecution of counter insurgency warfare and as an innovator of protective measures for the massive number of contract steamboats which churned the Ohio, Cumberland, and Tennessee rivers supplying the advancing Union armies." Duty-bound and indomitable, Fitch was not a flamboyant man and he has not received the recognition that he deserves, Smith said. In service the entire war, the energetic Fitch served well at Island No. 10, Fort Pillow, Memphis, Dover, on the Ohio during Morgan's famous raid, on the Upper Tennessee River, and during the 1864 Nashville campaign.

Steamboat historian Douglas said of Fitch: "He was the officer who did more than anyone else to keep the Cumberland open." Porter said of Fitch after his death: "The gallant Fitch never shrunk from the performance of any duty however hazardous."

Fitch learned about counterinsurgency from his half-brother Graham Newell Fitch, who was 25 years older than him and outlived him by 17 years. A former U.S. Senator, the elder Fitch raised the 46th Indiana Volunteers and led it into battle at Fort Pillow and Memphis. In June 1862, the elder Fitch was witness to the destruction of the *USS Mound City* ironclad in Arkansas. While the gunboat was disabled and under tow, Confederates fired into the steam drum and then shot survivors as they struggled in the water. Eighty-two sailors were either shot to death or scalded to death by steam, with another 43 drowned. Fitch vowed to retaliate against any persons firing on boats from shore and destroy their residences and property.

Lt. Commander LeRoy Fitch

The younger Fitch devised the strategy of engaging and holding Confederates on the shore with gunboats while another gunboat or transport disembarked Union cavalry to ride hard and engage the enemy from behind. Although a sound tactic, the Confederates always posted pickets or lookouts and they were never really surprised or routed. Besides, several rounds of canister from a 32-pounder was usually enough to persuade cavalry, especially units without field artillery, to disperse.

Fitch was much more successful in devising methods of escorting convoys with gunboats. By January 1863 Fitch's flotilla numbered six gunboats, and each one of them carried powerful eight-inch naval guns that outclassed any Confederate field artillery in the region. Borrowing from army doctrine, Fitch placed the slowest steamers in the front of the convoy, with the most valuable cargos in the middle, and the fastest boats in the rear. The gunboats were dispersed along the line, with one always in the lead and one trailing. In strong currents, a light-draught might be lashed to one of the larger transports. Following the *Hastings* affair, naval headquarters ordered that at least two gunboats escort every convoy. Each convoy to

Nashville would take a week, with boats leaving Smithland or Dover each Monday. While the transports were unloading at the Nashville wharf, the gunboats would conduct patrols on the upper Cumberland River all the way to Carthage.

On Jan. 23, 1863, a 22-boat return convoy left Nashville with the escorts *Brilliant* and *St. Clair*. At Betsy's Landing, raiders used three field artillery pieces to fire down on a transport, the *R.B. Hamilton*, and placed a shot into the vessel. The *St. Clair*, under Acting Volunteer Lt. Charles Perkins, steamed up and engaged the guerrillas, scattering them with several well-placed shells.

From January 24 to March 15, 1863, seven escorted convoys consisting of 180 steamers and 30 barges successfully made the trip between Smithland/Dover and Nashville. Soon, however, such success promoted complacency. On April 3, a convoy under the command of Acting Volunteer Lt. Jacob Hurd steamed toward Nashville with the most valuable boats up front and the slowest in the rear (contrary to orders). The convoy included the steamers *Eclipse* and *Lizzie Martin* lashed together, the gunboat *St. Clair*, the transport *Luminary*, the towboats *Charles Miller* and *J.N. Kellogg*, each drawing barges, and the slow gunboat *Fairplay*. The convoy reached Palmyra (between Dover and Clarksville) at 10:30 pm. From a bluff, Confederate gunners under Lt. Col. Thomas G. Woodward opened up with a 10-pounder Parrott rifle and a 12-pounder smoothbore. At 400 yards, the *Luminary* was hit with balls from 60 musketmen and the *St. Clair* was hit by small arms, canister, and at least six shells, one of which severed the steam supply pipe and disabled the gunboat. The executive officer's right knee was shattered by a six-pounder shell. The *Luminary* took the gunboat under tow. The *Kellogg* ended up towing the disabled gunboat back to Smithland, where Fitch was informed of the attack. He telegraphed headquarters: "I leave in 10 minutes for Palmyra with all the boats. Will whip them out."

The timberclad *Lexington* and the four tinclads in the avenging flotilla reached Palmyra the afternoon of April 4. While Fitch generally maintained a lenient attitude toward occupants of the surrounding countryside, in this case he agreed with the other

## Civil War in Charlotte, Tennessee

In 1860, 300 people lived in Charlotte, the Dickson County seat. During the war, the residents witnessed considerable military activity, beginning February 17, 1862, when Confederate Col. Nathan Bedford Forrest arrived here to re-equip his men and horses after escaping the surrender of Fort Donelson. Late in 1862 and early in 1863, local guerrillas used Charlotte as a base. Col. Thomas G. Woodward's band of partisans and Gen. Joseph Wheeler's Confederate cavalry raided the Union transportation center at Harpeth River Shoals on the Cumberland River, 6 miles northeast. In 1863 and 1864, Federal forces built the Nashville and Northwestern Railroad from Nashville to the Tennessee River.

*Historical Marker located at the Charlotte Co. Courthouse, 22 Court Square, Charlotte, TN 37036*

naval officers that Palmyra should pay the price. The village had the reputation as "one of the worst secession places on the river" and as a notorious gathering place for guerrillas, bushwhackers, and other scoundrels. Guerrilla attacks were organized at meetings held in the saloons on the court square in Charlotte, seat of Dickson County. The town was equidistant from Palmyra to the north and Harpeth Shoals to the northeast. A landing party was sent ashore under Acting Master James Fitzpatrick with orders to burn down Palmyra but not to loot. Residents of the village were given notice to evacuate immediately. One Federal officer wrote later: "It was clean work — every building was in flames and falling." Fitch reported that they had "burned the town; not a house left; a very bad hole; best to get rid of it and teach the rebels a lesson."

An amphibious force of gunboats and infantry set out from Clarksville to pursue the partisans at Betsy's Landing upstream, but the rebels were forewarned and disappeared. Fitch had hoped to employ his counterinsurgency technique to bag the bushwhackers. He intended to engage the rebels on the shore and hold them long enough so that the Union cavalry and infantry could sneak up behind and attack them against the river.

On April 9, two small steamers, *Saxonia* and *R.M.C. Lovell,* left Dover without waiting for gunboat escorts and were captured at nightfall 15 miles downstream from Clarksville by Woodward's 2nd Kentucky Cavalry and local guerrillas. The boats and their cargoes were burned and eight blacks from the crew were shot and killed. When the captain of the *Lovell* protested, he also was shot and killed. Rear Admiral Porter noted that the transport captains "paid the penalty of disobedience."

In six weeks time, Woodward, commanding the 2nd Kentucky Cavalry, White's Texas Battalion, and King's Missouri Battery, sank two gunboats and four armed transports, crippled six other transports, killed 157 men, and destroyed $250,000 worth of property, according to Confederate records.

Despite the relative success of the convoy system and the constant presence of the Union gunboats, the pro-Southern local population remained resistant. Nannie Haskins, 16, belonged to a prominent family in Clarksville whose house overlooked the river. At dusk on May 12, 1863, Nannie wrote in her diary, "Those hateful gun boats! They look like they are from the lower regions. Now this the second night that four of them have been anchored in the river opposite our house. I know they are frightened, they have placed their gunboats so that if an attack is made, they can shell the town. Poor cowards, I can just turn my head now and see them crawling about on the boats like so many snakes." The teenager added: "The whole county is alive with robbers, every night we hear of a new robbery and perhaps a murder. Every minute of the day we hear of something startling, which four years ago would have made us 'shake in our shoes,' now merely give them a passing thought. War has hardened us."

Brevet Brigadier General Lewis B. Parsons served as the efficient quartermaster stationed at St. Louis. For the fiscal year ending July 30, 1863, Parsons estimated that steamboats had brought 136,000 troops and 338 million pounds of goods through Nashville, while the rails handled 193,000 troops and 153 million pounds of goods. By March

of 1864, there were 50 steamer transports tied at the wharf at Nashville, the largest number ever, according to the *Nashville Times* newspaper.

How effective were the guerrillas against river shipping? According to Parsons, direct guerrilla action against river transports on all the Western rivers (Mississippi, Tennessee, Cumberland) during the entire war resulted in the sinking of 28 vessels weighing 7,065 tons and costing $355,000. Regular Confederate forces sank another 19 vessels weighing 7,925 tons and valued at $518,500. Most effective of all, Confederate secret agents using incendiaries sank double the tonnage (18,500) and 29 boats worth $891,000.

Confederate cavalry raids diminished after the spring of 1863. "Confederate overconfidence, combined with the inventiveness and flexibility of Federal commanders in confronting the raiding threat, negated raiding as a strategy in 1863," according to historian John Mackey. "After that summer, the Confederacy tried other raids, but when facing a veteran Union cavalry, fortified rail lines, the overwhelming material might of the north, and the slow attrition of their own mounted units, they had little chance of changing the course of the war. The summer of 1863 was the last real opportunity for organized raiding by conventional cavalry forces…"

No one person exemplified the deadly impact of the partisan guerrilla than Jack Hinson, the lone sharpshooter whose vengeance against the occupying Federal forces resulted in dozens of kills, according to Hinson's biographer, Tom C. McKenney, who noted, "Elements of nine regiments, both cavalry and infantry, and an amphibious task force of specially built navy boats with a special-operations Marine brigade targeted the elderly man with a growing price on his head. They never got him."

Captain Jack Hinson, as he was known, was in his late 50s when he ordered a specially made .50-caliber rifle (the gunsmith was William E. Goodman of Lewis County) and began targeting Union officers for death. One of his favorite shooting dens was at Towhead Chute on the Tennessee River near Hurricane Creek in Benton County, Tenn.

As the river flows northward through the narrow channel, the current increases significantly, and the paddlewheelers headed upstream worked hard against the current, barely moving. A Union officer might stand on the deck, admiring the view in his navy blue uniform. Hinson aimed between the shiny brass buttons of the victim's jacket. For each kill, he would stamp a round notch onto the octagonal barrel of his heavy rifle. By war's end, the plain-looking rifle was adorned with 36 notches (McKenney estimated that Hinson's actual kill total was close to 100).

What had motivated this lone sharpshooter to seek such vengence? Hinson was a wealthy landowner and farmer in the area between the rivers, now known as the Land Between the Lakes. At first, he was a Unionist, opposed to secession, even though he owned slaves. The invasion and occupation of his homeland, and the increasingly harsh treatment of locals by the Yankees, forced him to change his mind. His estate was called Bubbling Springs, located three miles southwest of Dover. General U.S. Grant at one time was a guest in the house of Hinson and his wife, Elisabeth. The couple had eight sons and two daughters. One son was a Confederate soldier stationed in Virginia, who was wounded and died in 1865. Two other sons were briefly imprisoned as spies during the Battle of Fort Donelson. The eldest son, Robert, was involved with a local guerrilla group. At one point, Robert was imprisoned at the county courthouse but escaped by jumping out a second-story window. His horsemen became known as Hinson's Raiders. He was captured a second time and questioned by authorities in Nashville who never realized exactly who he was. He managed to either escape or he was paroled. On Aug. 6, 1863, Hinson's men attacked Fort Henry and seized the telegraph station.

One morning in the fall of 1862, two of Jack Hinson's younger sons were out on horseback, armed and hunting game, when set upon by a roving Federal cavalry patrol. The Hinsons, ages 17 and 22, were assumed to be spies. They were tied to trees and summarily executed by firing squad. Their lifeless bodies were put on display in the courthouse square in Dover. Then the lieutenant commander of the patrol beheaded the bodies with his saber. As the patrol made its way to Bubbling Springs to confront Jack Hinson, they placed the severed heads of his sons on the gateposts at the Hinson home. A doctor and friend of the family was able to subdue the enraged Jack Hinson and save him from being killed or imprisoned by the patrol, which eventually left the scene. At this point, Hinson, of Scots-Irish descent, determined to save his family and vowed vengeance, however long it might take. He needed time to secure his family and estate, order his custom-made sharpshooter rifle, obtain supplies, and scout shooting locations.

Hinson's first victim was the lieutenant of the patrol that killed his sons. Hiding and waiting in the woods, Hinson shot him in the saddle while leading a patrol. A short time later, Hinson was out and about and sighted a Yankee patrol which included the sergeant who had placed the boys' heads on the gateposts. On the patrol's return to base, Hinson was waiting. With cool efficiency, he shot and killed the sergeant and made his escape.

Eventually the Hinson family was forced to abandon Bubbling Springs, which was burned to the ground by soldiers, and relocate. Hinson took his position at Towhead Chute and began picking off Union naval officers on the gunboats. At one point, Hinson's shots were so devastating that the captain of one gunboat "surrendered" his vessel before realizing that there were no Confederate troops to accept his surrender.

Jack Hinson died peacefully nine years after the war at the age of 67. Hinson's rifle is now owned by a judge in Murfreesboro, Tennessee.

– Chapter Twelve –

# Paducah

*"As an honorable officer, I must, therefore, respectfully decline surrendering as you may require"*

On Sept. 4, 1861, the same day that Brig. Gen. U.S. Grant assumed command at the naval base at Cairo, Illinois, Confederate President Jefferson Davis ordered Gen. Leonidas Polk and 1,500 men to occupy the Kentucky town of Columbus on the steep banks of the Mississippi River, thereby violating that state's tenuous neutrality (Federal troops were already being trained at Camp Dick Robinson in Kentucky). The Mississippi River was of vital importance to the Confederacy and garnered much more attention, manpower, and funding than either the Tennessee or Cumberland rivers. In time, the heavily fortified cliffs at Columbus would be called the "Gibralter of the West." When he heard the news, Grant acted swiftly and without orders moved up the Ohio 45 miles and seized the river port of Paducah, Ky. (pop. 4,600) at the mouth of the Tennessee River. "There was a large number of steamers lying at Cairo and a good many boatmen were staying in town," Grant wrote in his memoirs. "It was the work of only a few hours to get the boats manned, with coal aboard and steam up." He said the pro-Southern citizens of Paducah were taken by surprise, expecting the arrival of Confederate troops. Grant recalled, "I never after saw such consternation depicted on the faces of the people. Men, women, and children came out of their doors looking pale and frightened at the presence of the invader."

Photograph of Paducah riverwall painting by artist Robert Dafford and his team.

The occupation force consisted of the timberclads *Conestoga* and *Tyler* and the transports *Graham, Platte Valley,* and *W.B. Terry.* Grant captured the town with two infantry regiments and one battery (the 9th Illinois of Brigadier General Eleazer Paine, the 12th Illinois of Colonel John McArthur, and a section of Smith's Chicago Artillery under Lt. Charley Willard). He issued a proclamation to the citizens assuring them of the Federals' peaceful intentions and put General Charles Ferguson Smith in charge of the garrison. Also, at this time, the Federals moved a force to occupy the village of Smithland at the mouth of the Cumberland River, about 15 miles up the Ohio.

Many of the residents left Paducah, fearing a confrontation that would lead to the gunboats shelling the town. "A perfect panic seemed to possess them," according to a Missouri newspaper correspondent, "which no assurance of our officers or troops could allay." Within two days, only about 100 families remained. Their fears were heightened when U.S. artillery crews opened battery practice

from the town square. They were justifiably horrified when an errant gunboat shell during a practice drill accidentally hit the ground floor of an unoccupied riverside house and exploded. Paducah was the hometown of Confederate General Lloyd Tilghman, who was to be taken prisoner while defending Fort Henry in February 1862 and was killed in action at Champion's Hill, near Vicksburg, in May 1863.

Throughout most of the war, Colonel Stephen G. Hicks was in charge of Paducah and the massive Union supply depots and dock facilities for the gunboats and supply ships that supported Federal forces along the Ohio, Cumberland, and Tennessee river systems. Fort Anderson was built west of the town and along the river, named for General Robert Anderson, the hero of Fort Sumter. It was an earthen fortification 160 feet wide by 400 feet long with 32-pounder siege cannon facing both the river and the city. The fort was constructed around a marine hospital, which later burned in the fall of 1863. The town was surrounded by six smaller forts

*(Continued on Page 127)*

# The Battle of PADUCAH

## MARCH 25, 1864

OHIO RIVER

Tennessee Island

TENNESSEE RIVER

Floating Battery. One 8-inch Columbiad mounted; second battery under construction

SHIRK

USS Peosta (36) (Smith)

USS Paw Paw (31) (O'Neill)

Col. Albert "Sam" Thompson

FORT

Col. Stephen G. Hicks (650 men)

Camp of the 12th Regt. Illinois Vols

Missouri Sappers & Miners

14th Regt. Ill. Vols

Chicago Dragoons

8th Regt. Missouri Vols.

Battery № 6

23rd Regt. Ind. Vols.

PADUCAH

11th Regt. Ind. Vols

2nd US Cavalry Co. I

Battery № 5

Powder Magazine

Battery № 4

9th Regt. Ill. Vols

Battery № 3

Powder Magazine

Battery № 2

Chicago Light Artillery

40th Regt. Illinois Vols

Palisades and Infantry Trenches

Buell's Missouri Light Artillery

Battery № 1

Powder Magazine

FORT ANDERSON

KENTUCKY

Forrest

ELIZABETH STREET
GEORGE STREET
NORTON STREET
JONES STREET
JENNINGS STREET
OHIO STREET
JACKSON STREET
ADAMS STREET
CLARK STREET
COURT STREET
WASHINGTON
BROADWAY
JEFFERSON STREET
MONROE STREET
MADISON STREET
HARRISON STREET
HOSPITAL STREET
TRIMBLE STREET
MAIN STREET
MARKET STREET
LOCUST STREET

N E S W

Mark Zimmerman © 2019

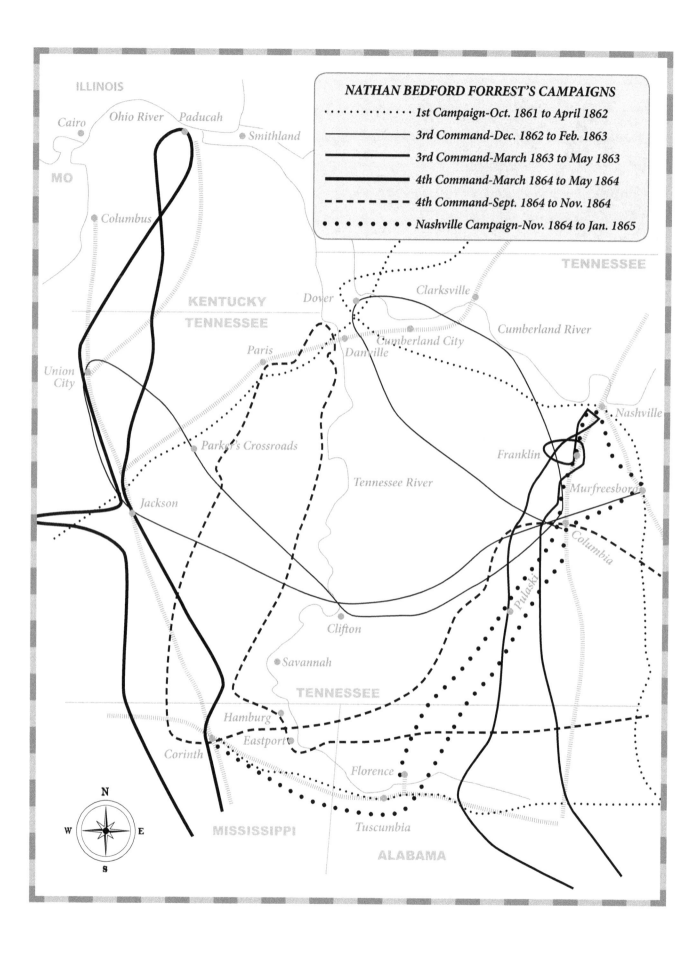

equipped with large 32-pounder siege cannon.

In the early months of 1864, as General William T. Sherman prepared to launch the Atlanta campaign, his nemesis, General Nathan Bedford Forrest, stormed through West Tennessee, capturing Union City and threatening the Kentucky river ports on the Mississippi and the Ohio.

On March 25, 1864, Forrest and his men raided Paducah. He intended to re-supply the Confederate forces in the region with recruits, ammunition, medical supplies, horses, and mules. And he hoped to disrupt Union domination of the region south of the Ohio River. The raid was successful in terms of the re-supply effort and in intimidating the Federals, but Forrest was forced to return south. According to his report, "I drove the enemy to their gunboats and fort; and held the city for ten hours, captured many stores and horses; burned sixty bales of cotton, one steamer, and a drydock, bringing out fifty prisoners."

Most of the Union garrison, 650 men consisting mainly of U.S. Colored Troops, retreated from the town into the safety of the fort, which at the time was guarded by two tinclads in the Ohio River — the USS Paw Paw, onstation and commanded by Acting Volunteer Lt. A.F. O'Neill, and the USS Peosta, newly arrived from Cairo and tcommanded by Acting Volunteer Lt. Thomas E. Smith. The Confederate raiders quickly had the run of the town and commenced to occupy houses and commercial buildings, shooting from the upper stories into the fort and at the gunboats.

Before attacking the fort, Forrest resorted to a common ploy. He sent an intimidating message to Colonel Hicks inside the fort: "Having a force amply sufficient to carry your works and reduce the place, and in order to avoid the unnecessary effusion of blood, I demand the surrender of the fort and troops, with all public property. If you surrender, you shall be treated as a prisoner of war; but if I have to storm your works, you may expect no quarter."

Hicks replied: "I can answer that I have been placed here by the Government to defend this post, and in this, as well as all other orders from my superiors, I feel it to be my duty as an honorable officer to obey. I must, therefore, respectfully decline

USS Peosta

surrendering as you may require."

A Paducah native, Confederate Colonel Albert P. "Sam" Thompson, led two futile unauthorized attacks against the fort. On the second attempt, as he led his men, waving his cap above his head, a shell struck him and tore him to pieces. His men retreated to nearby houses and began sniping. The Confederates were thwarted by water-filled ditches surrounding the fort and the shelling from the two gunboats stationed in the Ohio. Reportedly the Union men inside the fort spent 27,000 of the 30,000 available rounds of ammunition during the fighting.

The Paw Paw stayed beside the fort while the Peosta, a side-wheeler, churned upriver to station herself beside the town and began firing at targets of opportunity up the length of Broadway. In due time, the Peosta dropped back to the fort to assist in resisting Thompson's first attack, but when Forrest and Hicks suspended the fighting to discuss a possible surrender, the Peosta ran upriver opposite the town again.

The citizens remaining in town were left to defend for themselves, with several women and children reportedly killed in the melee. A wharfboat full of civilians managed to make it across the river to Metropolis, Illinois, where they watched parts of their town go up in flames.

The Confederate riflemen, many stationed in warehouses and other structures on Front Street, peppered the gunboats, especially the Peosta, with rifle fire. "While it lasted, their balls came pretty thick as some of them came in our portholes and some clean through the casemates..." reported one of the sailors on the *Peosta*.

Then the *Peosta*, armed with three 30-pounder rifles and eleven smoothbores, opened the ball on the riverfront. Lt. Smith said that he "reluctantly opened upon them, demolishing the Continental Hotel and brewery and setting several other buildings on fire." A Confederate rifleman said the shells sent "shingles, brick chimneys and window glass in wild profusion upon our heads."

Firing from the fort ceased at 8:30 pm. Thirty minutes later, the *Paw Paw* fired several shells but the enemy did not return fire. At 10:30 pm it was reported that Forrest's men were burning quartermaster warehouses and commissary buildings in preparation for departure. The *Peosta* churned upriver once again and lobbed shells into the Confederate troopers. Forrest withdrew his men, declaring victory. The U.S. suffered 90 casualties, the Confederates 50.

During the battle, the *Peosta* fired 530 rounds and was hit by rifle fire 200 times. Two sailors were wounded. The *Paw Paw* fired 177 rounds, with no casualties. Lt. O'Neill on the *Paw Paw* did report a scratch from a bullet on his right cheek and that "a ball went through his pantaloons."

Commander James Shirk arrived at Paducah the next morning and reported that the gunboat shelling did much damage to the town. Approximately 100 buildings were damaged or destroyed, including the hospital, gas works, customs house, post office, railroad depot, and tobacco warehouses. That morning, Colonel Hicks, expecting another rebel attack, ordered all buildings near the fort to be torched. One observer stated that one-fourth of the river port had been burned down. According to naval historian Jack Smith, the majority of the damage was committed by the two gunboats. Since Paducah was considered to be pro-Southern, with local merchants profiting from Union largess, the naval commanders were not too dismayed at the extensive damage.

Later having read in the newspapers that 140 horses had escaped confiscation during the raid, Forrest sent Brigadier General Abraham Buford back to Paducah to get the horses and to keep Union forces busy there while he attacked Fort Pillow on the Mississippi River. On April 14, Buford's men found the horses hidden in a Paducah foundry, as reported by the newspapers. Buford rejoined Forrest with the spoils, leaving the Federals in control of Paducah until the end of the war.

–Chapter Thirteen–

# Eastport

*Kelley's gunners turn a Federal amphibious
landing into an ambush and frenzied chaos*

In October 1864, about a month or so after Sherman finally captured Atlanta, a Federal task force was formed in West Tennessee to move against the Memphis & Charleston Railroad, which was being used by Major General Nathan Bedford Forrest to supply his troops at Cherokee, Alabama. In late September-early October 1864, Forrest roamed north from Alabama nearly to Nashville in an effort to disrupt Sherman's communication (supply) lines. The Federals planned to seize the railroad and wait two days for reinforcements to arrive. This operation was launched to prevent cavalry forces under Forrest from crossing the Tennessee River in northern Alabama and to provide an outpost against an expected advance by Confederate General John Bell Hood. The Yankee task force congregated at Clifton, Tennessee, and planned to move up the Tennessee River and disembark at Eastport, Mississippi, the only suitable landing in the vicinity. The leader of the 1,300-man task force, Colonel George B. Hoge, commanded the 113th and 120th Illinois regiments, the 61st U.S. Colored Troops, 30 dismounted Missouri cavalrymen, and Company G of the 2nd Missouri Light Artillery. The U.S. troops would be transported upriver by the steamers *Aurora, Kenton,* and *City of Pekin,* and escorted by the tinclad gunboats *USS Key West* and *USS Undine.*

According to ancient seafaring mythology, an undine is a female sea creature who constantly searches for a male of the human species so that she can marry him and thus gain a soul. The gunboat of the same name began life as the steamer *Ben Gaylord* in 1863. She was purchased by the U.S. Navy in March 1864 at Cincinnati for $35,000. She was finished at Mound City and armed with eight 24-pounder Dahlgren smoothbore howitzers. The No. 55 tinclad joined the Mississippi Squadron and was deployed in May 1864 on the Mississippi River. She soon left the Mississippi and operated during early July 1864 on the Tennessee River in support of Union forces ashore who were under sporadic attack by Colonel Jacob Biffle's 19th Tennessee Cavalry. While standing off the village of Clifton on July 25, the *Undine*, Acting Master John L. Bryant in command, snagged a tree, tearing a two-foot-long hole in the bottom, and sank at an angle in water ranging from fifteen to four feet deep. Her crew rescued two of her howitzers and mounted them in a stockade on the riverbank. On July 30, 1864, Biffle's troopers demanded surrender of the Clifton post, but Major James M. Dickerson of the 2nd Tennessee (US) Mounted Infantry refused and Biffle backed off. The *Undine* was successfully refloated on August 1 after the arrival of the pump steamer *Little Champion*.

Now, two months later, at mid-morning on Oct. 10, 1864, the *Undine*, *Key West* and the convoy of U.S. soldiers reached Eastport to prepare for another successful, uncontested amphibious landing.

Unfortunately for the Federals, that ole devil Forrest caught wind of the impending expedition. He chose his "Fighting Parson," Colonel David C. Kelley, to intercept the Yankees with 300 cavalrymen and a section of Hudson's artillery battery under Captain E.S. Walton. Thoroughly familiar with the layout of the river, Kelley knew exactly where Hoge was going to land and disembark. He also knew exactly what to do. "Kelley had been dealing with Yankee gunboats since 1861 and had long since lost his sense of awe at the appearance and the firepower of these vessels," according to his biographer Michael Bradley.

Kelley used earthworks abandoned earlier in the war to position a 10-pounder cannon on either side of the draw up the steep bank of the river. Dismounted riflemen were placed out-of-sight at the top of the draw. Kelley reckoned correctly that the tinclad gunboats could not elevate their guns high enough to hit his forces up on the banks, especially at so close a distance.

The *Key West* was a 207-ton sternwheeler purchased at Cairo in May 1863 for $33,800. She was 156 feet long, 52 feet at the beam, and drew 4.6 feet. Her main deck bristled with six 24-pounder Dahlgren smoothbore howitzers. The *Key West* steamed upriver past the Eastport landing, and seeing nothing suspicious, gave the all-clear signal. The three transports, "blue with Yankees," were unloaded and led ashore by two lieutenants on horseback, the U.S. Colored Troops in the van. Once they reached the top of the 20-foot riverbank, the Confederates in hiding let loose. First to face the music were the U.S. Colored Troops and three artillery pieces that had been off-loaded first. A well-placed rebel cannon shot disabled the *Undine*. Flustered, the captain of the *Key West* steamed a ways downriver, leaving the Union men unprotected. The transports *Aurora* and *Kenton* were also hit and set ablaze. One shot exploded in the engine room of the *Kenton*, ruptured a steam line, and killed a crewman. Capt. J.H. Dunlap withdrew the *Kenton* from the riverbank and extinguished the fire. On the *Aurora*, Capt. Patterson Marshall was killed along with 20 soldiers onboard. Many blueclad soldiers fell into the river and drowned. Meanwhile, the tinclads continued to fire harmlessly into the riverbank. According to a *Chicago Daily Tribune* correspondent who witnessed the debacle, "The worst feature of the whole inglorious defeat" was that the gunboats "killed more of our own troops and did more damage to ours than to the enemy."

In his after-action report, Acting Master Bryant of the *Undine* stated, "The transports were struck several times, exploding a caisson on board the *Aurora* and *Kenton*, and setting them on fire, causing great confusion among the troops, burning several of them, and mortally wounding the captain of the *Aurora*. Many of the troops jumped overboard from

*(Continued on Page 132)*

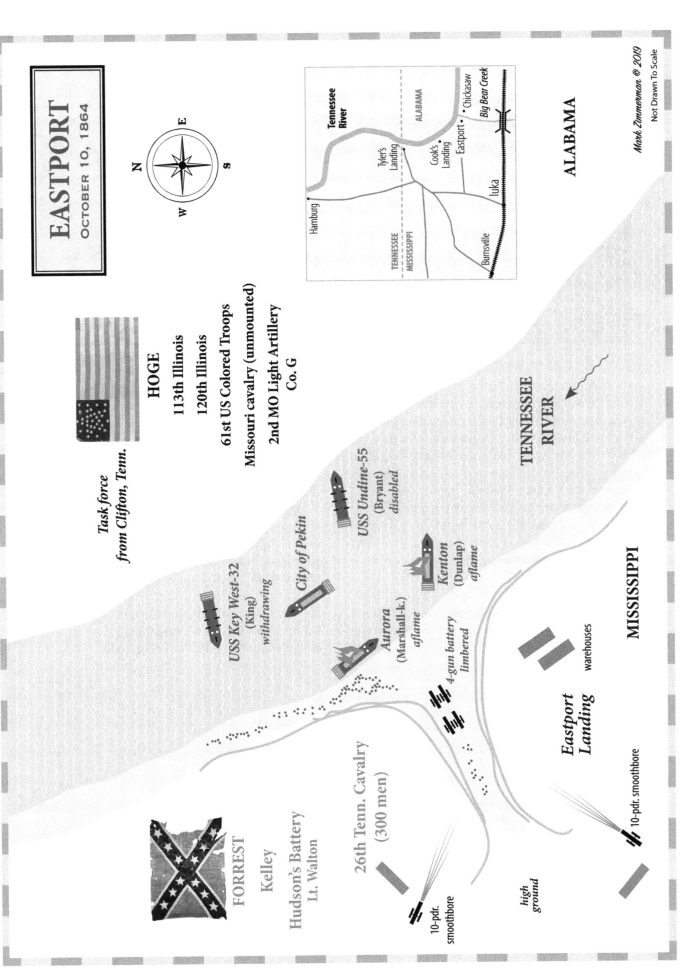

# EASTPORT

## OCTOBER 10, 1864

Tennessee River

Tyler's Landing

Hamburg

Cook's Landing

Eastport

Chickasaw

Big Bear Creek

ALABAMA

Iuka

Burnsville

TENNESSEE
MISSISSIPPI

ALABAMA

Mark Zimmerman © 2019

Not Drawn To Scale

N
E
S
W

**HOGE**

113th Illinois
120th Illinois

61st US Colored Troops

Missouri cavalry (unmounted)

2nd MO Light Artillery
Co. G

*Task force
from Clifton, Tenn.*

USS Key West-32
(King)
*withdrawing*

City of Pekin

USS Undine-55
(Bryant)
*disabled*

Aurora (Marshall-k.)
*aflame*

Kenton (Dunlap)
*aflame*

4-gun battery
*limbered*

TENNESSEE
RIVER

Eastport
Landing

warehouses

MISSISSIPPI

10-pdr. smoothbore

**FORREST**

Kelley

Hudson's Battery
Lt. Walton

26th Tenn. Cavalry
(300 men)

10-pdr.
smoothbore

*high
ground*

10-pdr. smoothbore

Confederate artillery demonstration

the burning steamers. A company that had been sent out as skirmishers immediately returned toward the boat. The other troops that were forming in line on the bank broke and fled in great disorder down the river. The battery of four guns was abandoned, the transports cut their lines and drifted downstream, *Aurora* and *Kenton* disabled."

Bryant wrote to Commander James Shirk, his superior at Paducah, "I am happy to inform you that during the engagement my officers and crew behaved gallantly and displayed coolness in every instance."

Hoge ordered his men into battle positions and ordered the third transport, *City of Pekin,* to withdraw from the landing. The Federal troops escaped by running along the shoreline and re-embarking on the transports downriver from Eastport.

In his report, Kelley noted 74 of the enemy killed, wounded, or captured. Three cannons and 60 horses were seized. The rebels suffered one man wounded. Later that day the Federal boats reached the safety of Paducah.

Sgt. John Darrough of Company F, 113th Illinois, was awarded the Medal of Honor for "saving the life of a captain." Darrough had been stranded on the riverbank, walking north, when he discovered a canoe in the reeds. Paddling out into the channel he heard shouts from behind him. He returned to the riverbank and picked up Captain A.W. Becket of Company B. The two men reached the safety of the east riverbank and fled the scene.

– Chapter Fourteen –

# Johnsonville

*Forrest creates his own gunboat navy*
*and destroys huge Tennessee River depot*

Convoys of top-heavy steam freighters winding their way down the Ohio and up the Tennessee, unloading their boxes and barrels and hogsheads at the depot cargo ramps, loading the railcars to be hauled over trestles and bridges to huge warehouses and fortified encampments, then forwarded behind belching locomotives through tunnels and up to the front in mule-drawn wagons. Laden with grain and gunpowder, bullets and beans, sacks of flour and sides of salted beef, shoes and blankets and rifles and a hundred varieties of munitions and supplies.

All of this continuous logistical activity, originating at Cincinnati and ending at Chattanooga, was to serve one goal—supplying the three armies led by General William T. Sherman during their advance and subsequent occupation of northern Georgia and Atlanta in the summer and fall of 1864.

The initial requirement was to stock enough provisions, food, forage, and ammunition for 100,000 soldiers and 35,000 horses for 70 days. As a result, Nashville became the largest Army depot on the face of the earth. At one point, Nashville warehouses bulged with enough foodstuffs to feed 200,000 soldiers three meals a day for four months. At the beginning of 1864 only 65 to 80 rail cars (600 tons) were reaching Chattanooga each day, but by the end of April, an average of 135 cars were making the daily trip.

Thirty thousand U.S. government employees worked in Nashville maintaining more than 220 locomotives and tending a coal yard that could hold four million bushels. Fifty wagons could be loaded or unloaded simultaneously at the huge Taylor and Eaton warehouses servicing the Tennessee & Alabama Railroad and the Nashville & Chattanooga Railroad, respectively. From November 1863 through August 1864, the following supplies passed through Nashville headed to the Atlanta campaign — 41,122 horses and 38,724 mules, 3,795 wagons, 445,355 pairs of shoes, 290,000 blankets, 529,000 tents, millions of bushels of corn and oats, and tens of thousands of tons of hay.

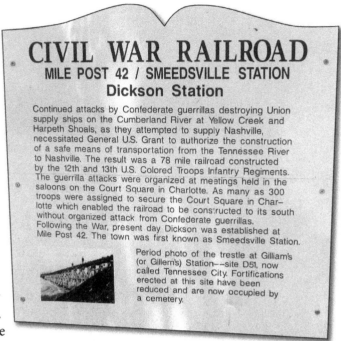

"No army in the world was ever better provided than Sherman's," proclaimed Gen. Robert Allen, chief quartermaster of the Western Theater. Such grand logistics could not have been accomplished solely through the use of the Louisville & Nashville Railroad and steamer transports on the erratic waters of the Cumberland River. Other means were necessary.

At the beginning of the war, the Nashville & Northwestern Railroad reached only 21 miles west to Kingston Springs when construction was halted. Incorporated in 1852, the railway was intended to run to Hickman, Kentucky. Instead, during 1863, work crews consisting of impressed blacks and Irish immigrants extended the line all the way west to the Tennessee River, where a supply depot was built. Later, many of the black workers who built the railroad were recruited into the U.S. Colored Troops and manned the blockhouses and redoubts that guarded the trestles and bridges of the military railroad, commanded by white officers. The 12th and 14th USCT infantry regiments guarded the trestles while the USCT artillery units were stationed at the river depot.

The depot was built on the hilly east bank of the Tennessee River at Knott's Landing, 78 miles due west of Nashville. The depot featured a railroad roundhouse and turntable, transfer sidings, a wide transfer building and warehouse with heavy lifting machinery, a narrow transfer building, open storage areas, a horse corral, a sawmill, housing for workers, huts for soldiers, civilian houses, a small fort (redoubt), rifle pits, and a blockhouse.

Work on the rail extension and depot began on Sept. 1, 1863, and by February 1864, crews were laying one-third to three-fourths of a mile of track each day. Construction was completed substantially in May. On the 19th of that month at 6:00 am, the first train of cars pulled out of Nashville and rolled westward to the Tennessee River to celebrate the newly completely railway and depot. Onboard were Military Governor Andrew Johnson, Nashville Mayor John Hugh Smith, Generals Gordon Granger and Alvan Gillem, and Colonel W.A. Browning. Arriving at their destination, Johnson got off the train, stood on top of a pile of crossties to make a speech, and promptly named the new depot Johnsonville. A self-made man and a tailor by trade, Johnson had risen up through the Democrat Party ranks as a pre-war Governor of Tennessee and the only U.S. Senator from a seceded state to remain loyal to the Union. He was pro-slavery and ruled wartime Tennessee with an iron fist. The fortified state capitol in Nashville was known as Fortress Johnson. In November 1864 he was elected Vice-President on the Union Party ticket as

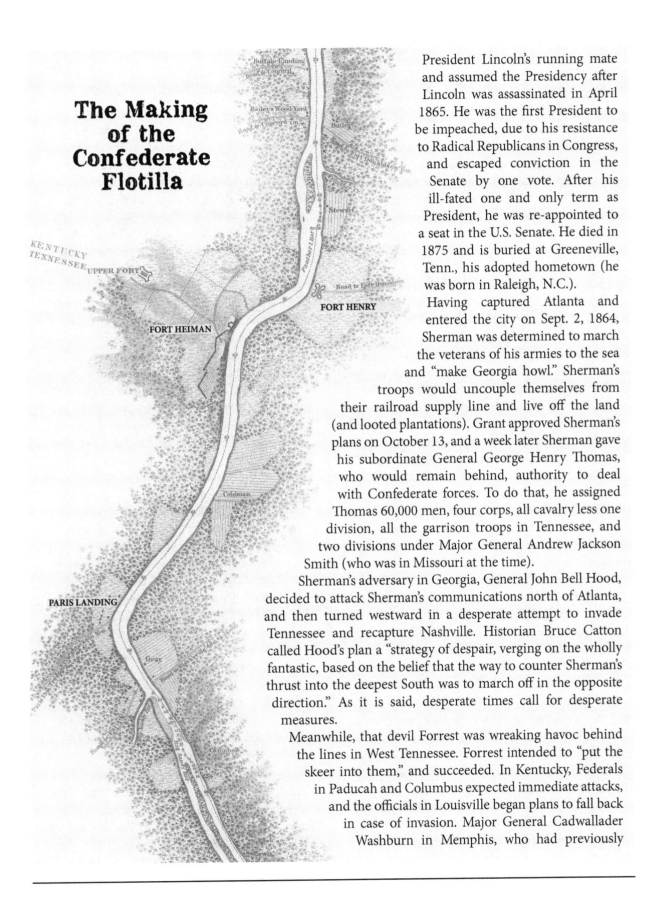

# The Making of the Confederate Flotilla

President Lincoln's running mate and assumed the Presidency after Lincoln was assassinated in April 1865. He was the first President to be impeached, due to his resistance to Radical Republicans in Congress, and escaped conviction in the Senate by one vote. After his ill-fated one and only term as President, he was re-appointed to a seat in the U.S. Senate. He died in 1875 and is buried at Greeneville, Tenn., his adopted hometown (he was born in Raleigh, N.C.).

Having captured Atlanta and entered the city on Sept. 2, 1864, Sherman was determined to march the veterans of his armies to the sea and "make Georgia howl." Sherman's troops would uncouple themselves from their railroad supply line and live off the land (and looted plantations). Grant approved Sherman's plans on October 13, and a week later Sherman gave his subordinate General George Henry Thomas, who would remain behind, authority to deal with Confederate forces. To do that, he assigned Thomas 60,000 men, four corps, all cavalry less one division, all the garrison troops in Tennessee, and two divisions under Major General Andrew Jackson Smith (who was in Missouri at the time).

Sherman's adversary in Georgia, General John Bell Hood, decided to attack Sherman's communications north of Atlanta, and then turned westward in a desperate attempt to invade Tennessee and recapture Nashville. Historian Bruce Catton called Hood's plan a "strategy of despair, verging on the wholly fantastic, based on the belief that the way to counter Sherman's thrust into the deepest South was to march off in the opposite direction." As it is said, desperate times call for desperate measures.

Meanwhile, that devil Forrest was wreaking havoc behind the lines in West Tennessee. Forrest intended to "put the skeer into them," and succeeded. In Kentucky, Federals in Paducah and Columbus expected immediate attacks, and the officials in Louisville began plans to fall back in case of invasion. Major General Cadwallader Washburn in Memphis, who had previously tangled with Forrest, packed his bags and went home to Wisconsin. Colonel Charles R. Thompson, the U.S. land forces commander at Johnsonville, expected Forrest to attack him. Thomas directed the entire XXIII Corps under General John Schofield to reinforce the depot, but as it turned out only a small party reached Johnsonville, too late to lend assistance. The end of September/beginning of October, Forrest hit the Nashville & Decatur Railroad, capturing 2,360 Federal soldiers and tons of supplies. Brigadier General James Chalmers of Forrest's command threatened Memphis with 1,000 cavalry.

On Oct. 16, 1864, Forrest moved north from Corinth, Mississippi, with 3,000 to 3,500 men. He re-established his headquarters at Jackson, Tennessee, where he was joined by General Chalmers. Forrest told his superior, General Richard Taylor, that the Union forces were deriving most of their supplies from the railroad connecting Johnsonville to Nashville. "It is my present design to take possession of Fort Heiman, on the west bank of the Tennessee River below Johnsonville, and thus prevent all communication with Johnsonville by transports."

He sent Brigadier General Abraham Buford to Fort Heiman, 40 miles north of Johnsonville, with the bulk of his force. On October 28, Jack Hinson, the well-known Southern guerrilla sharpshooter, led General Buford straight to Fort Heiman, one of Hinson's haunts.

Fort Heiman was on the west bank of the Tennessee River, almost directly across the water from old Fort Henry. Paris Landing, at the mouth of the Big Sandy River, was also on the west bank, four miles south of Fort Heiman. Buford created a trap for U.S. transports steaming south (upriver) towards the Johnsonville depot. He positioned two 20-pounder Parrott rifles (newly arrived from Mobile, Alabama) at Fort Heiman under Captain E.S. Walton. He then placed four guns at Paris Landing under master artillerist Captain John Morton of General Tyree Bell's command. Soon thereafter, four empty transports came into view northbound from Johnsonville. Buford ordered silence, knowing that the boats were empty. He told his men to wait until loaded boats came southward.

## Fort Heiman Changes Hands

Following the fall of Confederate Fort Henry on Feb. 6, 1862, the Tennessee River completely inundated the fortification, and although the river would recede in the following weeks, the fortress was ruined and never used again. (Today it sits submerged under the waters of Kentucky Lake.) According to a report by the National Park Service, "The task of occupying Fort Heiman fell to Colonel W. W. Lowe and the Iowa Fifth Cavalry regiment, also known as the Curtis Horse. Although no battles or skirmishes were fought at Fort Heiman during their occupation of the post, the Curtis Horse's time in Kentucky and Tennessee was not uneventful. Federal soldiers at Heiman were often bothered by Confederate sympathizing bushwhackers and partisans, not to mention regular Confederate cavalry, while on patrol. And, several times Union forces engaged assembled Confederate troops in Paris, Tennessee, usually suffering numerous casualties. During one particularly deadly exchange that occurred on March 11, 1862, the Fifth suffered nine deaths. Military records compiled for the Iowa Fifth Cavalry during the war also identify 14 others as being among the men who died while at Fort Heiman. Though adequately staffed to hold the fort itself, the Curtis Horse was never able to maintain control of the region surrounding Fort Heiman. Ultimately, the Iowa Fifth Cavalry remained at Fort Heiman for one year and four months, leaving on June 25, 1863. After remaining unoccupied for over a year, Fort Heiman was reoccupied in the autumn of 1864 by Confederate General Nathan Bedford Forrest, his 3,500 soldiers, and a battery of artillery under Captain John Morton."

The next day, on October 29, the 184-ton transport *Mazeppa* appeared, towing two supply barges upstream on her maiden voyage from

*(Continued on Page 138)*

**"Horse Marines"** by John Paul Strain, artist. Generals N.B. Forrest, J.R. Chalmers, and the captured *USS Undine* at Paris Landing, Oct. 31, 1864. As rain clouds began to form, Gen. Forrest congratulates Gen. Chalmers on their success. Draped across the general's saddle is the flag from the *Undine,* a rare prize indeed. Seeing a Confederate flag on a gunboat for the first time in two years, Forrest's men made the air "ring with cheer upon cheer."

## TABLE OF FIRE
### 20-PDR. PARROTT GUN
Charge, 2 lbs. of Mortar Powder

| ELEVATION in degrees | PROJECTILE | | RANGE in yards | TIME OF FLIGHT in seconds |
|---|---|---|---|---|
| 1 | Case Shot, | 19½ lbs. | 620 | 1⅞ |
| 2 | Case Shot, | 19½ lbs. | 950 | 3⅛ |
| 3⅝ | Shell, | 18¾ lbs. | 1,500 | 4¾ |
| 5 | Shell, | 18¾ lbs. | 2,100 | 6½ |
| 10 | Shell, | 18¾ lbs. | 3,350 | 11¼ |
| 15 | Shell, | 18¾ lbs. | 4,400 | 17¼ |

### CARE OF AMMUNITION CHEST

1st. Keep everything out that does not belong in them, except a bunch of cord or wire for breakage; beware of loose tacks, nails, bolts, or scraps.

2nd. Keep friction primers in their papers, tied up. The pouch containing those for instant service must be closed, and so placed as to be secure. Take every precaution that primers do not get loose; a single one may cause an explosion. Use plenty of tow in packing.

This sheet is to be glued to the inside of the Limber Chest Cover.

Cincinnati. She slipped past Fort Heiman, but three shots from the Paris Landing battery disabled her; Captain Lee Pettit grounded the boat on the east bank and fled. One enterprising Confederate cavalryman swam across the river naked, gunbelt around his neck, boarded the abandoned transport, and brought back a small boat. A landing party attached a line and the rebels pulled the captured prize to the west bank. The *Mazeppa* contained 700 tons of cargo, including 9,000 pairs of shoes, blankets, winter clothing, and food. Inspecting the haul, General Buford, holding aloft a bottle, told his men, "Plenty of meat, plenty of hardtack and clothes for the boys, but just enough brandy for the general!" Unloaded, the hardluck *Mazeppa* was burned just as three U.S. Navy gunboats approached from the south but did not engage.

The next day, the 110-ton sidewheeler transport *Anna* managed to slip by the batteries, feigning surrender. When the ploy was discovered, the rebel guns opened and damaged the steamer, which managed to limp home to Paducah and sound the alarm. The *Anna* had been escorted by the USS *Undine* tinclad gunboat, which had turned around to head back to Johnsonville before hearing the Confederate guns and turning about again to steam back northward. After the *Undine* passed Paris Landing, the shore gunners opened fire, four shots penetrating the gunboat's forward casemate,

breaking the steam escape pipe, and killing four sailors and wounding three others. After an hour-long fight, Acting Master John Bryant aboard the *Undine* went to shore on the east bank between the rebel batteries and continued shelling them. Meanwhile the Confederates moved their field artillery directly across the river from the *Undine* and continued their shelling.

Then, another U.S. transport, the 230-ton *Venus* commanded by Captain John Allen, came up and steamed past Paris Landing with a squad of the 34th New Jersey Infantry aboard. After the boat's captain was killed by musket fire, the transport was steered to the side of the *Undine* on the east bank. The empty transport *J.W. Cheeseman* (Capt. Thad Wirthlihn) came up and was grounded by guns on the west bank and captured. (The captain of the *Cheeseman* was later exonerated by a board of inquiry.)

Colonel D.C. Kelley's 26th Tennessee Cavalry battalion and Colonel T.C. Logwood's 15th Tennessee were sent to contest the *Undine*, along with two 10-pounders of Hudson's battery. Logwood and the cannons took on the *Undine* at 100 yards, while Kelley and his riflemen shot up the *Venus*. Both boats were abandoned after a three-hour fight. Kelley and two men rowed a skiff to the *Venus*, where Capt. Allen and three men were still on board. The captain refused to cooperate until

*(Continued on Page 140)*

# TENNESSEE RIVER

## The Affair at Reynoldsburg Island

### NOVEMBER 3, 1864

identities of Federal gunboats

Victory

Brilliant

Curlew

Moose

Paw-Paw

Fairy

**FITCH**

rocks

Reynoldsburg Island

Rebel Battery, masked, 1 gun

Rebel Battery, masked, 1 gun

rocks

Rebel Battery, masked, 1 gun

Rebel Battery, masked, 2 guns

very shoal

Cyprus Creek

**KELLEY**

heavy timber

Undine

Four Guns (Rebel)

**Waverly Landing**

Key West

**KING**

⬥⬥ **Reynoldsburg**

N

W — E

S

fallen timbers

channel

Johnsonville

*Mark Zimmerman © 2019*

Kelley held a pistol to his head and ordered him to steam over to the *Undine*, tie to the gunboat, and tow them back across the river.

During the melee, the tinclad *USS Tawah* under Acting Master James B. Williams came down from Johnsonville but stayed out of range of the guns.

Overall that day, the U.S. forces suffered eight killed, 11 wounded, and 43 captured, while one Confederate was wounded. Bryant surrendered all three boats (he also was exonerated by a board of inquiry).

The last day of October, Forrest himself arrived on the scene. While the *Cheeseman* was burned, the Confederates gladly loaded their two 20-pounder Parrott rifles aboard the *Venus* (the big guns had been extremely difficult to pull along the muddy riverbank), in addition to the captured goods from the *Mazeppa*. The *Undine*, armed with eight 24-pounder howitzers, was manned by the Confederate "horse marines." Thus was born the Confederate cavalry's gunboat navy on the Tennessee River. Captain Morton declined the invitation to command the flotilla. Captain Frank M. Gracey of the 3rd Kentucky Cavalry, a former steamboat captain, was given command of the *Undine* and Lt. Colonel William A. Dawson assumed command of the *Venus* and was named "Commodore."

As the mounted Forrest watched from the riverbank, the *Undine's* flag draped over his saddle, the newly appointed "sailors" hoisted the Confederate flag up the standard and practiced maneuvers on the river for two hours to the yelps and shouts of the delighted men. Far away, Federal officials worried that Forrest had possession of the *Undine's* codebook (however, the Confederates made no mention of the codebook in their reports).

On November 1, the Confederate force moved southward along the muddy bank of the river, Chalmers in the lead and Buford taking up the rear. At night they camped near the Danville bridge.

At Johnsonville, Federal commander Thompson wired Thomas in Nashville that he feared Forrest would attack, and added, "I have not now, nor have had any idea of surrendering. Will fight to the last if attacked. I feel confident that I can hold the place."

By November 2, Forrest was six miles from the riverbank directly across from Johnsonville. That afternoon, the *Venus* steamed ahead of the column, came around a bend at 3:30 pm, and faced two Union gunboats, the *Tawah* and the *Key West*, at Green Bottom Bar near Reynoldsburg Island. In a 20-minute engagement, the *Venus* was grounded at shore, with the crew taking to the woods, not bothering to set it afire. The Confederates aboard the *Undine* pulled back from the action. The *Venus* with its two Parrott guns was recaptured by the Federal tinclads and arrived back at Johnsonville by 6:30 pm.

Lt. E.M. King, commander of the gunboat flotilla at Johnsonville and aboard the *USS Elfin*, wired Lt. Commander James Shirk at Paducah: "All anxious about this place. Please send up more gunboats at once. We won't allow this place to fall into enemy hands, if our forces can prevent, but please send up more gunboats."

On November 3, Lt. Commander LeRoy Fitch set out from Paducah with a six-vessel rescue flotilla consisting of the tinclads *Paw Paw, Fairy, Curlew, Brilliant, Victory,* and *Moose*. After shelling the Confederate position at Paris Landing, the gunboats approached the Reynoldsburg Island sector, where the Confederates had placed five batteries, most of them masked. The east channel past the island was too shoal for any boats to pass; in the deeper main channel the *Undine* sat waiting, bait for the trap. As Fitch moved south, King steamed north. Cautious, King held back his three tinclads, sensing an ambush. By this time, at noon, Forrest noted that the *Undine* was nearly out of coal for its steam engines. No other actions were undertaken that day.

That night, Captain Jack Hinson led Forrest's troopers through the Cypress Creek swamp to favorable artillery positions across the river from Johnsonville. According to historian Michael Bradley, Colonel Kelley knew that the steep banks of the river made it impossible for the guns aboard the U.S. boats to hit targets on top of the banks because the targets were so far above the water. When the boat crews elevated their guns to hit targets on top of the high banks, the shells went over the top and landed far inland. The guns in the U.S. redoubt

*(Continued on Page 144)*

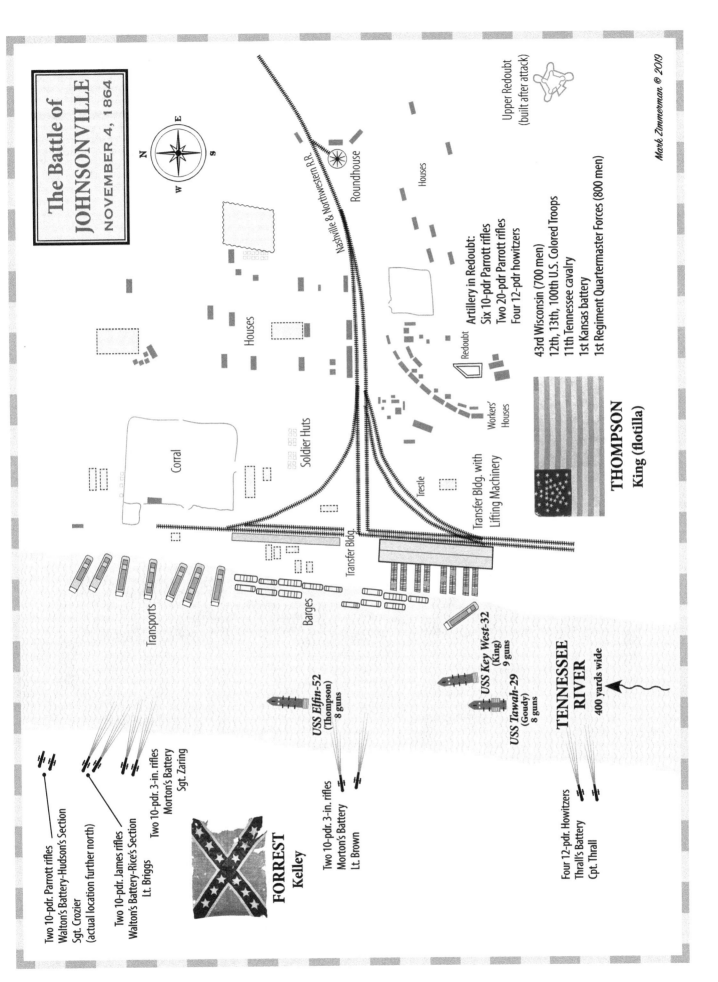

# The Battle of JOHNSONVILLE
## NOVEMBER 4, 1864

Nashville & Northwestern R.R.

Roundhouse

Houses

Houses

Corral

Soldier Huts

Houses

Workers' Houses

Redoubt

Transfer Bldg.

Transfer Bldg. with Lifting Machinery

Trestle

Upper Redoubt
(built after attack)

**Artillery in Redoubt:**
Six 10-pdr Parrott rifles
Two 20-pdr Parrott rifles
Four 12-pdr howitzers

43rd Wisconsin (700 men)
12th, 13th, 100th U.S. Colored Troops
11th Tennessee cavalry
1st Kansas battery
1st Regiment Quartermaster Forces (800 men)

**THOMPSON**
King (flotilla)

Mark Zimmerman © 2019

Transports

Barges

*USS Elfin-52*
(Thompson)
8 guns

*USS Key West-32*
(King)
9 guns

*USS Tawah-29*
(Goudy)
8 guns

**TENNESSEE RIVER**
400 yards wide

**FORREST**
Kelley

Two 10-pdr. 3-in. rifles
Morton's Battery
Lt. Brown

Four 12-pdr. Howitzers
Thrall's Battery
Cpt. Thrall

Two 10-pdr. Parrott rifles
Walton's Battery-Hudson's Section
Sgt. Crozier
(actual location further north)

Two 10-pdr. James rifles
Walton's Battery-Rice's Section
Lt. Briggs

Two 10-pdr. 3-in. rifles
Morton's Battery
Sgt. Zaring

# JOHNSONVILLE

Opposite page, top: U.S. Colored Troops artillery units looking eastward from the riverside transfer building, showing the muddy barren landscape, railroad sidings, soldiers' huts, and in the distance the horse corral.

Opposite page, bottom: U.S Military Railroad locomotive at Sullivan's Branch No. 2 trestle on the Nashville & Northwestern Railroad in Cheatham County, 10 miles west of Bellevue Station.

Above left: Statue of Andrew Johnson at the Tennessee State Capitol (photo by author).

Above right: Hillside view of buildings at Johnsonville.

Below: The huge transfer building at the depot showing the loading platforms for the rail freight cars. The Tennessee River would be just out of view to the right.

Photos courtesy of Tennessee State Library and Archives.

behind and high above the depot were also ineffective. As Morton told Forrest: "The fort is so elevated that they can't depress their guns sufficiently to affect me, and the gunboats are so much more below in the river that they will fire over me, and I'll be in an angle of comparative safety."

Meanwhile, on November 4, back at Reynoldsburg Island, Capt. Gracey aboard the *Undine* was caught between Fitch's flotilla to the north and King's gunboats to the south. Most of the Confederates had moved on to Johnsonville, so about 8:00 am Gracey guided their prized Yankee gunboat, nearly out of fuel, to shore, set the torch to it, and blew it up with a gunpowder charge. Abandoned in three feet of water 75 yards from Reynoldsburg Island, the *Undine* burned down to waterline and then exploded spectacularly. During a melee with the remaining Confederate batteries of Hudson and Rice, the *Key West* was hit 10 times in the upperworks, seven through the decks, and two in the hull. The *Elfin* was also damaged. By mid-morning King's three gunboats returned to the depot. Assistant Quartermaster Henry Howland later reported: "The *Key West,* in advance, ran into a battery of heavy guns within two miles of Johnsonville and but a short distance above where the *Undine* was lying. She received 19 shots from 20-pounder guns, which passed entirely through her, before she could escape from this newly discovered battery."

North of the island, aboard the *USS Moose*, Fitch moved up at 2:30 pm after hearing cannon fire and engaged for 15 minutes with Hudson's guns, then fell back. For all day on the fourth, Fitch refused to run through the narrow channel gauntlet. Fitch wrote: "I thought it mere folly to attempt such a hazardous move, as I am almost confident that not over two boats out of six would have got through, and they never could have got back again." According to biographer Jack Smith: "The enemy batteries, narrownesss of the channel, shoal water, and the possibility of a damaged vessel blocking the passage mitigated against any decision (by Fitch) to proceed (upriver)." Fitch's decision not to proceed was highly debatable, according to historian Edward

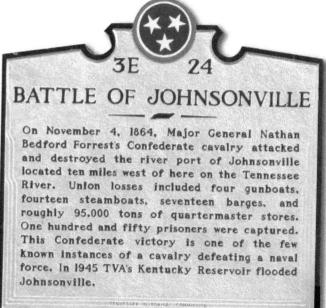

Williams III, who claimed that Fitch was stopped by "only his imagination." Fitch's flotilla of six gunboats arrived back at Fort Heiman on Nov. 4 at 10:30 pm.

Meanwhile, back near the depot, the Confederates were getting ready for action. Setting up his cannon, unnoticed by the enemy, master artillerist Morton peered 400 yards across the river at the Johnsonville depot. He noted that "two gunboats with steam up were moored at the landing … a third plied almost directly beneath the bluff." There were "a number of barges clustered around; negroes were loading them, officers and men were coming and going, and passengers could be seen strolling down to the wharf. The river banks for some distance back were lined with quantities of stores, and two freight trains were being made up. It was an animated scene, and one which wore an air of complete security."

Although warned of imminent attack, the Federal authorities at Johnsonville apparently did little to prepare for that eventuality.

At the depot were the three Union tinclads, *Key West, Tawah,* and *Elfin*, commanded by King, with a total of 25 guns. The Union redoubt, perched 100 feet above and behind the river depot, sported six 10-pounder Parrott rifles of the 1st Kansas Battery, two 12-pounder Napoleons of the 2nd USCT Artillery, two 12-pounder Napoleons of the 1st Regiment Quartermaster Forces, and the two 20-pounder Parrott rifles seized from the *Venus*.

The Parrotts were capable of firing a 19-pound shell more than a mile at five degrees of elevation. The U.S. armed forces consisted of 700 infantry of the 43rd Wisconsin, 400 men of USCT 12th, 13th and 100th regiments, and 800 armed quartermaster corpsmen.

Across the river, the Confederate cavalry consisted of Colonel Mabry's brigade, Colonel Rucker and the 7th Alabama Cavalry, Lt. Col. Kelley and the 26th Tennessee Battalion, and Lt. Col. Logwood and the 15th Tennessee Cavalry. Forrest's artillery, arranged from north to south, consisted of the following:

- Sgt. Crozier commanded Hudson's section of Walton's Battery several miles north of Johnsonville, consisting of two 10-pounder Parrott rifles. These guns were not involved in the destruction of the depot.

- Lt. Brigg's section of Walton's Battery, consisting of two 10-pounder James rifles (U.S. guns captured at Brice's Crossroads)

- Sgt. Zarring of Morton's Battery, consisting of two 10-pounder 3-inch rifles

- Lt. Brown of Morton's Battery, consisting of two 10-pounder 3-inch rifles (directly across the river from the depot)

- Capt. Thrall's Battery of four 12-pounder howitzers

Precisely at 2:00 pm, ten field artillery pieces went off as one, aimed directly at the Federal gunboats. Howland testified that "…the cannonading was the most terrific I have ever witnessed," speculating that the rebels manned up to 36 pieces of artillery. Within 40 minutes, the gunboats were abandoned. The *Key West* got underway but its paddlewheel fouled on a cable. The *Tawah* took the *Key West* in tow to a point upriver but eventually Commander King ordered all three boats abandoned and fired for fear of capture. Aboard the *Tawah*, the smallest of the three gunboats and known as "a miserable ship," one hundred shells exploded in a deafening cacophony. The gunners in the U.S. redoubt played no role in the battle. They were inexperienced and didn't respond to the attack because they couldn't see through the smoke.

Depot commander Thompson evidently assumed the Confederates would be crossing the river. He ordered Quartermaster Howland to set fire to the barges at the wharf to prevent them from being captured. Fire from the barges spread to the depot warehouses and by 4:00 pm the entire depot was an inferno. Howland said the warehouses ignited with the bursting of a rebel shell and "the intense heat of the burning boats (barges), which had been driven against the wharf by the strong wind, fired the stores in another place." He ordered the fires extinguished, but nobody obeyed his orders. The supplies in the wooden warehouses burned with a certain fury. A torrent of spilled whiskey ran ablaze from the warehouse down to the river.

Forrest said later: "By night the wharf for nearly one mile up and down the river presented one solid sheet of flame."

Boat crews fled to the fort and interfered with the gun crews there. Four hundred Federals scrambled onto a freight train and chugged off eastward for Nashville. Twelve miles later, at Waverly, the railroad agent uncoupled the overloaded cars and sped to Nashville with just the locomotive. The abandoned Federal troops commenced to looting the railcars.

Back on the west bank, Forrest was in an unusually festive and feisty mood. Jostling with his gunners, he tried his hand at firing a cannon. "Elevate the breach of that gun lower," he commanded to his grimacing gunners. He said he wanted to rickety-shey a shell off the water. Needless to say, the gunners were not impressed with their commander's artillery skills.

That night Forrest moved his men six miles to the south. The Confederates did not cross the river. The next morning, he and Morton returned to the previous day's artillery positions to survey the damage. The depot was still smouldering and lay in ruins. The destruction totaled $1.5 million to $6.7 million, including the gunboats (more than $100 million in 2018 dollars). The Federals lost eight men killed and wounded.

Forrest told Morton: "There is no doubt we could soon whip old Sherman off the face of the earth, John, if they'd give me enough men and you enough guns."

Forrest later reported that the Federals lost four gunboats, 14 steamboats, 17 barges, quartermaster stores of 75,000 to 120,000 tons, and 150 prisoners. Forrest reported two killed, nine wounded, and two Parrott guns lost. On November 7, Forrest put 400 cavalrymen across the river at Perryville and soon linked up with Hood's army approaching Nashville.

After the Johnsonville debacle, rumors abounded throughout the North, including one that had Forrest approaching Chicago, where the local militia was called out. On Nov. 30, 1864, the Johnsonville depot was abandoned and never used again, although the Federals did construct a redoubt on the ridge high above the river. The depot wreckage was not cleaned up for months.

News of the Confederate cavalry's exploits were received by Sherman, who on November 15th pushed off from Atlanta on his March to the Sea with the sardonic comment, "That devil Forrest was down around Johnsonville, making havoc among the gunboats and transports."

Commander King was court-martialed in May 1865 for burning the three tinclads, but he was acquitted of the charges. Witnesses testified that even if the gunboats had been scuttled in five feet of water (instead of burned) the Confederates could have salvaged them. Fitch reported, "The *Key West, Tawah,* and *Elfin* fought desperately and were handled in magnificent style, but it is impossible for boats of this class, with their batteries, to contend successfully against heavy rifled field batteries in a narrow river full of bars and shoals, no matter with what skill and desperation they may be fought."

Although Johnsonville was probably the most destructive raid of the war, and the result provoked near-hysteria in the North, the attack was too little too late to affect Sherman or any other Federal offensive operation.

–Chapter Fifteen–

# Bell's Bend

*Fitch and Kelley clash at Nashville*
*in the ultimate battle between gunboats and cavalry*

On Tuesday, Nov. 29, 1864, at noon, the villagers of Dover witnessed an amazing sight—the tinclad gunboat *USS Moose* leading a continuous procession of 60 steamers loaded with blueclad soldiers churning and chugging its way up the Cumberland River. The convoy was escorted by the City Class ironclad *Carondelet*, the river monitor *Neosho*, and the tinclads *Volunteer, Peosta, Fairplay, Silver Lake, Brilliant, Springfield, Reindeer,* and *Victory*. As promised, the convoy was delivering to Nashville the 10,000 veteran XVI Corps troops of Major General Andrew Jackson Smith. The well-traveled soldiers, known as Smith's Guerrillas, had journeyed by land from western Missouri and then by river from St. Louis. The flotilla included the steam transports *Albert Pearce, Havana, James Raymond, Julia, Lilly Martin, Maggie Hayes, Victory, Marmora, Camelia, Silver Cloud, Arizona, J.F. McComb, Mercury, Financier, Lilly, New York, Lady Franklin, Pioneer, Magnet, Prima Donna, Wananita, America, Thomas E. Tutt, Mars, Omaha, Olive, Silver Lake, Kate Kearney, Spray, Mollie McPike,* and *Prairie State*. When the mighty flotilla reached Nashville without incident the next day, commanding General George Thomas engaged in an unusual show of emotion by hugging General Smith heartily. Smith's reinforcements were desperately needed at Nashville as the Yankees were waiting for the arrival of the Confederate Army of Tennessee under General John Bell Hood.

Navy Lt. Commander LeRoy Fitch, who was standing in for the sick 10th District chief James Shirk, now commanded two ironclad gunboats, the heavy gunboat *Peosta*, and at least eight tinclad gunboats, "the greatest fleet of gunboats ever to appear on the Cumberland during the war," according to historian Byrd Douglas. Fitch was notified of his new assignment by Acting Rear Admiral Samuel Phillips Lee, who had assumed command of the Mississippi Squadron at a brief ceremony on November 1 at Mound City aboard the flagboat *Black Hawk*, replacing Rear Admiral David Dixon Porter, who went to the North Atlantic Blockading Squadron.

Meanwhile, 18 miles south of Nashville at Franklin, Hood had caught up with the small army of General John Schofield, which had been trying to reach the safety of the Nashville fortifications. In a spectacular frontal assault over two miles of open ground against fortified fieldworks, Hood's valiant soldiers suffered horrendous casualties, especially in its officer corps. Twelve Confederate generals were either killed, wounded, or captured.

The next day, on Thurs., Dec. 1, Schofield managed to fall back to Nashville and its fortifications. Hood's soldiers followed. The Confederates set up a four-mile seige line that fell about three miles short of encircling the southern part of Nashville (the northern half of Nashville was enclosed by a giant bend in the Cumberland River). Brigadier General James Chalmers' division of 1,500 troopers was positioned at the extreme left flank of the Confederate line while Forrest took the bulk of his cavalry, under orders from Hood, to raid U.S. positions at nearby Murfreesboro.

On December 2, Lt. Colonel David Campbell Kelley and the 26th Tennessee Battalion of 300 men set up field artillery at two positions on bluffs overlooking the river opposite the grist mills at Bell's Bend. The artillery consisted of two 10-pound

## Medal of Honor Citation

*USS Neosho* pilot John Ferrell's official Medal of Honor citation (June 22, 1865) reads:

"Served on board the U.S. Monitor *Neosho* during the engagement with enemy batteries at Bells Mills, Cumberland River, near Nashville, Tenn., 6 December 1864. Carrying out his duties courageously during the engagement, Ferrell gallantly left the pilothouse after the flag and signal staffs of that vessel had been shot away and, taking the flag which was drooping over the wheelhouse, make it fast to the stump of the highest mast remaining although the ship was still under a heavy fire from the enemy."

Parrott rifles of Lt. H.H. Brigg's section of Capt. T.W. Rice's artillery, plus two 12-pounder howitzers from Walton's battery. The site, known as Davidson's Landing, was four miles by land from downtown Nashville and 17 miles downriver. Between Bell's Bend and Nashville was a staging area at Davidson Island and Hyde's Ferry. Two miles downriver from Bell's Bend was the Hillsboro Landing. Beyond that was the infamous Harpeth Shoals. Kelley's batteries were in excellent position to contest any Federal gunboats and blockade the river. The confrontations in the next few days would constitute the heaviest engagements of Confederate cavalry versus U.S. Navy gunboats during the war. Unfortunately for the Confederates, Hood's army arrived one day too late to contest the arrival of Smith's massive convoy.

Meanwhile, Thomas was worried that Hood might try to ford the Cumberland above Nashville and get behind his lines. He instructed Fitch to direct a patrol up the river 100 miles to Hartsville consisting of the *USS Springfield* (Acting Volunteer Master Edmund Morgan) and the U.S. Army gunboat *Newsboy*.

On Sat., Dec. 3, 1864, while U.S. gunboats conducted routine patrols below Nashville, the rebel batteries at Bell's Bend fired upon two transports,

*(Continued on Page 150)*

# The Battle of
# BELLS BEND
### DEC. 4 AND 6, 1864

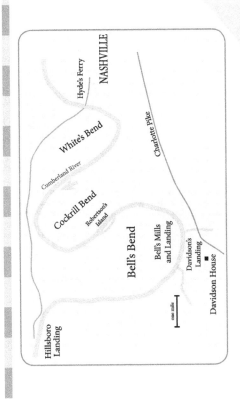

NASHVILLE

Hyde's Ferry

White's Bend

Cumberland River

Cockrill Bend

Robertson's Island

Bell's Bend

Bell's Mills and Landing

Davidson's Landing

Charlotte Pike

Davidson House

Hillsboro Landing

one mile

Cumberland River

*Silver Lake-23 (Coyle)*

**Forced back to Nashville (Dec. 6):**
Transports *Metamora, Prima Donna, Arizona, J.F. McComb, Mercury, Financier, Lilly, New York, Lady Franklin, Pioneer and Magnet;* Tinclads *Moose, Reindeer, Fairplay,* and *Silver Lake.*

Charlotte Pike (Nashville)

Mark Zimmerman. © 2019

*Carondelet* (Miller)
Dec. 6 action

*Reindeer-35*
(Glassford)

*Two 12-pdr. Howitzers
Walton's Battery*

Davidson Branch

*Moose-34* (Fitch)

*Davidson's
Landing*

**FITCH**

*Neosho* (Howard)
Dec. 6 action

*Two 10-pdr.
Parrott rifles*

*Capt. T.W. Rice
Lt. H.H. Brigg's section*

**KELLEY**

**Col. Edmund Rucker**
(300 infantrymen)

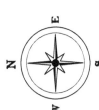

*Caronelet* (Miller)

*Two 10-pdr.
Parrott rifles
from Biffle's
Brigade
(Dec. 6 only)*

*Fairplay-17* (Groves)

N
E
S
W

the *Prairie State* and the *Prima Donna*, and drove them to the riverbank. Kelley's men captured 56 of the crew, 200 horses and mules, and many sacks of grain. The steamers were taken several miles downriver to Hillsboro Landing. At about this time, the naval supply steamer *Magnet* ran the batteries and was hit several times. Her captain, named Harrol, grounded his boat and managed to hightail it back to Nashville to report the batteries to Lt. Commander Fitch. At 12:45 am on December 4, Fitch responded by leading an attack column consisting of the *USS Carondelet* (commanded by Acting Volunteer Master Charles Miller), the tinclad *Fairplay* (Acting Volunteer Lt. George J. Groves), the flagboat *Moose* (Acting Volunteer Master Washington C. Coulson), the *Reindeer* (Acting Volunteer Lt. Henry Glassford), and the *Silver Lake* (Acting Volunteer Ensign J.C. Coyle). The *Neosho* and the *Brilliant* were left at Hyde's Ferry to protect the Union right flank. It should be noted that during the military maneuvers around Nashville during December 1864 that the City Class ironclad *USS Cincinnati* was stationed at Clarksville and did not participate.

Cumberland River from Kelley's Point Battlefield overlook

The *Silver Lake* was typical of a U.S. navy tinclad gunboat. The 236-ton sternwheeler, constructed at California, Pa. in 1862, was 155 feet long with a beam of 32 feet and a six-foot draft. Her two boilers and two steam engines produced six knots of speed. The tinclad was armed with six 24-pound brass Dahlgren howitzers.

That night was "cool, cloudy, and devoid of natural light," according to historian Jack Smith, "and hence the Confederates did not spot the Yankee craft..." At 12:45 am on December 4, the ironclad *Carondelet* opened up with grape shot and canister against Kelley's lofty field artillery batteries. The *Fairplay* was slightly below the upper battery, the *Moose* directly opposite it, the *Reindeer* 50 yards above, and the *Silver Lake* trailing. The Confederates responded with volleys that were "rapid and warm." The *Carondelet* steamed past, turned hard about, and churned past the batteries. After 20 minutes of sharp exchanges, Kelley's gunners drew back. The ironclad lobbed shells at the Confederate positions until 2:30 am and withdrew.

One Union sailor later wrote about "the thundering of the mighty guns, the shells screeching through the air back and forth, from one side to the other; sometimes bursting in the air, sometimes in the water, throwing the water high in the air."

The *Carondelet* fired 26 rounds. The *Fairplay* fired 37 rounds and received two hits (the shells did not explode and caused minor damage). The *Moose*, which almost collided in the narrow channel (80 yards wide) with the *Reindeer*, was hit three times while expending 59 rounds. To avoid the collision, the *Reindeer*'s captain ran the bow of his boat into the bank so the current would swing the stern downstream, and then chugged upriver to get back into position. The *Silver Lake*, only lightly involved, fired six rounds of canister. Amid the noise, smoke, and confusion, Kelley's batteries retreated, either to regroup or for want of ammunition. Fitch attributed the silencing of the rebel guns to the gunnery skills of the *Moose's* crew and Acting Volunteer Master

The *USS Neosho* battles Confederate batteries at Bell's Bend.

Coulson. The tinclad flagboat was lucky. One enemy shell nearly hit the gunpowder magazine and did not explode, while another would have torn through the bottom of the *Moose* if not deflected by a deck beam.

The *Carondelet* and *Fairplay* reached the two captured transports downstream at Hillsboro Landing and thwarted attempts by the Confederates to torch them. After hasty repairs, all five of the U.S. gunboats returned to Nashville safely with the *Prairie State* and *Prima Donna*. Fitch reported to Thomas that he had fought with Buford's brigade of Forrest's cavalry, part of a strong Confederate left flank ending at the river. In fact, the Confederate line did not reach the river; Buford and Forrest were at Murfreesboro; and the men he fought were commanded by Kelley, the "devil's parson." The major consequence of the duel at Bell's Bend were orders by Federal officials to stop all river traffic between Clarksville and Nashville. In essence, the Confederates had effected a blockade.

In a later report to Chalmers, his superior, Lt. Col. Kelley stated that the Confederate officers and men assigned to the captured U.S. transports at Hillsboro Landing commenced to looting the boats and consuming confiscated whiskey "too freely." The men in question were Company B of the 3rd Tennessee Cavalry commanded by Captain James G. Barbour. Kelley said he found it necessary to clear the boats of looters "myself with a drawn sabre." Kelley personally stood guard for two hours to prevent the return of the plunderers. He posted Capt. Chandler to act as guard, caught some sleep, and then went off to look for the "lost squadron" after he awoke. The company was called upon to go back and protect the captured boats but "such was the delay occasioned by drunkenness that the boats had been removed before I could reach them." Chandler said he set fire to the boats but "someone hidden on board extinguished them." Kelley admitted that "Capt. Chandler had evidently been drinking, but I am not prepared to say that this prevented his executing orders." This correspondence was contained in a copy of a manuscript letter in General Chalmers' papers at the National Archives found by Nashville historian Paul Clements and brought to the attention of the Battle of Nashville Preservation Society.

The *Carondelet,* a City Class casemate ironclad with 13 gunports, was the most famous of all the Western river gunboats, having participated in 15 engagements, including a duel with the Fort Donelson batteries and another duel with the Confederate ironclad *CSS Arkansas.* Despite its fame, it was also known as one of the slowest gunboats on the rivers.

The *Neosho* ironclad was one of only two gunboats of its kind built during the Civil War. Built in 1863 by James Eads at a cost of $195,000, the 523-ton behemoth was 180 feet long, 45 feet wide, and drew only four feet of water. With a crew of 100, she could make 12 knots at top speed but was difficult to maneuver. Low-board to the water, the distinguishing characteristics were a cylindrical rotating turret in the bow fitted with two 11-inch Dahlgren smoothbores and protected with iron plating six inches thick, the enclosed paddlewheel at the stern, and the wooden pilothouse superstructure and single chimney in-between. Fake gunports were painted on the iron turret to confuse the enemy. Along with the *USS Osage,* the *Neosho* was the only river monitor powered by paddlewheel.

The *Neosho's* guns, 13 feet long and each weighing nearly eight tons, used a 15-lb. powder charge to fire a 166-lb. solid shot or a load of canister balls.

A planned reconnaissance down the river on December 5 was postponed by the ominous sound of heavy cannon fire in the distance that Fitch speculated might be the beginning of a major Confederate assault on the city. He therefore kept his gunboats close at hand. The noise was actually Confederate assaults against railroad blockhouses south of the city.

Commanded by Acting Volunteer Lieutenant Samuel Howard, the strange-looking *Neosho* led a convoy of transports and gunboats downstream from Nashville on Tuesday, Dec. 6, 1864 at 9:30 in the morning. Following behind her, in order, were the *Metamora* transport, the tinclads *Moose* and *Reindeer* lashed together, the *Prima Donna* and *Arizona* transports, the *J.F. McComb* and *Mercury* sidewheeler transports, the tinclad *Fairplay,* the transports *Financier, Lily, New York* and *Lady Franklin,* the tinclad *Silver Lake,* the *Pioneer* and *Magnet* transports, and finally the *Carondelet.*

By this point in time, Kelley had positioned three batteries of field artillery on the south banks of the river opposite Bell's Mills, having added two more 12-pounder howitzers. Because Kelley made a practice of actively repositioning his guns and firing

many salvos, U.S. Commander Fitch reported that he was facing at least 14 rebel guns instead of the actual six.

At 11:15 am, the middle battery opened on the *Neosho* at the point-blank range of 20 to 30 yards. The *Neosho* responded with deadly canister loads from its two powerful Dahlgrens. Despite the pounding, the *Neosho* remained at station; the Confederate barrage blew away all of the ironclad's wooden superstructure like a blast of wind. The U.S. flag fell to the deck. Amid the conflagration, Quartermaster John Ditzenbach and civilian pilot John H. Ferrell climbed out onto the deck and attached the flag to a shortened but upright spar. For their bravery, Ditzenbach and Ferrell were awarded the Medal of Honor. Ferrel is one of only a handful of civilians ever so honored. A native of Tennessee, Ferrell had been residing in Illinois when hired by the U.S. Navy. He survived the war and died in 1900.

The December 6 firefight lasted for two and a half hours with Kelley "doing good work and thoroughly enjoying himself with his guns on the river bank." The firepower of the rebel batteries was too much for the convoy; at 3:10 pm all but the *Neosho* and *Carondelet* retired upriver. The two ironclads took a break but returned to Bell's Bend at 4:30 in the afternoon. The *Carondelet* tied fast to the north bank just upstream from the batteries and commenced to firing its starboard and stern guns. The apparently indestructible *Neosho* steadied itself in the channel opposite the middle battery, drew a bead on the Confederate gunners, and disabled two of the rebel 12-pounder artillery pieces. The afternoon exchange lasted only an hour. Similar to the situation at Johnsonville, the Union gunboats were forced to elevate their guns to aim at the Confederates on the bluffs and their shells flew harmlessly overhead. Afterwards, it was determined that the *Neosho* had been hit at least 100 times that day with only superficial damage. "Some six or eight men in the turret of the *Neosho* were somewhat bruised and scratched in the face by a shell striking the muzzle of one of the guns and exploding." Other injuries were too trivial to mention. It could have been much worse. An unexploded Confederate shell was found in the *Neosho's* gunpowder magazine.

December 7th was spent coaling and repairing the damages to the ironclads and tinclads. On December 8, the two ironclads along with the *Moose* and *Reindeer*, lashed together, steamed downriver to Davidson's Landing and for 90 minutes leisurely shelled a brick house believed to be occupied by Confederate soldiers.

As it turned out, at the time of Fitch's bitter fights with Kelley's batteries, the U.S. convoy could not have made the trip to Clarksville anyway — the water level at Harpeth Shoals had fallen so much in the previous week that no boats could have gotten through!

Bitter winter weather, low water, and other considerations limited gunboat activity until a thaw in the weather on December 14 foretold the movement of Federal troops out of their fortifications the next day.

Thomas' Federal armies moved out of their fortifications around Nashville on Thursday, Dec. 15, 1864 and brought the fight to Hood's waiting troops. The U.S. 6th Cavalry Division under General Richard Johnson was late moving out the Charlotte Pike against the Confederate left flank due to dense fog and entanglements with U.S. infantry troops. Finally, Johnson moved out and engaged with Chalmers' cavalry near the Belle Meade plantation. Kelley had moved four guns back a half-mile from the river and fired at the *Neosho* on the Cumberland River and at the advancing U.S. horsemen. After dark, Kelley retreated southeastward to Brentwood; Fitch reported erroneously that U.S. cavalry had captured Kelley's guns. During the two-day Battle of Nashville, Thomas drove Hood back to the point where a concentrated attack on Shy's Hill collapsed most of the Confederate resistance and forced a rout. Only a determined stand by relatively fresh troops on the Franklin Pike prevented the total destruction of the Confederate Army of Tennessee. Thus began the tragic 10-day, 100-mile fighting retreat of Hood's army in an effort to safely cross the Tennessee River in northern Alabama. During this time, the bulk of Forrest's command disengaged at Murfreesboro and linked up with the army at Columbia, and then fought effectively as the retreating army's rear guard. It was estimated that 10,000 horses perished in the harsh winter conditions.

The Confederates could not cross the Tennessee River at Florence, Ala. but established a pontoon bridge at Bainbridge, six miles above Florence at the foot of Muscle Shoals. Due to the rainy weather, the river level was up and many officers believed that the odds of U.S. gunboats reaching the pontoon bridge "not improbable." On December 20, Acting Rear Admiral Samuel P. Lee led a flotilla of gunboats up the Tennessee towards Florence, where the Confederates had established an artillery battery. Lee's squadron boasted more guns than Fitch had at Nashville, and included the ironclads *Neosho, Carondelet, Pittsburg,* and the timberclad *Lexington.* Even with the rising waters, the *Carondelet* and *Pittsburg* had to be left behind at Eastport, Mississippi, while the *Neosho* and the tinclads *Reindeer* and *Fairy* engaged with two four-gun rebel batteries at Florence. The Confederates stopped firing after 30 minutes and the gunboats drifted back downstream. The next day another futile engagement resulted in the *Neosho* being hit 27 times and the Union flotilla suffering three killed and five wounded. By the evening of December 27, all of Hood's retreating troops had crossed the Tennessee River to safety. Lee was determined to disrupt the enemy's movements and ordered the *Neosho* monitor up the river, but a "sudden and rapid fall of the river" convinced the gunboat's pilot to stop short of Little Muscle Shoals.

Hood's failed 1864 offensive was the last major combat in the Western Theater, but U.S. Navy gunboat operations continued on the Tennessee and the Cumberland with some guerrilla resistance encountered. "The guerrilla war continued, having a logic of its own, even though the military purposes were negligible," noted historian Richard Gildrie.

On April 29, 1865, almost three weeks after Robert E. Lee surrendered to U.S. Grant at Appomattox, the tinclad *Moose* successfully thwarted a Confederate attempt to cross the Cumberland River in order to burn down the town of Eddyville, Kentucky. The *Moose*, captained by the veteran riverman W.C. Coulson, all of 25 years old, heard news of the movement while moored at Tennessee Rolling Mills. The acting master of the

U.S. steamer *Albiona* had sighted 16 guerrillas at Centre Furnace, two miles from the river, at the crack of dawn. Five hours later, a courier reported a force of 150 to 200 men moving north to cross the river. Put immediately to full steam downriver, the *Moose* rounded the big bend at Eddyville and interrupted two boats of Confederates shoving off the shore. "They were taken completely by surprise and offered but little resistance," reported Coulson. Upon seeing the gunboat, the Confederates jumped out of the boats into the water. The forward gun on the upper deck of the *Moose* let loose, along with small arms fire from riflemen on the tinclad. The men on the shore, most armed only with revolvers, scattered. Few made it across the river. A landing party pursued, shot and killed four and wounded the same number. They captured six rebels, along with 19 horses and three mules. Coulson reported that the Confederate force was under Major Hopkins of Buford's command, but historian Jack Smith refutes this assertion, stating there is no record of a Major Hopkins serving under General Abraham Buford. Often, guerrilla bands would pose as well-known military units to confuse the enemy. Two of the prisoners were found to be civilians impressed as guides, and were released. Coulson did report that 60 men eventually made it north of the Cumberland. "I shall continue to cruise this vicinity, keeping a good lookout for them, and convoying transports by dangerous places." Coulson also told his superiors: "Great praise is due to Mr. Rowley, the pilot on watch, for his coolness and quick handling of the vessel, which assisted greatly to our success." The Eddyville affair was the last significant naval counter-insurgency action on the Western waters.

In the 12 months of 1864 Forrest had fought in 50 battles and skirmishes and had killed, captured, or put out of action three times his number of the enemy. His men captured 48 guns and destroyed about the same number, captured or destroyed five locomotives and 75 rail cars, 2,000 animals, 350 wagons, 10,000 small arms, four gunboats, and 14 transports, and tore up 100 miles of railroad track. In 1865, in response to calls for continued guerrilla resistance, General Forrest, as fierce a warrior as was ever seen, stated emphatically, "Any man who is in favor of a further prosecution of this war is a fit subject for a lunatic asylum, and ought to be sent there immediately."

In 1868, David Campbell Kelley, Forrest's "Fighting Parson," took a D.D. degree from Cumberland University and served the Methodist Episcopal Church in Gallatin and other towns in the Nashville area. Kelley was one of the founders of Vanderbilt University in 1873 and served on its board of trustees from 1875 to 1891. He held several posts in the church hierarchy and ran unsuccessfully as the Prohibition Party candidate for Tennessee governor in 1890. Kelley died in Nashville on May 14, 1909. According to John E. Fisher, Kelley was "a vocal force in urging upon whites reasoned and informed views of blacks and relations between the races." Forrest said, "He displayed all the dash, energy, and gallantry which has so long made him an efficient officer."

Lt. Commander LeRoy Fitch taught at the U.S. Naval Academy for a year, commanded a gunboat in the Atlantic and Caribbean for a year, and became superintendent of the Pensacola Naval Yard with the rank of Commander. He retired to his hometown of Logansport, Indiana, due to illness and died in obscurity in 1876 at the age of 39.

Following the cessation of hostilities, the U.S. military began disassembling the Mississippi Squadron and much of the infrastructure along the river shores. The mighty gunboats of the inland rivers were decommissioned and converted back to steamers or wharf boats, or sold for scrap. The tale of the *Carondelet*, the most celebrated ironclad on the Western waters, was a particularly sad one. She was decommissioned at Mound City in June 1865 and sold there in November 1865. In 1873, shortly before she was to be scrapped, a flood swept the *Carondelet* from her moorings at Gallipolis, Ohio. She drifted approximately 130 miles down the Ohio River, where she grounded and sank near Manchester, Ohio. Her grave remained unknown until a May 1982 search operation by the National Underwater and Marine Agency pinpointed and confirmed the location of the wreckage, two days after a dredge passed directly over the site, unintentionally demolishing the wrecked vessel.

–Chapter Sixteen–

# Conclusion

*The Confederate response to the Federal gunboats
was often effective, but the efforts were too little and too late*

The story of the Federal army/navy invasion of Middle Tennessee in 1862 is an amazing one with little precedent. The building of a freshwater navy began with the conversion of steam-powered paddlewheelers into heavily armed gunboats. These so-called timberclads and later the tinclads proved to be too fragile to confront fortifications with seige artillery, so an innovative program was established to build ironclad gunboats. Even these behemoths were vulnerable to concentrated firepower; the ultimate result was the river monitor, equipped with a revolving gun turret and almost impenetrable armor. Most of the ironclads, however, were slow and not very maneuverable. So it could be concluded that the Federal navy never did develop an entirely suitable river gunboat during the Civil War. And yet, the rapid and tortured establishment of a river gunboat flotilla from converted steamers and mostly inexperienced crews was a marvel in and of itself. There was little precedent for such a force and no written manuals to consult. Of course, it must be noted that much of the success of the Union riverboat flotilla on the Tennessee and Cumberland rivers was due to the fact that the Confederates had no gunboats of their own to confront them.

The river forts built by the Confederates proved to be inadequate. Fort Henry was sited so low that it was half submerged during battle. Nevertheless, the gunboats suffered extensive damage, especially the *Essex*. At Fort Donelson, the Confederate gunners turned back the Union flotilla in a show of force. The fort was lost anyway, due to incompetence in the high command. At that time, the Phelps raiders cruised far up the Tennessee, taking prizes and destroying Confederate stores. More importantly, perhaps, the raid instilled fear into the Confederates by penetrating so far into the rebel heartland. The raid influenced the thinking of the Confederate high command at Fort Donelson, Clarksville, Nashville, and Pittsburg Landing.

The Confederates built three forts at Clarksville and one below Nashville, all abandoned before the Federal flotilla could engage in battle. It would be interesting to speculate what the outcome would have been had those forts been manned, in addition to a rebel river battery established at Pittsburg Landing, as apparently was planned but not realized.

The control of the Tennessee River reaped many rewards for the Federal armies at Shiloh and greatly contributed to the close Federal victory there.

The rivers served as advantageous transportation routes for the advancing Federal forces, which required an enormous amount of supplies. The role of the Confederate cavalry, led by such raiders as Forrest, Kelley, Morgan, Van Dorn, and Wheeler, was to disrupt the flow of freighters on the rivers. Although the rebel cavalry, along with irregulars and even guerrillas, proved to be a powerful thorn in the side of Federal officials, they did not and could not turn the tide of the war.

The Federal army campaigns to capture Vicksburg and Chattanooga were delayed by many months due to the actions of the Confederate cavalry, but it was attacks against garrisons, railroads, and depots at Murfreesboro and Holly Springs that caused the delays, not action against the river convoys. It was much easier to disable a railroad, especially at tunnels, trestles, and bridges, than to blockade a river.

The Federals were unable to thwart the Confederate river attacks through counter-insurgency methods. The most effective method of discouraging attacks was to seize property and/or burn down houses and villages along the shore where the attacks occurred. Ironically, the most effective counter-insurgency episode occurred on the Tennessee River by the strange Mississippi Marine Brigade under Ellet. The marine force completely surprised the Confederate raiders and drove them a dozen miles inland. The Union did not learn from or build on the success of this skirmish, and it was not to be repeated.

As it happened, several times during the war, the Confederate raids, however successful, were too little too late to have significant impact.

The most successful effort by the Confederate cavalry by far was Forrest's Johnsonville campaign, beginning with the ambush at Eastport, continuing with the creation of a Confederate gunboat navy at Paris Landing and the complete destruction of the Federal river depot at Johnsonville, and culminating in the successful confrontation and river blockade at Bell's Bend. If these events had occurred during the summer of 1864 rather than November/December of that year, the destruction may have had great impact upon the progress of Sherman's campaign in Georgia. In fact, the spectacular raid had hardly any impact at all on Sherman's actions, although it caused near-hysteria among Union loyalists in the Ohio River Valley. The skirmishing at Nashville in December 1864 was the ultimate clash between well-trained Confederate cavalry (armed with field artillery) and the Federal flotilla, consisting of a City Class ironclad, several tinclads, and a river monitor. The Confederates had arrived a day late to prevent a large convoy of Federal reinforcements from reaching Nashville, but they did repel attempts by convoys to travel downriver. The blockade had little real impact and the Federal convoy could not have made it past the Harpeth Shoals anyway due to low water.

From the very beginning of the war in 1861, the U.S. army and navy discovered that they needed to cooperate to make any advancement. The army didn't know anything about river gunboats and the navy preferred to conduct saltwater operations. Hardly anyone in the service knew about the rivers

*USS Neosho* river monitor. Watercolor illustration.

themselves. Cooperation proved irksome at first but improved over time. Grant and Foote set the tone with their amphibious operations at Belmont, Fort Henry, Fort Donelson, and Shiloh. Although the protection of freight convoys was vital to the Union cause, Federal resources were allocated elsewhere (e.g., the Lower Mississippi), causing some Federal army commanders to become too cautious in their campaigns. Although the U.S. Army was expressly prohibited from operating river gunboats, they did so anyway, although to a limited extent and with dubious results.

The successful use of civilian resources was incalcuable. Rivermen of vast experience were needed to survey the rivers, inventory the available resources, and design and produce the unique river gunboats. Each and every U.S. Navy gunboat carried at least one civilian pilot to negotiate the treacherous, mysterious, and ever-changing rivers. They knew full well that they were a prime target for Confederate gunners and riflemen. The bravery of those pilots is difficult to fathom.

By the end of the war, the Federal interservice cooperation had reached its zenith. "It is difficult to find anywhere in the history of the American Civil War a better demonstration of combined operations in which the army and the navy worked together with fewer problems and more impressive results," stated U.S. Admiral Samuel P. Lee's biographer in regards to the repulse of Hood's 1864 offensive. Ironically, the Confederate army, what was left of it after the defeat at Nashville, had to flee 100 miles southward to the safety of a river.

Following the end of hostilities, the proud Federal fleet was scrapped or converted to wharfboats, and the naval shipyards and facilities disassembled. Few traces remain. It was the end of an era. Never again would a brown-water navy be needed on the western rivers.

–Chapter Seventeen–

# Travel Guide to Battle Sites

*Tremendous progress has been made in recent years*
*preserving and interpreting the river sites*

Much of the landscape has changed in the 150 years since the Civil War, most notably the rivers themselves. Dams built by the Tennessee Valley Authority and the U.S. Army Corps of Engineers in the 20th Century created huge serpentine reservoirs for recreation and power generation, opened up navigation, and alleviated most seasonal flooding. The Great Muscle Shoals are no longer an impediment to navigation. University of Tennessee football fans can navigate their small vessels from West Tennessee all the way to the side of Neyland Stadium in Knoxville. Near the Ohio River, dams created Kentucky Lake on the Tennessee River and Lake Barkeley on the Cumberland River. The land between the rivers is now the Land Between the Lakes National Recreation Area, which feaures a bison meadow, HomePlace 1840 living history farm, and the limestone stacks of abandoned ironworks. Boats of all sizes cruise Kentucky Lake; there are even sailboats. Barges laden with coal or sand wind their way along the Cumberland, pushed by diesel-powered tugboats. A canal near Eddyville links the Cumberland to the Tennessee, cutting miles off the route to the Ohio River.

Paducah features a historic district, river museum, and a floodwall of 50 panels painted by artist Robert Dafford depicting historic events. The shipyards at Carondelet, now incorporated as a neighborhood of St. Louis, and Mound City, site of a national cemetery, are long gone with only a few traces remaining. Cairo has seen better days, its historic commercial district blighted and resembling a ghost town. The view of the confluence of the Ohio and Mississippi rivers at Fort Defiance is still impressive, but the state park there is ramshackle due to lack of funding and maintenance. Cairo does still feature several magnificent mansions such as Magnolia Manor, built by businessmen enriched by the war.

Fort Henry slipped under the waters of Kentucky Lake decades ago although remnants of the rifle pits remain. The area is best known for its numerous hiking trails. The ruins of the Johnsonville depot are also submerged all the way inland to the point where the railroad turntable used to stand. This area is home to TVA's coal-fired steam plant and numerous industries. The railroad bridge at Danville is long gone but the approaches remain, along with the upper structure of an abandoned riverside grain elevator. River erosion at Shiloh has been a problem, threatening the prehistoric Indian mounds there.

The river at Johnsonville is expansive, with numerous sloughs and false channels. It would be unrecognizable to men such as Forrest and Fitch. Upstream at Shiloh, however, the river channel remains much as it looked in Civil War days. At Dover, the Cumberland River is swollen from impoundment, looking much as it did during the heavy rains and flooding preceding the battle at Fort Donelson.

There are numerous bridges over the river at Nashville now although the stone piers from the old railroad bridge remain. The wharf at Nashville is now Riverfront Park, home of concerts and other gatherings, while Nissan Stadium, home of the NFL Tennessee Titans, sits across the river at Edgefield.

Interest in the Civil War has grown steadily since the war's centennial in the 1960s. Civil War historic sites had been badly neglected through the years in many cases, but tremendous strides have been made in the past few decades to preserve our history.

At the top of the tourism list would be Fort Donelson National Battlefield at Dover and Shiloh National Military Park at Pittsburg Landing.

Fort Donelson National Battlefield is located on the banks of the Cumberland River (Lake Barkley) in Stewart County. The 1,007-acre park, created in 1928 and operated by the National Park Service, is visited by 700,000 people each year. The re-creation of the water batteries, featuring authentic artillery along with replicas, is most interesting. The 15-acre National Cemetery was built in 1867 on the site of the old Union fort at Dover. It contains 670 burials, many unknown, arranged in circular rows. The Confederate dead were buried in trenches on the battlefield, the locations of which are unknown. The Visitors Center features a museum about the 1862 battle, including an orientation video, and a bookstore. The self-guided battlefield tour is six miles long by vehicle and features 11 stops, including monument, surrounding earthworks, the fort itself, the river batteries, the national cemetery, and the Dover Hotel (Surrender House). A replica of the swivel gun used in the February 1863 Battle of Dover is displayed in the town square. Fort Henry is located 12 miles west of Fort Donelson on the Tennessee River. The fort lies beneath the waters of Kentucky Lake but some surrounding rifle pits are visible. Remnants of Fort Heiman are visible on the western bank of Kentucky Lake opposite the Fort Henry site.

Shiloh National Military Park, preserved much as it appeared in 1862 and extensively interpreted with markers and signage as well as dozens of impressive monuments, is a history buff's dream. Just as during the war, the site is well off the beaten path. One has to drive a few miles to get there. The 2,400-acre park, designated in 1894, features a self-driving tour, visitor's center and museum, well-stocked bookstore, U.S. National Cemetery, prehistoric Indian mounds, and knowledgeable park rangers. Those interested in naval history should attend the annual living history demonstrations, featuring the U.S. Naval Landing Party and the Navy & Marine Living History Association. Nearby is Pickwick

*(Continued on Page 162)*

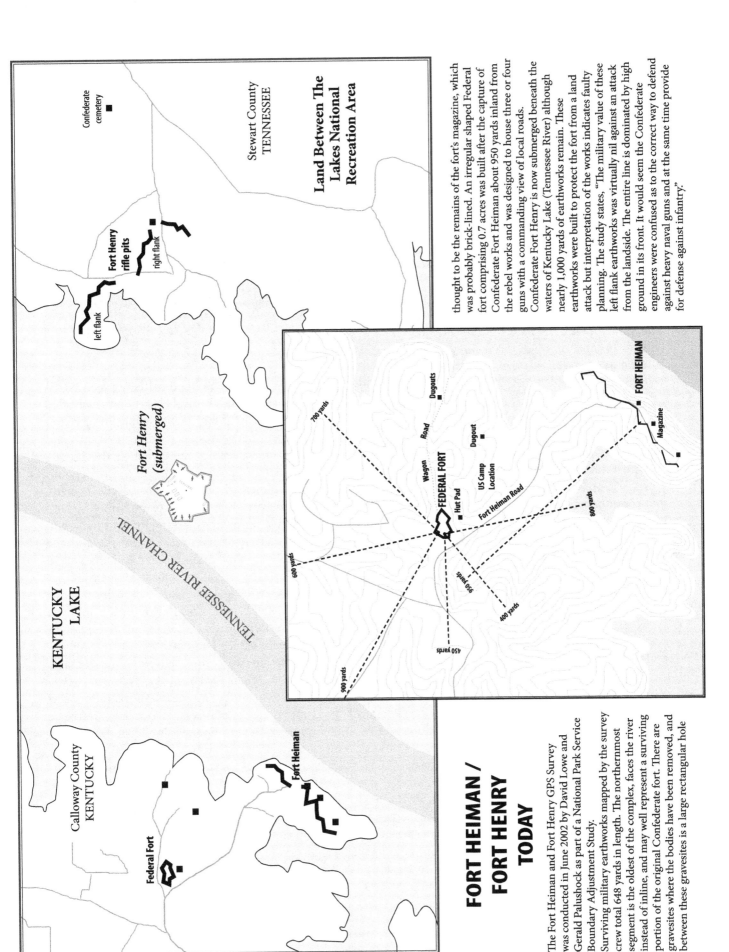

thought to be the remains of the fort's magazine, which was probably brick-lined. An irregular shaped Federal fort comprising 0.7 acres was built after the capture of Confederate Fort Heiman about 950 yards inland from the rebel works and was designed to house three or four guns with a commanding view of local roads.

Confederate Fort Henry is now submerged beneath the waters of Kentucky Lake (Tennessee River) although nearly 1,000 yards of earthworks remain. These earthworks were built to protect the fort from a land attack but interpretation of the works indicates faulty planning. The study states, "The military value of these left flank earthworks was virtually nil against an attack from the landside. The entire line is dominated by high ground in its front. It would seem the Confederate engineers were confused as to the correct way to defend against heavy naval guns and at the same time provide for defense against infantry."

## FORT HEIMAN / FORT HENRY TODAY

The Fort Heiman and Fort Henry GPS Survey was conducted in June 2002 by David Lowe and Gerald Palushock as part of a National Park Service Boundary Adjustment Study.

Surviving military earthworks mapped by the survey crew total 648 yards in length. The northernmost segment is the oldest of the complex, faces the river instead of inline, and may well represent a surviving portion of the original Confederate fort. There are gravesites where the bodies have been removed, and between these gravesites is a large rectangular hole

Landing State Park. Associated with Shiloh is the modern Corinth Civil War Interpretive Center in Mississippi which interprets the 1862 battles fought there.

Speaking of Mississippi, the only extant U.S. Navy river gunboat from the Civil War, the *USS Cairo,* can be viewed at the Vicksburg National Military Park (see special section in this book for details).

The 1,500-acre Johnsonville State Historic Park in Humphreys County commemorates the Battle of Johnsonville and the historic town that existed from 1864-1944 prior to the formation of Kentucky Lake. The park features the upper and lower redoubts, the original Federal breastworks (rifle pits), and 10 miles of hiking trails. In 2012, the park opened a new Visitors Center, museum, and gift shop. Each year on November 4th, the anniversary of the Battle of Johnsonville, park staff leads a walking tour. What impresses the visitor here, among other things, is the steepness of the hills along the river.

In 1864 the *USS Undine* sank near Johnsonville and efforts have been made to salvage her. According to consultants, the *Undine* has been "heavily salvaged of all her guns and armor," and "very little remains of the burned vessel but her lower hull," which lies buried under eight feet of sediment.

Across the river from Johnsonville lies Nathan Bedford Forrest State Park, comprising 2,587 acres, and Pilot Knob, the highest elevation in West Tennessee. Camping and hiking are the main activities here. The obelisk monument to General Forrest and the Tennessee River Folklife Interpretive Center and Museum can be seen at Pilot Knob as well as an impressive view of the Tennessee River (much wider now than it was during the war).

At Nashville, the Fort Negley Visitor's Center serves as the focal point for Civil War tourism. The battlefield at Nashville has been consumed by commercial and residential development although a couple dozen compact sites remain to be seen. The historic sites of Nashville are examined and mapped in the author's 2019 book, *Guide to Civil War Nashville, 2nd Ed.*

Fort Defiance Interpretive Center

The site of the Bell's Bend battle between Fitch's gunboats and Kelley's cavalry went undiscovered until members of the Battle of Nashville Preservation Society identified the site, finding grapeshot and other expended ammo embedded in the muddy riverwalls. In a unique example of cooperation among commercial developers, local government, historic preservationists, and private donors, land was set aside for a park, parking lot, and trail, with the preservation of wartime earthworks and the building of a river overlook. Kelley's Point Battlefield is now part of the city's Brookmeade Greenway.

In Clarksville, several years ago, a local judge asked a college professor if overgrown land he owned overlooking the Cumberland River might have historic value. Hidden amongst the jungle-like vegetation were the well-preserved remains of the Fort Defiance earthworks. Following some heavy bushhogging and years of planning and fundraising, the 1,500-square-foot Fort Defiance Interpretive Center opened in 2008, telling the story of Clarksville during the Civil War. The outer earthworks, powder magazine, and gun platforms of the fort are still discernible. Sevier Station, the old frontier home of town founder Valentine Sevier, can be viewed a few blocks away.

Historic sites and interpretive signage can be found on maps produced by the non-profit Civil War Trails (www.civilwartrails.org). Most of the attractions mentioned in this chapter are open and free of charge to the public. Consult the appropriate websites for visitation guidelines.

# Timeline of Events

## 1861

| | |
|---|---|
| April 13, 1861 | Fort Sumter in Charleston, S.C. harbor. |
| April 23, 1861 | State troops occupy Cairo, Ill. at the confluence of the Mississippi and Ohio rivers. |
| May 16, 1861 | John Rodgers named commander of Western Gunboat Flotilla. |
| June 8, 1861 | Tennessee votes 105,000 to 47,000 to secede from Union. |
| June 21, 1861 | Battle of Bull Run (Manassas), Va. |
| Aug. 7, 1861 | Contract signed between US Army and Eads for construction of seven City Class ironclads. |
| Aug. 30, 1861 | Andrew H. Foote named commander of Western Gunboat Flotilla. |
| Sept. 3, 1861 | Confederate Gen. Polk occupies Columbus, breaking Kentucky's neutrality. |
| Sept. 6, 1861 | Grant occupies Paducah and Smithland, Ky., at the mouths of the Tennessee and Cumberland. |
| Oct. 12, 1861 | First City Class ironclad USS Carondelet launched at St. Louis, Mo. |
| Nov. 7, 1861 | Grant attacks Confederate camp at Belmont, Mo. using timberclads and transports. |
| Nov. 19, 1861 | Henry Halleck named commander of the Department of the Missouri. |
| Nov. 20, 1861 | Canton, Ky. skirmish between USS Conestoga under Phelps and Forrest's cavalry under Kelley. |

## 1862

| | |
|---|---|
| Jan. 15, 1862 | Foote accepts the seven City Class ironclads from contractor Eads. |
| Feb. 6, 1862 | Fort Henry on Tennessee River falls to ironclad gunboats under Foote. |
| Feb. 6-11, 1862 | Phelps raid up Tennessee River to Florence, Ala. by three timberclads. |
| Feb. 14, 1862 | Confederate gunners at Fort Donelson defeat Foote's ironclad gunboats. |
| Feb. 16, 1862 | Fort Donelson on Cumberland River falls to Grant's army. |
| Feb. 19, 1862 | Clarksville, Tenn. occupied by Federal troops. |
| Feb. 25, 1862 | Nashville, capital of Tennessee, occupied by Union forces under Buell. |
| March 1, 1862 | First Battle of Shiloh. Lexington and Tyler skirmish with rebel infantry at Pittsburg Landing. |
| March 8, 1862 | 40th Illinois Infantry Regiment, vanguard of 40,000, reaches Savannah, Tenn. by river. |

# Timeline of Events

| | |
|---|---|
| March 9, 1862 | Battle of Hampton Roads, Va. between the ironclads *USS Monitor* and *CSS Virginia*. |
| April 6-7, 1862 | Battle of Shiloh (Pittsburg Landing). *Tyler* and *Lexington* shell Confederate troops. |
| May 9, 1862 | Charles H. Davis named commander of Western Gunboat Flotilla. |
| June 6, 1862 | Battle of Memphis on Mississippi results in surrender of town and destruction of CSA fleet. |
| Aug. 12-13, 1862 | John Hunt Morgan's men block South Tunnel on Louisville & Nashville Railroad near Gallatin. |
| Aug. 18, 1862 | Clarksville recaptured by Confederates. |
| Aug. 25, 1862 | Woodward attacks Federal garrison at Dover. |
| Oct. 1, 1862 | Army hands Western Gunboat Flotilla over to US Navy; renamed Mississippi River Squadron. |
| Oct. 15, 1862 | David D. Porter named commander of Mississippi River Squadron. |
| Dec. 7, 1862 | Fort Negley in Nashville is completed using contraband labor. |

## 1863

| | |
|---|---|
| Jan. 2, 1863 | Battle of Stones River (Murfreesboro) ends with Confederate retreat. |
| Feb. 3, 1863 | Battle of Dover, Tenn. Wheeler's cavalry defeated as Fitch's gunboats intervene. |
| Feb. 7, 1863 | Gen. Gordon Granger's convoy from Louisville reaches Nashville. |
| April 8, 1863 | Confederate troops capture and burn the steamers *Saxonia* and *Lovell* near Clarksville. |
| April 26, 1863 | Mississippi Marine Brigade chases Texas Rangers on the Tennessee at Duck River. |
| July 3, 1863 | Battle of Gettysburg. Lee's Army of Northern Virginia defeated. |
| July 4, 1863 | Confederates surrender Vicksburg on Mississippi River to Grant. |
| Sept. 10, 1863 | Bureau of U.S. Colored Troops opens in Nashville. |

## 1864

| | |
|---|---|
| March 25, 1864 | Forrest attacks Paducah, repelled in part by US gunboats on Ohio River. |
| April 12, 1864 | Fort Pillow on Mississippi River captured by Forrest, massacre alleged. |
| May 7, 1864 | Sherman begins Atlanta campaign through northern Georgia. |
| May 10, 1864 | Nashville & Northwestern Railroad to Johnsonville depot completed. |

# Timeline of Events

| | |
|---|---|
| July 1864 | Alexander M. Pennock named commander of Mississippi River Squadron. |
| Sept. 2, 1864 | Sherman's armies capture Atlanta, Ga. after four-month campaign and seige. |
| Oct. 14, 1864 | Eastport, Miss. ambush of US troops, gunboats by Kelley's cavalry and artillery. |
| Oct. 16, 1864 | Forrest begins month-long raid of West Tennessee. |
| Oct. 29-30, 1864 | Forrest captures Union gunboats at Paris Landing, Tenn. |
| Nov. 1, 1864 | Samuel P. Lee named commander of Mississippi River Squadron. |
| Nov. 4, 1864 | Forrest destroys Johnsonville depot on Tennessee River. |
| Nov. 8, 1864 | Lincoln re-elected President with Tennessean Andrew Johnson as Vice-President. |
| Nov. 15, 1864 | Sherman leaves Atlanta and begins his March to the Sea. |
| Nov. 21, 1864 | Hood marches north from Florence, Ala. |
| Nov. 30, 1864 | Battle of Franklin-Confederate Army of Tennessee smashed. |
| Dec. 3-4, 1864 | Transports captured by Kelley at Bell's Bend are seized by Fitch's gunboats. |
| Dec. 6, 1864 | Kelley's artillery battles *USS Carondelet* and *USS Neosho* at Bell's Bend. |
| Dec. 15-16, 1864 | Battle of Nashville. Kelley skirmishes with Union cavalry under Gen. Richard Johnson. |
| Dec. 21, 1864 | Sherman marches into Savannah, Ga. on the seacoast. |
| Dec. 25, 1864 | Hood retreats across the Tennessee River; Union gunboats decline to intervene. |

## 1865 ∙∙∙∙∙∙∙∙∙∙∙∙∙∙∙∙∙∙∙∙∙∙∙∙∙∙∙∙∙∙∙∙∙∙∙∙∙∙∙∙∙∙∙∙∙∙∙∙∙∙∙∙∙∙∙∙∙∙∙∙

| | |
|---|---|
| April 9, 1865 | Lee surrenders to Grant at Appomattox, Va. |
| April 14, 1865 | Lincoln shot at Ford's Theater in Washington, D.C. and dies the next day. |
| April 26, 1865 | Gen. Joseph Johnston surrenders to Gen. William T. Sherman at Bentonville, N.C. |
| April 29, 1865 | *USS Moose* turns back Confederate attack on Eddyville, Ky. |

# Bibliography

Allyn, John, "The Naval Battle of Nashville," Battle of Nashville Preservation Society, 2011, www.bonps.org/the-battle/nashville-naval-battle/

Ambrose, Stephen E., *The Campaigns for Fort Donelson*, Eastern Acorn Press, 1993.

American Society of Mechanical Engineers, *U.S.S. Cairo Engine & Boilers* booklet, 1990.

Ash, Stephen V., "Sharks in an Angry Sea: Civilian Resistance and Guerrilla Warfare in Occupied Middle Tennessee 1862-65," *Tennessee in the Civil War Vol. 1,* Tennessee Historical Quarterly, 2011.

Bearss, Edwin C., *Hardluck Ironclad: The Sinking and Salvage of the Cairo*, Louisiana State University Press, 1980.

_____, *The Fall of Fort Henry,* Eastern National, 1999.

_____, "The Construction of Fort Henry and Fort Donelson," *West Tennessee Historical Society Papers* 21 (1967): 24-27

_____, "A Federal Raid Up the Tennessee River," *Alabama Review* 17 (October 1964): 261-70

_____, "The Ironclads at Fort Donelson," *Register of the Kentucky Historical Society* (Jan.-Apr.-July 1976)

Biggs, Greg, "Stopping Hood: The Navy in the Tennessee Campaign," Battle of Nashville 153rd Anniversary Symposium, Dec. 16, 2017.

Bradley, Michael R., *Forrest's Fighting Preacher: David Campbell Kelley of Tennessee,* The History Press, 2011.

Castel, Albert, *Decision in the West: The Atlanta Campaign of 1864,* University Press of Kansas, 1992.

Civil War Trust, "Ulysses S. Grant: The Myth of Unconditional Surrender Begins at Fort Donelson," *Civil War Times Magazine* (historynet.com), www.civilwar.org/battlefields/fortdonelson/fort-donelson -history-articles/ulysses-s-grant-the-myth-of.html

Cooling, Benjamin Franklin, *Forts Henry and Donelson: The Key to the Confederate Heartland,* University of Tennessee Press, 1987.

Crandall, Warren D. and Isaac D. Newell, *History of the Ram Fleet and the Mississippi Marine Brigade in the War for the Union on the Mississippi and Its Tributaries,* Society of Survivors, St. Louis, 1907.

Davison, Eddy and Foxx, Daniel, *Nathan Bedford Forrest: In Search of the Enigma,* Pelican Publishing Co., 2007.

Douglas, Byrd, *Steamboatin' on the Cumberland,* Tennessee Book Co., 1961.

Durham, Walter T., *Nashville: The Occupied City,* Tennessee Historical Society, 1985.

Gott, Kendall D., *Where the South Lost the War: An Analysis of the Fort Henry-Fort Donelson Campaign, February 1862,* Stackpole Books, 2003.

Grant, U.S., *Personal Memoirs of U.S. Grant,* Da Capo Press, 1982.

## Bibliography (continued)

Groom, Winston, *Shiloh 1862,* National Geographic Society, 2012.

_____, *Shrouds of Glory: From Atlanta to Nashville, the Last Great Campaign of the Civil War,* Atlantic Monthly Press, 1995.

_____, *Vicksburg 1863,* Alfred A. Knopf, 2009.

Hearn, Chester G., *Ellet's Brigade: The Strangest Outfit of All,* Louisiana State University Press, 2000.

Hoobler, James A., *Cities Under the Gun: Images of Occupied Nashville and Chattanooga,* Rutledge Hill Press, 1986.

Horn, Stanley F., *The Decisive Battle of Nashville,* Louisiana University Press, 1956.

Hunter, Louis C., *Steamboats on Western Rivers: An Economic and Technological History,* Harvard University Press-Cambridge, 1949.

Hurst, Jack, *Nathan Bedford Forrest, A Biography,* Vintage Books, 1994.

Jobe, James, "The Battles for Fort Henry and Donelson," *Blue & Gray Magazine,* Vol. XXVIII No. 4, 2011.

_____, "Forts Heiman, Henry, and Donelson," Civil War Trust, www.civilwar.org/battlefields/fortdonelson /fort-donelson-history-articles/donelsonjobe.html

Joiner, Gary D., "Soul-Stirring Music to Our Ears," *The Shiloh Campaign,* Southern Illinois University Press, 2009.

Jones, Terry L., "The Mississippi Marine Brigade," *The New York Times,* May 17, 2013. https://opinionator.blogs. nytimes.com/2013/05/17/the-mississippi-marine-brigade/

Jordan, Thomas, *The Campaigns of General Forrest* (1868), Da Capo Press, 1996.

Kirkpatrick, Jim, "Boom Town: Cairo's Strategic Location in the Civil War," *The Southern,* Oct. 18, 2010, thesouthern.com/progress/section3/boom-town-cairo-s-strategic-location-in-the-civil-war/ article_html

Kitchens, Ben Earl, *Gunboats and Cavalry: A History of Eastport, Mississippi,* Iuka Battlefield Commission, 2010.

Knight, James R., "Nothing but God Almighty Can Save that Fort: Fort Donelson's Path to Unconditional and Immediate Surrender," *Hallowed Ground Magazine,* Civil War Trust, Winter 2011.

Lovett, Bobby L., "Nashville's Fort Negley: A Symbol of Blacks' Involvement with the Union Army," *Tennessee in the Civil War Vol. 1,* Tennessee Historical Quarterly, 2011.

Luther, Edward T., *Our Restless Earth,* University of Tennessee Press, 1977.

Mackey, Robert R., *The Uncivil War: Irregular Warfare in the Upper South 1861-65,* University of Oklahoma Press, 2004.

Mariner's Museum and Park, Newport News, Va., "Jefferson's Gunboat Navy," https://www.marinersmuseum.org/sites/micro/usnavy/07.htm

## Bibliography (continued)

McDonough, James Lee, *Nashville: The Western Confederacy's Final Gamble,* University of Tennessee Press, 2004.

McKenney, Tom C., *Jack Hinson's One-Man War: A Civil War Sniper,* Pelican Publishing Co., 2014.

Missouri Civil War Museum, "St. Louis' Ships of Iron," mcwm.org

Morris, William R., "The War In The Backwaters," *The Wayne County Historian,* Vol. 2, No. 2, June 1989.

Morton, John Watson, *The Artillery of Nathan Bedford Forrest's Cavalry,* Publishing House of the M.E. Church, 1909.

*Nashville Press & Times,* "Our Trip over the Northwestern Railroad," October 30, 1867, http://nashvillenwrr.tripod.com/id1.html

Naval History and Heritage Command, "River Warfare During the Civil War," www.history.navy.mil/library/online/riverine.htm

*Official Records of the Union and Confederate Navies in the War of the Rebellion,* Series I Vol. 26, Naval Forces on Western Waters.

Page, Dave, *Ships Versus Shore: Civil War Engagements Along Southern Shores and Rivers,* Rutledge Hill Press, 1994.

Parsons, Timothy A., "Rivers and Rifles: The Role of Fort Heiman in the Western Theater of the Civil War," National Park Service, 2002.

Pearson, Charles E., "Great Expectations for an Ill-Fated Ironclad," *Naval History,* U.S. Naval Institute, Vol. 31, No. 1, February 2017.

Perry, John C., "Forrest's Navy: The Raid on Johnsonville," *Confederate Veteran,* Jan.-Feb. 1993.

Quertermous, Grant, "Summary of Excavations at Fort Star: Archaeology of a Union Civil War Fortification," *Ohio Valley Historical Archaeology,* Vol. 14, 1999.

Rush, Linda, "Mound City Shipyards: Marine Ways Kept Them Sailing Through Civil War, Two World Wars," *The Southern,* Oct. 18, 2011.

Scales, John R., *The Battles and Campaigns of Confederate General Nathan Bedford Forrest,* Savas Beatie, 2017.

Slagle, Jay, *Ironclad Captain: Seth Ledyard Phelps & the U.S. Navy 1841-64,* Kent State University Press, 1996.

Smith, Myron J. "Jack", *Le Roy Fitch: The Civil War Career of a Union River Gunboat Commander,* McFarland & Co., Inc., 2007.

_____, "Le Roy Fitch Meets the Devil's Parson," *North & South Magazine,* Vol. 10 No.4, 2008.

_____, *The Timberclads in the Civil War: The Lexington, Conestoga and the Tyler on the Western Waters,* McFarland & Co., Inc., 2008.

_____, *The U.S.S. Carondelet: A Civil War Ironclad on Western Waters,* McFarland & Co., Inc., 2010.

## Bibliography (continued)

_____, *The Tinclads in the Civil War: Union Light-Draught Gunboat Operations on Western Waters 1862-65*, McFarland & Co., Inc., 2010.

Smith, Timothy B., *Grant Invades Tennessee: The 1862 Battles for Forts Henry and Donelson*, University Press of Kansas, 2016.

Sons of Confederate Veterans Camp 28 and Fort Heiman Camp 1834, signage at Mt. Olivet Cemetery, Nashville.

Stuart, Reginald C., "Cavalry Raids in the West: Case Studies of Civil War Cavalry Raids, Nathan Bedford Forrest and the Confederate Cavalry," *Tennessee in the Civil War Vol. 5*, Tennessee Historical Quarterly 2013.

Suhr, Robert Collins, "Saving the Day at Shiloh," *America's Civil War Magazine*, January 2000.

Sword, Wiley, *The Confederacy's Last Hurrah*, University Press of Kansas, 1992.

Taylor, Lenette S., *The Supply for Tomorrow Must Not Fail: The Civil War of Captain Simon Perkins, Jr., A Union Quartermaster*, Kent State University Press, 2004.

Tennessee Historical Society, *Tennessee Encyclopedia of History and Culture*, Editor-in-Chief Carroll Van West, Rutledge Hill Press, 1998.

Toll, Ian W., *Six Frigates: The Epic History of the Founding of the U.S. Navy*, W.W. Norton & Co., Inc., 2006

Tucker, Spencer C., "Capturing the Confederacy's Western Waters," *Naval History*, June 2006.

Veit, Chuck, "First Shiloh," Navy & Marine Living History Association, www.navyandmarine.org

Walke, Henry, "Henry Walke's Account of the Battle of Fort Henry," Feb. 6, 1862, Civil War Trust, www.civilwar.org/education/history/navy-hub/navy-history/primary-sources/the-battle-of-fort-henry.html

Walker, Thomas E., "*The Origins of the Mississippi Marine Brigade: The First Use of Brown Water Tactics by the United States in the Civil War*," Thesis, Texas Christian University, May 2006.

Weller, Jac, "Nathan Bedford Forrest: An Analysis of Untutored Military Genius," *Nathan Bedford Forrest and the Confederate Cavalry, Tennessee in the Civil War Vol. 5*, Tennessee Historical Quarterly 2013.

White, Ronald C., *American Ulysses: A Life of Ulysses S. Grant*, Random House, 2016.

Williams III, Edward F., "The Johnsonville Raid and Nathan Bedford Forrest State Park," *Nathan Bedford Forrest and the Confederate Cavalry, Tennessee in the Civil War Vol. 5*, Tennessee Historical Quarterly 2013.

Wills, Brian Steel, *The Confederacy's Greatest Cavalryman: Nathan Bedford Forrest*, University Press of Kansas, 1992.

Zimmerman, Mark, *Guide to Civil War Nashville, 2nd Ed.*, ZIMCO Publications LLC, 2019.

_____, *God, Guns, Guitars & Whiskey: An Illustrated Guide to Historic Nashville, Tennessee, 2nd Ed.*, ZIMCO Publications LLC, 2019.

## Bibliography (continued)

### Map, Photo, and Illustration Credits:

All modern photographs by Mark Zimmerman © 2019 unless otherwise noted.
All original maps drawn by Mark Zimmerman © 2019 unless otherwise noted.
All other photos, maps, illustrations, unless otherwise noted, from OR Atlas, Library of Congress, or Wikipedia.

Page 3: Paddlewheel linkage, USS Cairo Exhibit, Vicksburg National Military Park.

Page 27: Map of Cairo, Ill. from Harper's Weekly of June 1861.

Page 31: Map based on map of Fort Star prepared by Andie Kellie of Murray State University.

Page 32: "Gun-Deck of One of the Mississippi Gun-Boats Engaged in the Attack on Fort Henry" engraving after a sketch by Alexander Simplot, published in Harper's Weekly, 1862.

Page 40: Boat Howitzer, Shiloh National Military Park.

Page 55: Portrait of Nathan Bedford Forrest, 1869, by Nicola Marschall, Marion, Ala., Tennessee State Museum Collection, Feb. 16, 2005. Photo by the author.

Page 55: Photo of Confederate cavalry re-enactors at Stones River National Battlefield living history demonstration.

Page 56: Portrait of Seth Ledyard Phelps from Library of Congress, reproduction of ink drawing by Carl Joseph Becker, 1841-1910

Page 57: Battle map adapted from map by Hal Jespersen in John Scales' book on Forrest, and charts from the US Army Corps of Engineers.

Page 60: "Battle of Fort Henry" by Andy Thomas. Used with permission. View Andy's historical artwork at www.andythomas.com.

Page 64: Photo of torpedo (naval mine) taken at Shiloh National Military Park living history demonstration of the Navy & Marine Living History Association. www.navyandmarine.org

Page 70: Swing bridge over Tennessee River at Danville from website of Houston County, Tennessee Library.

Page 78: "Exchanging Iron Valentines," by Andy Thomas. Used with permission. View Andy's historical artwork at www.andythomas.com.

Pages 86-87: City of Nashville and Edgefield 1860 map and prominent buildings published by Haydon & Booth civil engineers.

Page 92: Close-up of the General Alfred Mouton Monument. (Photo taken by Eric Scott on November 21, 2013.) "General Alfred Mouton Monument," Acadiana Historical, accessed April 8, 2016, http://acadianahistorical.org/items/show/87

Page 93: Map of First Shiloh based on map by Chuck Veit, "First Shiloh," Navy & Marine Living History Association, www.navyandmarine.org

## Bibliography (continued)

### Map, Photo, and Illustration Credits:

Page 107: Duck River engagement illustration from *History of the Ram Fleet and the Mississippi Marine Brigade in the War for the Union on the Mississippi and Its Tributaries,* Society of Survivors, St. Louis, 1907.

Page 109: Map of Duck River Affair adapted from *History of the Ram Fleet and the Mississippi Marine Brigade in the War for the Union on the Mississippi and Its Tributaries,* Society of Survivors, St. Louis, 1907.

Page: 117: Photos of field artillery at the Chickamauga National Battlefield Visitor's Center.

Page 119: Commander LeRoy Fitch, 1870, from Naval Historical Center.

Page 124: Photograph by author of "The Battle of Paducah at Fort Anderson," one of the 50 riverwall paintings "Portraits from Paducah's Past," by renowned artist Robert Dafford and the Dafford Murals Team. The murals can be seen at the Paducah-Ohio river waterfront.

Page 132: Photograph of Confederate artillery re-enactors by the author at vicinity of Shy's Hill, Nashville.

Page 137: "Horse Marines" by John Paul Strain. Artwork used with permission. Artist's gallery can be viewed at www.johnpaulstrain.com.

Page 139: Map of Reynoldsburg Island affair based on map drawn by Lt. Commander LeRoy Fitch.

Pages 142-143: Photographs of old Johnsonville courtesy of Tennessee State Library and Archives. Photo of Andrew Johnson statue at Tennessee State Capitol by the author.

Page 157: *USS Neosho* river monitor. Watercolor by Dr. Oscar Parkes, London, 1936. U.S. Naval History and Heritage Command. NH-60617.

Page 161: Map based on map produced by National Park Service historian David Lowe.

### About the Author

Mark Zimmerman is a retired newspaperman and publications manager who resides in Nashville, Tennessee. In addition to operating Zimco Publications LLC, he is a member of the American Battlefield Trust, Battle of Nashville Preservation Society, Nashville Civil War Roundtable, Save the Franklin Battlefield, Civil War Fortification Study Group, and other historical preservation groups. He enjoys traveling to historic sites and museums, a good joke, and collecting books and old bottles of whiskey. More information available at www.zimcopubs.com.

# NOTES

# NOTES

# NOTES

# NOTES

# NOTES

CPSIA information can be obtained
at www.ICGtesting.com
Printed in the USA
LVHW010040081019
633404LV00001B/297